THE LAW OF TRAFFIC STOPS AND OFFENSES IN NORTH CAROLINA

SHEA RIGGSBEE DENNING

CHRISTOPHER TYNER

JEFFREY B. WELTY

The School of Government at the University of North Carolina at Chapel Hill works to improve the lives of North Carolinians by engaging in practical scholarship that helps public officials and citizens understand and improve state and local government. Established in 1931 as the Institute of Government, the School provides educational, advisory, and research services for state and local governments. The School of Government is also home to a nationally ranked Master of Public Administration program, the North Carolina Judicial College, and specialized centers focused on community and economic development, information technology, and environmental finance.

As the largest university-based local government training, advisory, and research organization in the United States, the School of Government offers up to 200 courses, webinars, and specialized conferences for more than 12,000 public officials each year. In addition, faculty members annually publish approximately 50 books, manuals, reports, articles, bulletins, and other print and online content related to state and local government. The School also produces the *Daily Bulletin Online* each day the General Assembly is in session, reporting on activities for members of the legislature and others who need to follow the course of legislation.

Operating support for the School of Government's programs and activities comes from many sources, including state appropriations, local government membership dues, private contributions, publication sales, course fees, and service contracts.

Visit sog.unc.edu or call 919.966.5381 for more information on the School's courses, publications, programs, and services.

Michael R. Smith, DEAN
Thomas H. Thornburg, SENIOR ASSOCIATE DEAN
Johnny Burleson, ASSOCIATE DEAN FOR DEVELOPMENT
Michael Vollmer, ASSOCIATE DEAN FOR ADMINISTRATION
Linda H. Weiner, ASSOCIATE DEAN FOR OPERATIONS
Janet Holston, DIRECTOR OF STRATEGY AND INNOVATION

FACULTY

Whitney Afonso
Trey Allen
Gregory S. Allison
David N. Ammons
Ann M. Anderson
Maureen Berner
Frayda S. Bluestein
Mark F. Botts
Anita R. Brown-Graham
Peg Carlson
Leisha DeHart-Davis
Shea Riggsbee Denning
Sara DePasquale
James C. Drennan
Richard D. Ducker

Norma Houston
Cheryl Daniels Howell
Jeffrey A. Hughes
Willow S. Jacobson
Robert P. Joyce
Diane M. Juffras
Dona G. Lewandowski
Adam Lovelady
James M. Markham
Christopher B. McLaughlin
Kara A. Millonzi
Jill D. Moore
Jonathan Q. Morgan
Ricardo S. Morse
C. Tyler Mulligan

Kimberly L. Nelson
David W. Owens
LaToya B. Powell
William C. Rivenbark
Dale J. Roenigk
John Rubin
Jessica Smith
Meredith Smith
Carl W. Stenberg III
John B. Stephens
Charles Szypszak
Shannon H. Tufts
Aimee N. Wall
Jeffrey B. Welty
Richard B. Whisnant

Contents

Chapter 3

Scope and Duration of Traffic Stops 49

Chapter 4

Driver's License and Vehicle Registration Laws 67

Preface

Jeff Welty wrote a popular paper on the law of traffic stops several years ago. Around the same time, Shea Denning began rewriting Ben F. Loeb, Jr. and James C. Drennan's 2000 book, *Motor Vehicle Law and The Law of Impaired Driving in North Carolina*. It occurred to Jeff and Shea that a single work addressing the law of traffic stops and the elements of traffic offenses might make sense, given that many cases concerning the legality of a traffic stop implicate both areas of law. They invited Christopher Tyner to help complete the connection by writing about the law of checkpoints. This book is the result of these combined efforts.

As with all School of Government publications, this book was improved by the contributions of colleagues. Retired faculty member Robert Farb reviewed draft chapters and provided substantive feedback. Editor Melissa Twomey scrutinized every sentence and footnote (and there are many) and suggested changes that improved the book's readability as well as its accuracy. Designers Diane O'Brien and Dan Soileau turned words in a manuscript into an appealing layout. The talented Robby Poore designed the cover. Kevin Justice shepherded the book through the publications process, providing weekly updates and gently nudging us to meet deadlines. He also encouraged us to come up with a title more catchy than *The Law of Traffic Stops and North Carolina Motor Vehicle Offenses*. We obliged. Of course, any remaining inaccuracies, oversights, and inartful phrases are exclusively the fault of the authors.

We hope that this book will assist law enforcement officers, prosecutors, defense attorneys, and judicial officials in carrying out their important work. We welcome your comments about the book's scope, organization, or content. Please contact us at welty@sog.unc.edu, denning@sog.unc.edu, or ctyner@sog.unc.edu.

Shea Denning
Christopher Tyner
Jeff Welty

Chapel Hill
September 2017

Introduction

Traffic enforcement is the Rodney Dangerfield of law enforcement duty assignments: it gets no respect. Citizens often resent being stopped for what they view as minor transgressions. Many officers would rather do more glamorous work investigating major crimes. Yet no other kind of interaction between officers and citizens is as common or as significant.

North Carolina officers conduct more than a million traffic stops each year.[1] In 2015, the State Highway Patrol alone made more than 625,000 stops.[2] The federal Bureau of Justice Statistics reports that approximately 44 percent of all face-to-face contacts between officers and citizens take place in the context of traffic enforcement.[3]

These interactions are significant even when they result in nothing more than a traffic citation, as about two thirds of all stops do.[4] Studies suggest that enforcing traffic laws changes drivers' behavior and improves roadway safety.[5] Of course, enforcement works precisely because receiving a traffic ticket is an unpleasant experience, with court costs for a motorist who is held accountable for a violation likely to approach $200,[6] plus the cost of any sanction and the potential expense of an attorney, not to mention possible insurance and licensure impacts and the stress and inconvenience of handling the citation.

---

1. Since 2002, state law has required that virtually all traffic stops be reported to the North Carolina Department of Public Safety (DPS). Chapter 143B, Section 903 of the North Carolina General Statutes (hereinafter G.S.). The data are available online, but only on an agency-by-agency basis, not in the aggregate. *See* DPS, Traffic Stop Reports (fillable tool for retrieving specified reports), http://trafficstops.ncsbi.gov/Default.aspx?pageid=2. However, researchers at the University of North Carolina at Chapel Hill (UNC) aggregated the DPS data collected from early 2000 through mid-2011 in the course of researching whether racial disparities exist in traffic stops. They found that officers made more than thirteen million stops in an eleven-year period. Frank R. Baumgartner & Derek Epps, *North Carolina Traffic Stop Statistics Analysis: Final Report to the North Carolina Advocates for Justice Task Force on Racial and Ethnic Bias* 4 (Feb. 1, 2012) (footnote omitted), www.unc.edu/~fbaum/papers/Baumgartner-Traffic-Stops-Statistics-1-Feb-2012.pdf ("From January 1st, 2000 through June 14th, 2011, various NC police departments reported 13,397,573 individuals involved in traffic stops.").

2. DPS, Traffic Stop Reports, *supra* note 1.

3. Christine Eith & Matthew R. Durose, U.S. Dep't of Just., Office of Just. Programs, Bureau of Just. Stats., Contacts between Police and the Public, 2008, Special Report 3 (Oct. 2011), www.bjs.gov/content/pub/pdf/cpp08.pdf) (finding that 44.1 percent of all contacts with police result from traffic stops).

4. Baumgartner & Epps, *North Carolina Traffic Stop Statistics Analysis*, *supra* note 1, at Table 6 (showing that just over 68 percent of traffic stops result in a citation).

5. *See, e.g.*, Tom Vanderbilt, *In Praise of Traffic Tickets*, Slate (Aug. 28, 2009), www.slate.com/articles/life/transport/2009/08/in_praise_of_traffic_tickets.html (summarizing research and concluding that traffic tickets "help keep people . . . alive" and "increase[] public safety").

6. *See generally* G.S. 7A-304.

Some traffic stops involve far greater consequences. Drivers may be charged with serious motor vehicle offenses, such as driving while impaired, or with non-motor-vehicle offenses detected during the stop, such as drug crimes. In such cases, custodial arrests are routine and prison sentences are possible. Non-motor-vehicle charges often come about after an officer searches a stopped vehicle, typically either by consent or based on probable cause. Between 3 and 4 percent of traffic stops in North Carolina result in searches of the stopped vehicle.[7]

The most serious potential consequences of traffic stops involve violence. According to FBI data, between 2005 and 2014, ninety-three officers were feloniously killed during traffic stops and pursuits, most often while the officer approached or interviewed a motorist.[8] An additional thirty-one officers were accidentally killed when they were struck by vehicles while conducting traffic stops or roadblocks.[9] Thousands of officers are assaulted during traffic stops each year.[10]

Officers are not the only ones injured or killed in violent confrontations during traffic stops. The *Washington Post* recently reported that more than 100 civilians were shot and killed by police during traffic stops in 2015 alone. About a third of those killed were African American, making a "roadside interaction one of the most common precursors to a fatal police shooting" for blacks.[11]

Given the important consequences of traffic stops, it is not surprising that they have received considerable attention in recent years. Controversies have erupted concerning whether observed racial disparities in traffic stops are unjustified;[12] whether limits should be placed on officers' authority to conduct consent searches during or after traffic stops;[13] and whether officers should be able to extend

---

7. Baumgartner & Epps, *supra* note 1, at Table 3 (showing that 3.37 percent of traffic stops result in searches, with vehicles driven by blacks and Hispanics more likely to be searched than vehicles driven by whites).

8. U.S. Dep't of Just., Fed. Bureau of Investigation (FBI), Crim. Just. Info. Servs. Div., 2014 Law Enforcement Officers Killed & Assaulted Table 22, "Law Enforcement Officers Feloniously Killed During Traffic Pursuits/Stops: Activity of Victim Officer at Scene of Incident, 2005–2014," www.fbi.gov/about-us/cjis/ucr/leoka/2014/tables/table_22_leos_fk_activity_of_victim_officer_at_scene_of_incident_2005-2014.xls.

9. FBI, Crim. Just. Info. Servs. Div., 2014 Law Enforcement Officers Killed & Assaulted Table 67, "Law Enforcement Officers Accidentally Killed: Circumstance at Scene of Incident, 2005–2014," www.fbi.gov/about-us/cjis/ucr/leoka/2014/tables/table_67_leos_ak_circumstance_at_scene_of_incident_2005-2014.xls.

10. FBI, Crim. Just. Info. Servs. Div., 2014 Law Enforcement Officers Killed & Assaulted Table 75, "Law Enforcement Officers Assaulted: Circumstance at Scene of Incident by Type of Assignment and Percent Distribution, 2014," www.fbi.gov/about-us/cjis/ucr/leoka/2014/tables/table_75_leos_asltd_circum_at_scene_of_incident_by_type_of_assignment_and_percent_distribution_2014.xls (showing more than 4,000 officers assaulted in 2014). In North Carolina, members of the State Highway Patrol reported encountering "physical force" 107 times in 2015. DPS, Traffic Stop Reports, *supra* note 1.

11. Wesley Lowery, *A Disproportionate Number of Black Victims in Fatal Traffic Stops*, Wash. Post (Dec. 24, 2015), www.washingtonpost.com/national/a-disproportionate-number-of-black-victims-in-fatal-traffic-stops/2015/12/24/c29717e2-a344-11e5-9c4e-be37f66848bb_story.html.

12. *See, e.g.,* Sharon LaFraniere & Andrew W. Lehren, *The Disproportionate Risks of Driving While Black*, N.Y. Times (Oct. 24, 2015), https://www.nytimes.com/2015/10/25/us/racial-disparity-traffic-stops-driving-black.html?_r=0 (analyzing North Carolina data and finding "wide racial differences in measure after measure of police conduct" regarding traffic stops but also noting officials' response that "more African-Americans live in neighborhoods with higher crime, where officers patrol more aggressively" in an effort to protect the public).

13. *See, e.g.,* Jim Wise, *Written Consents Are Fayetteville Policy*, News & Observer (Sept. 3, 2014), http://www.newsobserver.com/news/local/counties/durham-county/article10049000.html (noting that in Fayetteville, officers may conduct consent searches of vehicles only with written consent and stating that Durham was considering adopting a similar policy).

traffic stops briefly to investigate matters unrelated to the initial purpose of the stop.[14] Courts have tackled some of these questions, while others have been addressed by municipal governing boards, law enforcement agency heads, or other actors.

In short, the law of traffic stops is important, contested, and changing. As one commentator put it, "[i]n recent years more Fourth Amendment battles have been fought about police activities incident to . . . what the courts call a 'routine traffic stop' than in any other context."[15]

This book is intended as a reference for anyone who deals with traffic stops regularly, including officers, lawyers, and judges. While it contains complete legal citations and analysis, it is written to be accessible to non-lawyers as well. Consistent with the mission of the UNC School of Government, it focuses mainly on North Carolina law, though the law in this area is heavily informed by federal constitutional considerations, and much of the book would be pertinent in any jurisdiction.

The book is organized as follows. Chapter 1 concerns when an officer may make a stop. It sets out the legal standard for doing so and summarizes how courts have applied that standard to several common fact patterns. Chapter 2 covers motor vehicle checkpoints. It addresses when they are permitted, how they must be operated, and how challenges to checkpoints have fared in the courts. Chapter 3 focuses on the scope and duration of traffic stops. It explains what an officer may and may not do during a stop, including what sorts of investigative strategies an officer may employ. Finally, chapter 4 covers North Carolina's driver's license and vehicle registration laws and the elements of many common traffic offenses. The offense of impaired driving and other alcohol-related traffic offenses are the subject of a separate publication and are therefore generally not discussed in this book.[16]

---

14. This issue, and the seminal case of *Rodriguez v. United States*, ___ U.S. ___, 135 S. Ct. 1609 (2015), are discussed in chapter 3 of this book.

15. 4 WAYNE R. LaFAVE, SEARCH AND SEIZURE § 9.3 (5th ed. 2012). It is worth noting that among officers, there is an "axiom that there is no such thing as a routine traffic stop." Amaury Murgado, *How to Approach Traffic Stops*, POLICE (Nov. 26, 2012), www.policemag.com/channel/careers-training/articles/2012/11/traffic-stops.aspx).

16. SHEA RIGGSBEE DENNING, THE LAW OF IMPAIRED DRIVING AND RELATED IMPLIED CONSENT OFFENSES IN NORTH CAROLINA (UNC School of Government, 2014).

Chapter 1

Making a Traffic Stop

Chapter 1

Making a Traffic Stop

This chapter discusses when a law enforcement officer may make a traffic stop. It addresses an officer's authority to investigate before making a stop; the legal standard for making a stop; and recurrent fact patterns that courts have deemed sufficient, or insufficient, to justify a stop.

I. Investigation before the Stop

A. Territorial Limits

Most law enforcement officers are authorized to enforce the law only within certain territorial limits. A complete discussion of officers' territorial jurisdiction is provided in another School of Government publication.[1] However, it is worth reviewing the most important considerations here.

City law enforcement officers, such as municipal police officers, generally may make stops and arrests[2] within the cities that they serve, including non-contiguous satellite territory; on property or rights of way owned or leased by their cities, wherever located; and within one mile of city limits.[3] A few cities are the subject of local acts expanding the one-mile radius.[4]

---

1. Robert L. Farb, Arrest, Search, and Investigation in North Carolina 14–18 (UNC School of Government, 5th ed. 2016).

2. The principal statute concerning officers' territorial jurisdiction is Chapter 15A, Section 402 of the North Carolina General Statutes (hereinafter G.S.), which addresses officers' authority to make arrests. In *State v. Harris*, 43 N.C. App. 346 (1979), the court of appeals reserved the question of whether the territorial limits in G.S. 15A-402 apply to investigative stops and other exercises of an officer's authority beyond arrests. This chapter assumes that the territorial limits do apply to exercises of authority other than arrests. *Cf.* G.S. 15A-247 (providing that search warrants may be executed by an officer "acting within his territorial jurisdiction," without detailing what territorial limits apply).

3. *See* G.S. 15A-402(b) ("Law-enforcement officers of cities and counties may arrest persons within their particular cities or counties and on any property and rights-of-way owned by the city or county outside its limits."); 160A-286 ("In addition to their authority within the corporate limits, city policemen shall have all the powers invested in law-enforcement officers by statute or common law within one mile of the corporate limits of the city, and on all property owned by or leased to the city wherever located."); 15A-402(c) ("Law-enforcement officers of cities may arrest persons at any point which is one mile or less from the nearest point in the boundary of such city.").

4. *See* Jeff Welty, *Police Jurisdiction in Satellite and Related Areas*, N.C. Crim. L., UNC Sch. of Gov't Blog (Nov. 3, 2014), www.sog.unc.edu/blogs/nc-criminal-law/police-jurisdiction-satellite-and-related-areas (noting such acts concerning Edenton and Weaverville; a comment on the post states that Rockingham is also the subject of such an act).

County law enforcement officers, such as sheriffs and their deputies, generally may make stops and arrests within their counties; on property or rights of way owned by their counties, wherever located; and anywhere in the state for felonies committed within their counties.[5] Importantly, county officers do not have a one-mile buffer like the one that pertains to city officers. County officers have law enforcement authority even in areas of the county that are incorporated, though as a matter of policy they often leave law enforcement in municipalities to city officers.

State law enforcement officers, such as members of the North Carolina Highway Patrol, have authority throughout the state.[6]

An officer's territorial jurisdiction may be expanded beyond the limits that would otherwise apply when the officer is engaged in continuous hot pursuit of a person who has committed a criminal offense.[7] Hot pursuit may continue across state lines for felonies and, in limited circumstances for certain impaired driving misdemeanors.[8]

An officer's territorial jurisdiction may also be expanded by G.S. 20-38.2, which provides that "[a] law enforcement officer who is investigating an implied-consent offense or a vehicle crash that occurred in the officer's territorial jurisdiction is authorized to investigate and seek evidence of the driver's impairment anywhere in-state or out-of-state, and to make arrests at any place within the State." Finally, an officer's territorial jurisdiction may be expanded by a mutual aid agreement between law enforcement agencies.[9]

When an officer makes a stop or an arrest outside his or her territorial jurisdiction, a defendant may seek to suppress evidence obtained as a result of the stop or arrest under the statutory exclusionary rule in G.S. 15A-974.[10] However, the appellate cases on point generally have not required suppression.[11] Furthermore, so long as the officer acted with reasonable suspicion (for a stop) or probable cause (for an

---

5. *See* G.S. 15A-402(b) ("Law-enforcement officers of cities and counties may arrest persons within their particular cities or counties and on any property and rights-of-way owned by the city or county outside its limits."); 15A-402(e) ("Law-enforcement officers of counties may arrest persons at any place in the State of North Carolina when the arrest is based upon a felony committed within [the officer's county].").

6. G.S. 15A-402(a) ("Law-enforcement officers of the State of North Carolina may arrest persons at any place within the State."); 20-188 (stating, among other things, that "the members of the Patrol . . . are . . . authorized to arrest without warrant any person who, in the presence of said officers, is engaged in the violation of any of the laws of the State regulating travel and the use of vehicles upon the highways, or of laws with respect to the protection of the highways, and they shall have jurisdiction anywhere within the State, irrespective of county lines," and that members "shall have the authority throughout the State of North Carolina of any police officer in respect to making arrests for any crimes committed in their presence and shall have authority to make arrests for any crime committed on any highway").

7. G.S. 15A-402(d) ("Law-enforcement officers of cities and counties may arrest persons outside the [territorial limits that normally apply] when the person arrested has committed a criminal offense within that territory, for which the officer could have arrested the person within that territory, and the arrest is made during such person's immediate and continuous flight from that territory.").

8. FARB, *supra* note 1, at 17–18.

9. *Id.* at 24–25.

10. The statute requires the suppression of evidence that "is obtained as a result of a substantial violation of the provisions of [G.S. Chapter 15A]." G.S. 15A-974(a)(2).

11. *See, e.g.,* State v. Scruggs, 209 N.C. App. 725 (2011) (even if a campus police officer made a stop and an arrest outside his territorial jurisdiction, the violation was not so substantial as to require suppression); State v. Melvin, 53 N.C. App. 421 (1981) (even if a city officer's stop of a vehicle in which the defendant was a passenger, along with the arrest of the defendant, took place outside the officer's territorial jurisdiction, the officer's actions were not unreasonable and suppression was not required); State v. Harris, 43 N.C. App. 346 (1979) (any territorial jurisdiction problem presented by a Stokes County deputy's stop of the defendant in Forsyth County was not so substantial as to require suppression).

arrest), a stop or an arrest conducted outside an officer's territorial jurisdiction is not unconstitutional, and no constitutional exclusionary rule requires the suppression of any evidence obtained as a result.[12]

B. Investigative Techniques

Officers use many different investigative techniques to identify motorists who are violating the law, including deploying radar devices, positioning themselves in concealed locations and observing traffic, and running computer checks based on the license plate numbers they observe. In general, motor vehicles traveling on public roads are in plain view, and these investigative techniques do not implicate the Fourth Amendment.

1. Radar Guns

Officers may use radar guns or other devices to measure a vehicle's speed. This is not a search for purposes of the Fourth Amendment because it does not intrude upon any reasonable expectation of privacy when a motorist is traveling on a public road.[13] Therefore, no warrant or individualized suspicion is required for an officer to use a radar gun or similar device.

Although not directly relevant to an officer's authority to use a radar gun at the investigative stage, it is worth noting that in order for the results of a "speed-measuring instrument" to be admissible, G.S. 8-50.2(b) requires that (1) the officer who operated the instrument was certified by the North Carolina Criminal Justice Education and Training Standards Commission, (2) the officer followed the "procedures established by the Commission for the operation of such instrument," (3) the instrument was approved by the Commission and the Secretary of Public Safety, and (4) the instrument was calibrated according to the Commission's standards.[14] When admitted, the results may be used "for the purpose of corroborating the opinion of a person as to the speed of an object" and may not stand alone as proof of speed.[15]

To the extent discussed below,[16] an officer may stop a motor vehicle for speeding based on the officer's visual estimate of the vehicle's speed. In other words, an officer is not required to use a radar gun or other device to measure a vehicle's speed.

---

12. *See generally* Virginia v. Moore, 553 U.S. 164 (2008) (a search incident to an arrest did not violate the Fourth Amendment where the arrest was constitutional because it was supported by probable cause, even though the arrest was not authorized by state statutory law); State v. Eubanks, 283 N.C. 556 (1973) (suppression of evidence was not required where an impaired driving arrest was constitutional but was conducted in violation of state statutory law).

13. State v. Jackson, 287 N.W.2d 853 (Wis. Ct. App. 1979) (unpublished) (stating that "readings as to defendant's speed obtained through the use of radar in no way constitute either a search or seizure of his automobile. . . . The privacy of the defendant is not affected by radar readings of the speed of his automobile."); People v. McGuirk, No. 2-11-0268, 2012 WL 6967585, at *6 (Ill. Ct. App. Mar. 23, 2012) (unpublished) (noting that "an officer parked on the shoulder of a road using a radar gun to detect speeders . . . would not qualify as a fourth amendment seizure").

14. The pertinent regulations of the Commission may be found in Chapter 9 of Title 12 of the North Carolina Administrative Code (hereinafter N.C.A.C.). For example, 12 N.C.A.C. 09C, § .0608 provides that the operating procedures for speed-measuring instruments are those outlined in a specific publication of the North Carolina Justice Academy.

15. G.S. 8-50.2(a); State v. Jenkins, 80 N.C. App. 491, 495 (1986) (citation omitted) ("By the express provisions of the statute, evidence of radar speed measurement is admissible only to corroborate testimony based on visual observation. . . . [T]he General Assembly has provided that the speed of a vehicle may not be proved by the results of radar measurement alone and that such evidence may be used only to corroborate the opinion of a witness as to speed, which opinion is based upon actual observation.").

16. *See infra* section II.B.1.

2. Concealed Locations

Officers may conceal themselves and their vehicles while looking for motorists who are breaking the law. A motorist has no reasonable expectation of privacy in his or her conduct on the road.[17] Thus, an officer's observation of a motorist is not a Fourth Amendment search, and there is no need to consider whether the officer's conduct in concealing himself or herself is reasonable or not.[18]

3. "Running Tags"

Sometimes, an officer will decide to conduct a computer check to determine whether the license plate on a vehicle is current and matches the vehicle and perhaps also whether the vehicle is registered to a person with outstanding warrants or to a person who does not have a valid license. When this is done randomly, without individualized suspicion, defendants sometimes argue that the officer has conducted an illegal search by running the tag. Courts have uniformly rejected this argument, finding that license plates are open to public view and not subject to a reasonable expectation of privacy.[19]

---

17. United States v. Knotts, 460 U.S. 276, 281 (1983) ("A person travelling in an automobile on public thoroughfares has no reasonable expectation of privacy in his movements from one place to another."); State v. Parker, 183 N.C. App. 1, 7 (2007) (same, quoting this language from *Knotts*).

18. *See generally* Lewis R. Katz, *"Lonesome Road": Driving Without the Fourth Amendment*, 36 Seattle U. L. Rev. 1413, 1435 (2013) ("Police surveillance of a motorist does not implicate the Fourth Amendment as long as it occurs 'unobtrusively and do[es] not limit defendant's freedom of movement by so doing.'" (quoting People v. Thornton, 667 N.Y.S.2d 705, 707 (App. Div. 1998))).

19. *See, e.g.*, State v. Chambers, 203 N.C. App. 373 (2010) (unpublished) ("Defendant's license tag was displayed, as required by North Carolina law, on the back of his vehicle for all of society to view. Therefore, defendant did not have a subjective or objective reasonable expectation of privacy in his license tag. As such, the officer's actions did not constitute a search under the Fourth Amendment."); Jones v. Town of Woodworth, 132 So. 3d 422, 424–25 (La. Ct. App. 2013) ("[A] survey of federal and state cases addressing this issue have concluded that a license plate is an object which is constantly exposed to public view and in which a person, thus, has no reasonable expectation of privacy, and that consequently, conducting a random license plate check is legal."); State v. Setinich, 822 N.W.2d 9, 12 (Minn. Ct. App. 2012) (rejecting a defendant's challenge to an officer's suspicionless license plate check because "[a] driver does not have a reasonable expectation of privacy in a license plate number which is required to be openly displayed"); State v. Davis, 239 P.3d 1002, 1006 (Or. Ct. App. 2010) (upholding a random license check and stating that "[t]he state can access a person's driving records by observing a driver's registration plate that is displayed in plain view and looking up that registration plate number in the state's own records"), *aff'd by an equally divided court*, 295 P.3d 617 (2013); State v. Donis, 723 A.2d 35, 40 (N.J. 1998) (holding that there is no reasonable expectation of privacy in the exterior of a vehicle, including the license plate, so an officer's ability to run a tag "should not be limited only to those instances when [the officer] actually witness[es] a violation of motor vehicle laws"). *Cf.* New York v. Class, 475 U.S. 106, 114 (1986) (finding no reasonable expectation of privacy in a vehicle's VIN number because "it is unreasonable to have an expectation of privacy in an object required by law to be located in a place ordinarily in plain view from the exterior of the automobile"). *See also infra* section II.B.9 (discussing the extent to which the identity of the driver may be inferred from the vehicle's registration information).

II. Making the Stop

A. Legal Standard

1. Generally

Although it is often said that driving is a privilege, not a right,[20] officers do not have unlimited authority to stop vehicles without suspicion in order to check for compliance with licensing requirements and other motor vehicle regulations.[21] Instead, "[r]easonable suspicion [is] the necessary standard for stops based on traffic violations."[22] Reasonable suspicion of an infraction or a criminal offense is sufficient to justify a stop.[23]

Reasonable suspicion is the same standard that applies to investigative stops made in connection with non-traffic criminal offenses.[24] Although it is "not possible" to state precisely what reasonable suspicion requires,[25] the standard is less than probable cause and considerably less than a preponderance of the evidence.[26] It does, however, require a minimal level of objective justification, based on articulable facts and circumstances rather than an officer's hunch or intuition.[27] A court reviewing an officer's determination regarding reasonable suspicion may consider the facts and circumstances as would a reasonable, cautious officer in light of the officer's experience and training.[28]

---

20. North Carolina's appellate courts have referred to this idea when addressing impaired driving, see, e.g., State v. Howren, 312 N.C. 454, 456 (1984) ("anyone who accepts the privileges of driving on the highways of this State has consented to the use of chemical analysis"), or licensure, see, e.g., State v. Hurley, 18 N.C. App. 285, 287 (1973) ("A person has no right to drive upon the highways after his driving privilege has been revoked").

21. Delaware v. Prouse, 440 U.S. 648, 662 (1979) ("[E]xcept in those situations in which there is at least articulable and reasonable suspicion that a motorist is unlicensed or that an automobile is not registered, or that either the vehicle or an occupant is otherwise subject to seizure for violation of law, stopping an automobile and detaining the driver in order to check his driver's license and the registration of the automobile are unreasonable under the Fourth Amendment").

22. State v. Styles, 362 N.C. 412, 415 (2008) (rejecting the argument that full probable cause is required for stops based on readily observable traffic violations). Other jurisdictions have generally adopted the same rule. See, e.g., United States v. Delfin-Colina, 464 F.3d 392 (3d Cir. 2006) (referencing Terry v. Ohio, 392 U.S. 1 (1968), and stating: "[W]e now join our sister circuits in holding that the Terry reasonable suspicion standard applies to routine traffic stops."); State v. Houghton, 868 N.W.2d 143, 147 (Wis. 2015) ("We hold that an officer's reasonable suspicion that a motorist is violating or has violated a traffic law is sufficient for the officer to initiate a stop of the offending vehicle."); Moore v. Commonwealth, 668 S.E.2d 150, 154 (Va. 2008) (noting that a defendant "erroneously relied on the wrong standard governing his Fourth Amendment claim because [his brief] invoked the 'probable cause' standard rather than the applicable 'reasonable suspicion' standard"). A few courts require probable cause for at least some types of traffic violations. See United States v. Lyons, 687 F.3d 754, 763 (6th Cir. 2012) ("In order to effect a traffic stop, an officer must possess either probable cause of a civil infraction or reasonable suspicion of criminal activity."). Cf. Wayne R. LaFave, The "Routine Traffic Stop" from Start to Finish: Too Much "Routine," Not Enough Fourth Amendment, 102 MICH. L. REV. 1843, 1852 (Aug. 2004) (arguing for requiring probable cause in cases of minor traffic infractions and stating that doing so "would be one significant step toward enhancing the Fourth Amendment rights of suspected traffic violators").

23. See, e.g., State v. McClendon, 130 N.C. App. 368 (1998) (stating that an officer may stop a vehicle based on a criminal offense or an infraction); State v. Braxton, 90 N.C. App. 204, 208 (1988) (stating that it is "unquestioned" that an officer has the authority to stop a motorist for speeding, even when the offense is "not a criminal violation but rather . . . merely an infraction").

24. Terry v. Ohio, 392 U.S. 1 (1968).

25. Ornelas v. United States, 517 U.S. 690 (1996).

26. State v. Styles, 362 N.C. 412 (2008).

27. Id.

28. State v. Maready, 362 N.C. 614 (2008).

Reasonable suspicion may be based on an officer's reasonable mistake of fact.[29] As the Supreme Court of the United States recently stated:

> [A] search or seizure may be permissible even though the justification for the action includes a reasonable factual mistake. An officer might, for example, stop a motorist for traveling alone in a high-occupancy vehicle lane, only to discover upon approaching the car that two children are slumped over asleep in the back seat. The driver has not violated the law, but neither has the officer violated the Fourth Amendment.[30]

Other mistake-of-fact cases have found reasonable suspicion where an officer stopped a vehicle for failure to display a license plate and no plate was attached to the rear bumper, even though it later turned out that a dealer plate was present in the rear window of the vehicle;[31] and where an officer stopped a vehicle when a computer check indicated that a driver's license was suspended, even though it later turned out that the computer was mistaken.[32]

Reasonable suspicion may also be based on an officer's reasonable mistake of law, i.e., when the officer reasonably believes that a given set of facts constitute a violation of law, even though the conduct in question is actually lawful. The U.S. Supreme Court so ruled in *Heien v. North Carolina*,[33] a case that began when an officer stopped a motorist for having a nonfunctioning brake light. The Court of Appeals of North Carolina ruled that the applicable statute required only one working brake light—which the vehicle had, notwithstanding the fact that the other brake light wasn't working—and that the stop was therefore unreasonable.[34] The Supreme Court reviewed the case and ruled that the brake light statute was sufficiently difficult to parse that the officer's interpretation was reasonable even if mistaken, rendering the stop reasonable also.

The majority opinion in *Heien* did not establish a standard for when an officer's mistaken interpretation of law is reasonable, but Justice Kagan's concurrence argued that such an interpretation is reasonable only when the law itself is "genuinely ambiguous."[35] In other words, it is not enough if the law is obscure or surprising, it must be unclear. Lower courts—including the Court of Appeals of North Carolina—have since adopted that reasoning.[36] Cases involving reasonable mistakes of law are likely to be rare.

---

29. *See generally* Williams v. Decker, 767 F.3d 734, 740 (8th Cir. 2014) ("However, reasonable suspicion of criminal activity can be based upon a mistake of fact so long as that mistake was objectively reasonable."); United States v. Herrera, 444 F.3d 1238 (10th Cir. 2006) (noting that the court has "consistently held" that an objectively reasonable mistake of fact may support reasonable suspicion).

30. Heien v. North Carolina, ___ U.S. ___, ___, 135 S. Ct. 530, 534 (2014).

31. United States v. Pena-Montes, 589 F.3d 1048, 1052 (10th Cir. 2009) (so holding and stating that "we may weigh objectively reasonable mistakes of fact made by the officer in favor of reasonable suspicion").

32. United States v. Coplin, 463 F.3d 96, 101 (1st Cir. 2006) (so holding and stating that "[s]tops premised on mistakes of fact . . . generally have been held constitutional so long as the mistake is objectively reasonable").

33. ___ U.S. ___, 135 S. Ct. 530.

34. The statute interpreted by the court of appeals is G.S. 20-129. It was amended by S.L. 2015-31, the effect of which is to require at least two working "stop lamps," one on each side of a vehicle.

35. ___ U.S. at ___, 135 S. Ct. at 540.

36. State v. Eldridge, ___ N.C. App. ___, 790 S.E.2d 740 (2016) (an officer noticed that an out-of-state vehicle lacked a working exterior mirror on the driver's side and stopped the vehicle on that basis; however, G.S. 20-126(b), which requires vehicles to have driver's side mirrors, applies only to vehicles registered in North Carolina; the trial court viewed this as a reasonable mistake of law, but the court of appeals disagreed, finding the statute "clear and unambiguous").

Questions sometimes arise about whether a specific interaction is a stop or something else. Generally, it is not a stop for an officer to park his or her vehicle near a stopped car and approach the car on foot. The driver of the car is, at least in theory, free to drive away.[37] If an officer makes a show of authority, such as activating his or her blue lights, and the motorist complies by stopping or by remaining in place, the interaction is no longer optional and may be categorized as a stop. Whether specific words or gestures constitute a show of authority is often clear but sometimes perplexingly difficult to determine.[38]

2. Pretextual Stops

If an officer has reasonable suspicion that a driver has committed a crime or an infraction, the officer may stop the driver's vehicle. This is so even if the officer is not interested in pursuing the crime or infraction for which reasonable suspicion exists but, rather, is hoping to observe or gather evidence of another offense.[39] Indeed, because courts focus on the objective facts surrounding a stop rather than on the officer's subjective motivations, it seems that a stop may be legally justified even where the officer is completely unaware of the offense for which reasonable suspicion exists and makes the stop based entirely on his or her incorrect belief that reasonable suspicion exists for another offense.[40] Because the officer's subjective intentions regarding the purpose of the stop are immaterial, whether "an officer conducting a traffic stop [did or] did not subsequently issue a citation is also irrelevant to the validity of the stop."[41]

If an officer makes a pretextual traffic stop and then engages in extensive investigative activity that is directed not at the traffic offense but at another offense for which reasonable suspicion is absent, the officer may exceed the permitted scope of the traffic stop. This issue is addressed in chapter 3, which considers the legal limits on an officer's investigative activity during a stop.

---

37. *See, e.g.*, State v. Veal, 234 N.C. App. 570, 575 (2014) (finding no seizure where an officer "parked his vehicle [near the defendant's but he] did not pull his vehicle in behind defendant's car, he did not activate his blue lights, and . . . he got out of his vehicle and approached defendant's truck on foot and asked to speak with defendant").

38. For example, in *State v. Wilson*, ___ N.C. App. ___, 793 S.E.2d 737 (2016), the court divided over whether an officer engaged in a show of authority when he "waved his hands back and forth just above shoulder level" at a motorist. The majority concluded that these motions were "not so authoritative or coercive that a reasonable person would not have felt free to leave," but the dissent thought that "any reasonable motorist . . . seeing a uniformed officer standing next to a marked patrol car waving his arms, gesturing to the motorist to stop . . . would feel compelled to stop."

39. Whren v. United States, 517 U.S. 806, 813 (1996) (emphasizing that the "[s]ubjective intentions" of the officer are irrelevant); State v. McClendon, 350 N.C. 630, 635–36 (1999) (adopting *Whren* under the state constitution).

40. *See, e.g.*, Devenpeck v. Alford, 543 U.S. 146, 153 (2004) (citations omitted) ("[A]n arresting officer's state of mind (except for the facts that he knows) is irrelevant to the existence of probable cause. That is to say, his subjective reason for making the arrest need not be the criminal offense as to which the known facts provide probable cause."); State v. Osterhoudt, 222 N.C. App. 620 (2012) (an officer stopped the defendant based on the officer's mistaken belief that the defendant's driving violated a particular traffic law; the court of appeals concluded that the law in question had no application to the defendant's driving but upheld the stop because the facts observed by the officer provided reasonable suspicion that the defendant's driving violated a different traffic law, notwithstanding the fact that the officer did not act on that basis).

41. State v. Parker, 183 N.C. App. 1, 8 (2007).

3. When Reasonable Suspicion Must Exist

Normally, a law enforcement officer will develop reasonable suspicion before instructing a motorist to stop. But sometimes an officer will not have reasonable suspicion at that point, yet will develop reasonable suspicion prior to the suspect's compliance with the officer's instruction. Such a stop is valid. In *California v. Hodari D.*,[42] the U.S. Supreme Court held that a show of authority is not a seizure until the subject complies. Because the propriety of a seizure depends on the facts known at the time of the seizure, events occurring after an officer's show of authority but before a driver's submission to it may be used to justify the stop. For example, an officer who activates his blue lights after observing a driver traveling 45 m.p.h. in a 55 m.p.h. zone may be without reasonable suspicion. But if the driver initially fails to respond to the blue lights, continues driving, and weaves severely before stopping, the seizure may be upheld because the driver's weaving, in addition to his slow rate of speed, provides reasonable suspicion of impairment.[43]

4. When Reasonable Suspicion Dissipates

Sometimes a stop will be supported by reasonable suspicion, but reasonable suspicion will dissipate shortly after the stop is made. For example, an officer may stop a vehicle because it is registered to a person with a revoked license if there is no reason to believe that the driver is someone other than the registered owner.[44] Suppose that an officer makes a stop on that basis but, as the officer approaches the vehicle, the officer is able to see that the driver is a female, while the registered owner is a male. May the officer nonetheless conduct the routine activities of a traffic stop, such as a license and registration check?

---

42. 499 U.S. 621 (1991).

43. State v. Mangum, ___ N.C. App. ___, ___, 795 S.E.2d 106, 116–17 (2016) (referencing Terry v. Ohio, 392 U.S. 1 (1968), and stating: "[D]efendant was not seized within the meaning of the Fourth Amendment until he stopped his vehicle on Pitt Street. When Lt. Andrews activated his blue lights, he asserted his authority and ordered defendant to pull over. Yet because defendant chose to continue driving, there was no submission to the officer's authority and therefore no seizure at that time. Rather, the *Terry* stop occurred approximately two minutes later, when defendant did in fact pull over. Accordingly, the trial court's reasonable suspicion inquiry properly took account of circumstances that arose after Lt. Andrews' activation of his blue lights but before defendant's actual submission to police authority."); State v. Atwater, ___ N.C. App. ___, 723 S.E.2d 582 (2012) (unpublished) (reasoning that "[r]egardless of whether [the officer] had a reasonable suspicion that defendant was involved in criminal activity prior to turning on his blue lights, defendant's subsequent actions [erratic driving and running two stop signs] gave [the officer] reasonable suspicion to stop defendant for traffic violations"); United States v. Swindle, 407 F.3d 562, 568–69 (2d Cir. 2005) (reluctantly concluding that a court may, in determining the constitutionality of a seizure, "consider[] events that occur[] after [a driver is] ordered to pull over" but before he or she complies); United States v. Smith, 217 F.3d 746, 750 (9th Cir. 2000) (relying on *Hodari D.* to reject the argument that "only the factors present up to the point when [the officer] turned on the lights of his patrol car can be considered in analyzing the validity of the stop"). *Cf.* United States v. McCauley, 548 F.3d 440, 443 (6th Cir. 2008) ("We determine whether reasonable suspicion existed at the point of seizure—not . . . at the point of *attempted* seizure."); United States v. Johnson, 212 F.3d 1313 (D.C. Cir. 2000) (similar). *Cf. generally* 4 Wayne R. LaFave, Search and Seizure § 9.4(d) n.198 (5th ed. 2012) (collecting cases).

44. State v. Hess, 185 N.C. App. 530, 534 (2007) ("[W]hen a police officer becomes aware that a vehicle being operated is registered to an owner with a suspended or revoked driver's license, and there is no evidence appearing to the officer that the owner is not the individual driving the automobile, reasonable suspicion exists to warrant an investigatory stop.").

Probably not. Most courts have ruled that the officer must let the driver go immediately,[45] perh ‿ps after a brief explanation of the nature of the mistake.[46] There is no North Carolina case squarely on point,[47] but in *State v. Kincaid*,[48] the court of appeals considered a situation where an officer stopped a motorist based on the officer's belief that the driver's license was suspended, then learned after a computer check that the license was valid. In passing, the court agreed with the defendant that "the reasonable suspicion the officer had in order to stop defendant for a possible revoked license would not be sufficient to detain defendant any longer than necessary to dispel the officer's suspicion."[49]

B. Common Fact Patterns

The appellate courts have issued rulings on whether certain common fact patterns involve reasonable suspicion sufficient to justify a traffic stop. This section summarizes some of those decisions.

1. Speeding

Many traffic stops based on speeding are supported in part by radar or other technological means as discussed above. However, an officer's visual estimate of a vehicle's speed is generally sufficient by itself to support a traffic stop for speeding.[50] If a vehicle is speeding only slightly or there are other reasons to doubt the officer's accuracy, an officer's visual estimate of speed may be insufficient to support a traffic stop.[51]

---

45. *See* 4 LaFave, *supra* note 43, § 9.3(c), at 510 n.162 (collecting cases); United States v. de la Cruz, 703 F.3d 1193, 1197 (10th Cir. 2013) (footnote omitted) (quoting United States v. Burleson, 657 F.3d 1040, 1045 (10th Cir. 2011)) (considering a case of this kind and concluding that "[o]nce reasonable suspicion has been dispelled, '[e]ven a very brief extension of the detention without consent or reasonable suspicion violates the Fourth Amendment' "). *But cf.* State v. Bonacker, 825 N.W.2d 916 (S.D. 2013) (distinguishing cases in which reasonable suspicion dissipated immediately and ruling that an officer did not violate the Fourth Amendment by asking to see a driver's license while investigating a suspected headlight violation; although the vehicle's occupants had explained that the vehicle's low beams were unusually bright and demonstrated that fact, the explanation was not so conclusive that the officer was required to terminate his investigation).

46. *See* 4 LaFave, *supra* note 43, § 9.3(c), at 510 n.162 (citing several cases so holding).

47. The issue was raised but not decided in *State v. Hernandez*, 227 N.C. App. 601 (2013) (not considering the issue on appeal because it was not preserved below).

48. 147 N.C. App. 94 (2001).

49. *Id.* at 98–99.

50. State v. Barnhill, 166 N.C. App. 228, 232 (2004) (upholding a traffic stop based on the estimate of an officer without any special training that the defendant was speeding 40 m.p.h. in a 25 m.p.h. zone, and stating that "it is well established in this State, that any person of ordinary intelligence, who had a reasonable opportunity to observe a vehicle in motion and judge its speed may testify as to his estimation of the speed of that vehicle"). *See also* United States v. Ludwig, 641 F.3d 1243, 1247 (10th Cir. 2011) (stating that "[i]t's long been the case that an officer's visual estimation can supply probable cause to support a traffic stop for speeding in appropriate circumstances," as where the officer "enjoyed a fine view" of the road and had substantial training and experience in speed enforcement). *Cf.* United States v. Gaffney, 789 F.3d 866, 868, 869–70 (8th Cir. 2015) (citation to trial court omitted) (noting that the court "has not resolved whether an officer's visual estimate of speed alone can furnish either probable cause or reasonable suspicion to stop a vehicle" but finding reasonable suspicion of speeding where an officer "was familiar with the area, thought [a driver] was speeding, and [the driver] 'braked hard' immediately after [the officer] u-turned to follow him," even though the officer had little experience with speeding stops and the trial court stated that it did "not place a great deal of confidence" in the officer's estimate).

51. *Compare* United States v. Sowards, 690 F.3d 583, 593–94 (4th Cir. 2012) (officer's visual estimate that the defendant was speeding 75 m.p.h. in a 70 m.p.h. zone was insufficient to support a traffic stop; the officer also expressed some difficulty with units of measurement), *with* United States v. Mubdi, 691 F.3d 334, 341 (4th Cir. 2012) (traffic stop was justified when two officers independently estimated that the defendant was speeding between 63 m.p.h. and 65 m.p.h. in a 55 m.p.h. zone), *vacated on other grounds*, ___ U.S. ___, 133 S. Ct. 2851 (2013).

2. Driving Slowly

Driving below the posted speed limit is not in itself unlawful. In fact, it is sometimes required by G.S. 20-141(a), which states that "[n]o person shall drive a vehicle on a highway or in a public vehicular area at a speed greater than is reasonable and prudent under the conditions then existing." On the other hand, in some circumstances driving slowly may constitute obstruction of traffic under G.S. 20-141(h) ("No person shall operate a motor vehicle on the highway at such a slow speed as to impede the normal and reasonable movement of traffic . . .") or may violate posted minimum speed limits under G.S. 20-141(c), which makes it unlawful to operate a passenger vehicle at less than certain minimum speeds indicated by appropriate signs. Furthermore, the fact that a driver is proceeding unusually slowly may contribute to reasonable suspicion that the driver is impaired.[52]

Whether slow speed alone is sufficient to provide reasonable suspicion of impairment is not completely settled in North Carolina. The state supreme court seemed to suggest that it might be sufficient in State v. Styles,[53] where the court stated that "law enforcement may observe certain facts that would, in the totality of the circumstances, lead a reasonable officer to believe a driver is impaired, such as weaving within the lane of travel or driving significantly slower than the speed limit." The court of appeals, however, stated that it is not sufficient in a subsequent unpublished decision, State v. Brown,[54] where it indicated that traveling 10 m.p.h. below the speed limit is not alone enough to create reasonable suspicion but found reasonable suspicion based on the combination of the defendant's speed, weaving, and the late hour. The weight of authority in other states suggests that slow speed alone is not sufficient to provide reasonable suspicion.[55]

It is also unclear just how slowly a driver must be travelling in order to raise suspicions. Of course, driving slightly under the posted limit is not suspicious.[56] Ten miles per hour under the limit, however, may be enough to contribute to suspicion.[57] Certainly, the more sustained and the more pronounced the slow driving, the greater the suspicion.

---

52. See, e.g., State v. Bonds, 139 N.C. App. 627, 628–29 (2000) (driver's blank look, slow speed, and the fact that he had his window down in cold weather provided reasonable suspicion; the opinion quotes the National Highway Traffic Safety Administration regarding the connection between slow speeds, blank looks, and driving while impaired (DWI)); State v. Aubin, 100 N.C. App. 628, 632 (1990) (fact that defendant slowed to 45 m.p.h. on I-95 and weaved within his lane supported reasonable suspicion of DWI); State v. Jones, 96 N.C. App. 389, 395 (1989) (although the defendant did not commit a traffic infraction, "his driving 20 miles per hour below the speed limit and weaving within his lane were actions sufficient to raise a suspicion of an impaired driver in a reasonable and experienced [officer's] mind").

53. 362 N.C. 412, 427 (2008).

54. 207 N.C. App. 377 (2010) (unpublished).

55. See, e.g., State v. Bacher, 867 N.E.2d 864, 867 (Ohio Ct. App. 2007) (holding that "slow travel alone [in that case, 23 m.p.h. below the speed limit on the highway] does not create a reasonable suspicion," and collecting cases from across the country).

56. State v. Canty, 224 N.C. App. 514 (2012) (fact that vehicle slowed to 59 m.p.h. in a 65 m.p.h. zone upon seeing officers did not provide reasonable suspicion).

57. Brown, 207 N.C. App. 377 (finding reasonable suspicion where defendant was driving 10 m.p.h. under the speed limit and weaving within a lane); State v. Bradshaw, 198 N.C. App. 703 (2009) (unpublished) (late hour, driving 10 m.p.h. below the limit, and abrupt turns provided reasonable suspicion).

3. Weaving

a. Across Lanes

G.S. 20-146(d)(1) requires that "[a] vehicle shall be driven as nearly as practicable entirely within a single lane and shall not be moved from such lane until the driver has first ascertained that such movement can be made with safety." Weaving across lanes of traffic generally violates this provision and supports a traffic stop.[58]

b. Within a Lane

Weaving within a single lane, by contrast, does not violate G.S. 20-146 and so is not itself a crime or an infraction. In some circumstances, however, weaving within a single lane may provide, or contribute to, reasonable suspicion that a driver is impaired or is driving carelessly.

Moderate weaving within a lane is to be expected from imperfect human drivers and so does not provide reasonable suspicion by itself. In *State v. Fields,*[59] the court of appeals held that an officer did not have reasonable suspicion that a driver was impaired where the driver "swerve[d] to the white line on the right side of the traffic lane" three times over a mile and a half. However, the court stated that weaving, "coupled with additional . . . facts," may provide reasonable suspicion.[60] The court cited cases involving additional facts, such as driving "significantly below the speed limit," driving at an unusually late hour, and driving in the proximity of drinking establishments as illustrations of the types of additional facts that might suffice.[61] Thus, *Fields* stands for the proposition that moderate weaving within a single lane does not provide reasonable suspicion, but that "weaving plus" may do so. *Fields* has been applied in cases such as *State v. Kochuk,*[62] where the court ruled that reasonable suspicion supported a stop where the defendant was weaving and it was 1:10 a.m.; *State v. Derbyshire,*[63] where the court held that weaving alone did not provide reasonable suspicion to support a stop, that driving at 10:05 p.m. on a Wednesday is "utterly ordinary" and insufficient to render weaving suspicious, and that having "very bright" headlights also was not suspicious; and *State v. Peele,*[64] where the court found no reasonable suspicion of DWI where an officer received an anonymous tip that defendant was "possibl[y]" driving while impaired, then saw the defendant "weave within his lane once."

---

58. *See, e.g.,* State v. Osterhoudt, 222 N.C. App. 620, 629 (2012) (where the "defendant crossed [a] double yellow line . . . he failed to stay in his lane and violated" G.S. 20-146(d)(1)); State v. Simmons, 205 N.C. App. 509, 525 (2010) (finding that a stop was supported by reasonable suspicion where the defendant "was not only weaving within his lane, but was also weaving across and outside the lanes of travel, and at one point actually ran off the road"). *But see* State v. Kochuk, 223 N.C. App. 301, 301 (2012) (dissent found reasonable suspicion but did so by applying the "weaving plus" framework discussed below, notwithstanding the fact that the defendant "cross[ed] over the dotted white line [separating freeway lanes], causing both wheels on the passenger side of the vehicle to cross into the right lane for [several] seconds, and then move[d] back into the middle lane"; state supreme court adopted analysis of dissenting opinion, see 366 N.C. 549 (2013)); State v. Derbyshire, 228 N.C. App. 670, 680 (2013) (footnote omitted) (holding that a stop was not supported by reasonable suspicion because it was based on only "one instance of weaving," even though "the right side of Defendant's tires crossed into the right-hand lane" during the weaving).

59. 195 N.C. App. 740, 741 (2009).

60. *Id.* at 744.

61. *Id.* at 746.

62. 366 N.C. 549.

63. 228 N.C. App. 670 (2013).

64. 196 N.C. App. 668, 669 (2009).

By contrast, severe weaving within a lane may be sufficient on its own to support reasonable suspicion. In *State v. Fields*[65]—a case unrelated to the case of the same name discussed in the preceding paragraph—the court of appeals upheld a traffic stop conducted by an officer who followed the defendant for three quarters of a mile and saw him "weaving in his own lane . . . sufficiently frequent[ly] and erratic[ly] to prompt evasive maneuvers from other drivers." The officer compared the defendant's vehicle to a "ball bouncing in a small room."[66] The pronounced extent of the weaving led the court of appeals to distinguish the precedents discussed in the preceding paragraph.[67] The courts have not yet firmly established the dividing line between moderate and severe weaving, but the fact that the weaving in the second *Fields* case impacted other motorists appeared to be a significant factor in the decision.

4. Sitting at a Stoplight

Remaining at a stoplight after the light turns green is not, in itself, a violation of the law. But, like weaving, it may provide or contribute to reasonable suspicion that the driver is impaired. The National Highway Traffic Safety Administration (NHTSA) posits:

> A driver whose vigilance has been impaired by alcohol also might respond more slowly than normal to a change in a traffic signal. For example, the vehicle might remain stopped for an unusually long period of time after the signal has turned green.[68]

When courts have considered motorists' delayed responses to traffic signals, they have typically given significant weight to the length of the delay, with a five- or ten-second delay causing much less concern than a more extended one.[69]

5. Unsafe Movement/Lack of Turn Signal

Under G.S. 20-154(a), "before starting, stopping or turning from a direct line[, a driver] shall first see that such movement can be made in safety . . . and whenever the operation of any other vehicle may be affected by such movement, shall give a signal as required." As discussed in greater detail in chapter 4, cases decided under this statute have focused on the phrase "the operation of any other vehicle may

---

65. 219 N.C. App. 385, 385–86 (2012).

66. *Id.* at 388.

67. *See also* State v. Otto, 366 N.C. 134, 138 (2012) (traffic stop justified by the defendant's "constant and continual" weaving at 11:00 p.m. on a Friday night).

68. U.S. Dept. of Transp., NHTSA, The Visual Detection of DWI Motorists 11 (Mar. 2010).

69. *Compare* State v. Barnard, 362 N.C. 244, 245 (2008) (determining that reasonable suspicion supported an officer's decision to stop the defendant where the defendant was waiting at a traffic light in a high-crime area, near several bars, at 12:15 a.m., and "[w]hen the light turned green, defendant remained stopped for approximately thirty seconds" before proceeding), *with* State v. Roberson, 163 N.C. App. 129, 134 (2004) (finding no reasonable suspicion where the defendant sat at a green light at 4:30 a.m., near several bars, for eight to ten seconds, and stating that "[a] motorist waiting at a traffic light can have her attention diverted for any number of reasons. . . . [Thus,] a time lapse of eight to ten seconds does not appear so unusual as to give rise to suspicion justifying a stop"). *See also* State v. Emory, 809 P.2d 522, 523–25 (Idaho Ct. App. 1991) (ruling that the fact that a driver "failed to move for five to six seconds" after a light turned green did not provide reasonable suspicion of impairment, notwithstanding an officer's testimony that "he was taught in training that forty percent of all people who have a slow response at a traffic signal may be under the influence of alcohol," because "[i]t is self-evident that motorists often pause at a stop sign or traffic light when their attention is distracted or preoccupied by outside influences").

be affected." Generally, the appellate courts have held that a driver need not signal when making a mandatory turn but must signal if the turn is optional and there is another vehicle following closely.[70]

6. Late Hour, High-Crime Area

The U.S. Supreme Court has held that presence in a high-crime area, "standing alone, is not a basis for concluding that [a suspect is] engaged in criminal conduct."[71] Although the stop in that case took place at noon, presence in a high-crime area at an unusually late hour is also alone insufficient to provide reasonable suspicion.[72] But the incidence of crime in the area and the hour of night are factors that, combined with others such as evasive action, may contribute to reasonable suspicion.[73] And when a place goes beyond merely being located in a high-crime neighborhood and instead rises to the level of being "a location with no use or purpose other than criminal activity," a person's presence at the place may weigh more heavily.[74]

7. Community Caretaking

The Court of Appeals of North Carolina recently recognized that officers may make some vehicle stops without reasonable suspicion of a crime or infraction, in the course of their responsibility to protect members of the community and to address potential safety threats. The court relied on this community caretaking doctrine as a basis for a vehicle stop in *State v. Smathers*.[75] In *Smathers*, an officer stopped the defendant to make sure that she was unharmed after her car hit a large animal that ran in front of her. The court held that in order for a stop to be justified under the community caretaking doctrine:

> [T]he State has the burden of proving that: (1) a search or seizure within the meaning of the Fourth Amendment has occurred; (2) if so, that under the totality of the circumstances an objectively reasonable basis for a community caretaking function is shown; and (3) if so, that the public need or interest outweighs the intrusion upon the privacy of the individual.[76]

---

70. *Compare* State v. Ivey, 360 N.C. 562, 565 (2006) (the defendant was not required to signal at what amounted to a right-turn-only intersection; a right turn was the "only legal movement he could make," and the vehicle behind him was likewise required to stop, then turn right, so the defendant's turn did not affect the trailing vehicle), *abrogated on other grounds by* State v. Styles, 362 N.C. 412 (2008) (discussed *infra* this note), *and* State v. Watkins, 220 N.C. App. 384, 389–90 (2012) (suggesting that there was insufficient evidence of unsafe movement where the defendant changed lanes without signaling while driving three to four car lengths in front of a police vehicle on a road with heavy traffic, because it was not clear that another vehicle was affected), *with Styles*, 362 N.C. at 416–17, (where the defendant changed lanes "immediately in front of" an officer, he violated the statute; "changing lanes immediately in front of another vehicle may affect the operation of the trailing vehicle"), *and* State v. McRae, 203 N.C. App. 319, 323 (2010) (similar).

71. Brown v. Texas, 443 U.S. 47, 52 (1979).

72. State v. Murray, 192 N.C. App. 684, 689–90 (2008) (no reasonable suspicion to stop defendant, who was driving in a commercial area with a high incidence of property crimes at 3:41 a.m.).

73. *Cf. In re* I.R.T., 184 N.C. App. 579, 585–86 (2007) (listing factors); State v. Mello, 200 N.C. App. 437, 446–47 (2009) (holding that the defendant's presence in a high-drug area, coupled with evasive action on the part of individuals seen interacting with the defendant, provided reasonable suspicion supporting a stop).

74. State v. Crandell, ___ N.C. App. ___, ___, 786 S.E.2d 789, 793 (2016) (discussing the defendant's presence at "Blazing Saddles," a burned-out building that an officer described as being "known for one thing and that is selling drugs and dealing in stolen property").

75. 232 N.C. App. 120 (2014).

76. *Id.* at 128–29.

The court further explained that in weighing the public need against the intrusion of privacy, a court should consider:

> (1) the degree of the public interest and the exigency of the situation; (2) the attendant circumstances surrounding the seizure, including time, location, the degree of overt authority and force displayed; (3) whether an automobile is involved; and (4) the availability, feasibility and effectiveness of alternatives to the type of intrusion actually accomplished.[77]

Applying this test, the court ruled that the stop was justified. Although the test established by the court is quite flexible and seems to have the potential to apply to many stops made by law enforcement officers, the court cautioned that the community caretaking doctrine should be applied narrowly. Therefore, the precise scope of the doctrine remains uncertain. The only North Carolina case applying *Smathers* in a motor vehicle context is *State v. Sawyers*,[78] where the court of appeals ruled that the community caretaking doctrine justified an officer's decision to stop a vehicle into which the defendant and another man, who appeared to be homeless, had dragged what appeared to be an intoxicated or unconscious woman.

Courts in other states have ruled that a stop was proper under the community caretaking doctrine when

- in the early morning, a passenger lifted her upper body through a vehicle's moonroof and waved her arms, possibly signaling distress or a need for assistance;[79]
- a vehicle "was traveling 20–25 miles per hour late at night on a deserted street with a posted speed limit of 40 miles per hour," causing an officer to worry that the driver may have had a stroke or suffered another medical problem;[80]
- a vehicle was in an "isolated location late at night" and had two flat tires;[81]
- an officer saw that the female passenger in a vehicle appeared to be unconscious and "did not look like she was in a sleeping position;"[82]
- a vehicle was parked near a curve, "half on the pavement, although [just] past the right fog line, and half off the road," with one turn signal flashing, causing an officer to believe that the vehicle was disabled.[83]

Other states' courts have found stops not to be justified under the community caretaking doctrine when

- a vehicle struck a metal object in the vehicle's lane of travel, causing "minor damage not affecting the drivability of the car;"[84]

---

77. *Id.* at 129.

78. ___ N.C. App. ___, 786 S.E.2d 753 (2016). Outside the motor vehicle context, the court of appeals recently ruled that the community caretaking doctrine did not justify an officer's decision to enter the backyard of a home and approach the back door after seeing a vehicle in the driveway with the doors standing open. State v. Huddy, ___ N.C. App. ___, 799 S.E.2d 650 (2017).

79. State v. Rohde, 864 N.W.2d 704 (Neb. Ct. App. 2015).

80. State v. Rinehart, 617 N.W.2d 842, 844 (S.D. 2000).

81. Dearmond v. State, 487 S.W.3d 708, 712 (Tex. App. 2016).

82. State v. Sheehan, 344. P.3d 1064, 1066 (N.M. Ct. App. 2014).

83. State v. Edwards, 945 A.2d 915, 916 (Vt. 2008).

84. State v. Kurth, 813 N.W.2d 270, 271 (Iowa 2012).

- an officer observed a pedestrian, walking unsteadily and sweating, enter the passenger side of a vehicle, and, although the passenger may have been ill, he exhibited only a "low level of distress" and did not present a serious danger to himself or others;[85]
- a vehicle was traveling 58–60 m.p.h. in the left lane of a 70 m.p.h. highway at 1:00 a.m. and did not move to the right lane when a trailing vehicle flashed its high beams several times.[86]

8. Tips

Whether information from a tipster provides reasonable suspicion to stop a vehicle depends on the totality of the circumstances. Whether the tipster is anonymous or identified is an important factor, so anonymous tips and non-anonymous tips are discussed separately below.

a. Anonymous Tips

Historically, courts have viewed anonymous tips with skepticism and have often found such tips insufficient to provide reasonable suspicion unless an officer has corroborated a significant portion of the information contained in the tip.[87] This approach was rooted in part in *Florida v. J.L.*,[88] a non–traffic stop case in which the U.S. Supreme Court stated that "[u]nlike a tip from a known informant whose reputation can be assessed and who can be held responsible if her allegations turn out to be fabricated . . . 'an anonymous tip alone seldom demonstrates the informant's basis of knowledge or veracity,' " and so rarely provides reasonable suspicion.[89]

However, the U.S. Supreme Court recently decided *Navarette v. California*,[90] in which it ruled that a motorist's 911 call, reporting that a specific vehicle had just run the caller off the road, was an anonymous tip that nonetheless sufficed to provide reasonable suspicion of impaired driving. The Court therefore upheld a stop of the described vehicle fifteen minutes later. In the course of its discussion, the Court first ruled that the tip was reliable. It reasoned that the caller claimed first-hand knowledge of the other vehicle's dangerous driving; that the call was "especially reliable" because it was contemporaneous with the dangerous driving; and that the call was made to 911, which "has some features [like the ability to record and caller ID] that allow for identifying and tracing callers, and thus provide some safeguards against making false reports with immunity."[91] Then the Court held that running another vehicle off the road "suggests lane-positioning problems, decreased vigilance,

---

85. People v. Madrid, 85 Cal. Rptr. 3d 900, 908 (Cal. Ct. App. 2008).

86. Trejo v. State, 76 So. 3d 684 (Miss. 2011).

87. State v. Coleman, 228 N.C. App. 76, 82 (2013) (a tip that the court treated as anonymous did not provide reasonable suspicion, in part because it "did not provide any way for [the investigating officer] to assess [the tipster's] credibility, failed to explain her basis of knowledge, and did not include any information concerning defendant's future actions"); State v. Blankenship, 230 N.C. App. 113, 114, 117 (2013) (taxi driver's anonymous call to 911, reporting that a specific red Ford Mustang, headed in a specific direction, was "driving erratically [and] running over traffic cones," was insufficient to support a stop of a red Mustang located less than two minutes later headed in the described direction; officers did not corroborate the bad driving and the tip had "limited but insufficient indicia of reliability"); State v. Johnson, 204 N.C. App. 259, 263 (2010) (stating that "[c]ourts have repeatedly recognized, as a general rule, the inherent unreliability of anonymous tips standing on their own" unless such a tip "itself possess[es] sufficient indicia of reliability, or [is] corroborated by [an] officer's investigation or observations"); State v. Peele, 196 N.C. App. 668, 673–74 (2009) (an anonymous tip that the defendant was driving recklessly, combined with an officer's observation of a single instance of weaving, was insufficient to give rise to reasonable suspicion).

88. 529 U.S. 266 (2000).

89. *Id.* at 270 (internal quotation marks, citation omitted).

90. 572 U.S. ___, 134 S. Ct. 1683 (2014).

91. *Id.* at ___, 134 S. Ct. at 1689.

impaired judgment, or some combination of those recognized drunk driving cues," and so provided reasonable suspicion of impairment.[92]

Because *Navarette* approvingly quoted the Court's prior statements to the effect that anonymous tips alone are rarely sufficient to provide reasonable suspicion, the opinion does not represent a complete change of course.[93] At the same time, the Court found reasonable suspicion based on a brief, anonymous 911 call that officers did little to corroborate, so *Navarette* signals a greater willingness to credit anonymous tips, if the totality of the circumstances support the credibility of a tip.[94]

Because the decision is relatively recent, it is unclear how far *Navarette* will extend. Will it apply when the tip is received through a means other than 911?[95] Will it apply when the tip concerns a completed traffic offense rather than an ongoing one like DWI?[96] These issues will need to be decided in future cases.

b. Non-Anonymous Tips

Where an informant identifies himself or herself in the course of providing a tip, or exposes his or her identity by speaking to an officer face to face, courts view the lack of anonymity as a factor supporting the reliability of a tip. For example, in *State v. Maready*,[97] a driver flagged down two officers to report that another vehicle was proceeding erratically. In the course of ruling that the officers' subsequent stop of the other vehicle was justified, the state supreme court stated:

> We reiterate that the overarching inquiry when assessing reasonable suspicion is always based on the *totality* of the circumstances. . . . When police act on the basis of an informant's tip, the indicia of the tip's reliability are certainly among the circumstances that must be considered in determining whether reasonable suspicion exists. . . .
> [W]e give significant weight to the fact that the minivan driver approached the deputies in person and gave them information at a time and place near to the scene of the alleged traffic violations. She would have had little time to fabricate her allegations

---

92. *Id.* at ___, 134 S. Ct. at 1691.

93. *Id.* at ___, 134 S. Ct. at 1688.

94. North Carolina's appellate courts could adhere to the previous line of authority by ruling that the North Carolina Constitution provides greater protection than the Fourth Amendment, but that is unlikely given the courts' repeated statements that the state and federal constitutions provide coextensive protection from unreasonable searches and seizures. State v. Verkerk, 229 N.C. App. 416, 432 (2013) (stating that "this Court and the [state] Supreme Court have clearly held that, as far as the substantive protections against unreasonable searches and seizures are concerned, the federal and state constitutions provide the same rights," and citing multiple cases holding that the two constitutions are coextensive in this regard), *rev'd on other grounds*, 367 N.C. 483 (2014).

95. In *United States v. Aviles-Vega*, 783 F.3d 69, 77 (1st Cir. 2015), the court found an anonymous tip from a motorist sufficiently reliable to provide reasonable suspicion even though the call was "made directly to the desk sergeant, rather than to a 911 operator." The motorist called to report that the occupants of another vehicle were passing a handgun back and forth, and the court believed that the circumstances suggested "that the caller was a concerned citizen, acting in good faith and reporting his direct observation of a crime committed in front of him."

96. In *State v. Rodriguez*, 852 N.W.2d 705, 714 (Neb. 2014), the court ruled that a 911 call by a person who claimed to have been pushed from a moving vehicle did not provide reasonable suspicion to support an investigative stop. The court distinguished *Navarette* in part as follows: "The caller did not report an ongoing crime and instead indicated an isolated past episode. The majority in *Navarette* found that the anonymous caller reported an ongoing crime, which finding was key to its decision. Such factor is not present in this case."

97. 362 N.C. 614 (2008).

against defendant. Moreover, in providing the tip through a face-to-face encounter with the sheriff's deputies, the minivan driver was not a completely anonymous informant. It is inconsequential to our analysis that the officers did not actually pause to record her license plate number or other identifying information. Not knowing whether the officers had already noted her tag number or if they would detain her for further questioning, and aware they could quickly assess the truth of her statements by stopping the silver Honda, the minivan driver willingly placed her anonymity at risk. This circumstance weighs in favor of deeming her tip reliable.[98]

The *Maready* court's focus on whether the informant "willingly placed her anonymity at risk" is consistent with how other courts have viewed information from an identifiable source.[99] Technological advances, including caller identification, have made it easier for law enforcement to determine the origins of many contacts, and citizens are generally aware of such technology. Thus, the argument for treating 911 callers who do not identify themselves by name as identifiable informants rather than anonymous tipsters is strengthening over time. For now, courts are wrestling with how to categorize such callers.[100]

9. Driver's Identity

"[W]hen a police officer becomes aware that a vehicle being operated is registered to an owner with a suspended or revoked driver's license, and there is no evidence appearing to the officer that the owner is not the individual driving the automobile, reasonable suspicion exists to warrant an investigatory stop."[101] Reasonable suspicion will not exist if it is apparent that the driver is not the owner—for

---

98. *Id.* at 619, 619–20 (footnote, citations omitted).

99. *See generally* United States v. Gomez, 623 F.3d 265, 270 (5th Cir. 2010) (noting "the presumption of reliability this court attaches to citizen reports to police" and noting the controversy regarding whether to classify a citizen who calls 911 and provides his first name to the operator as an anonymous tipster); United States v. Quarles, 330 F.3d 650, 655 (4th Cir. 2003) (noting that "[t]he fact that [a caller] was identifiable lends support to his credibility and reliability" because an identified caller can be held accountable if he or she provides false information).

100. *Compare* State v. Hudgins, 195 N.C. App. 430, 435 (2009) (a driver called the police to report that he was being followed, then complied with the dispatcher's instructions to go to a specific location to allow an officer to intercept the trailing vehicle; when the officer stopped the second vehicle, the caller also stopped briefly; the defendant, who was driving the second vehicle, was impaired; the stop was proper, in part because "by calling on a cell phone and remaining at the scene, [the] caller placed his anonymity at risk"), *with* State v. Blankenship, 230 N.C. App. 113, 114, 116 (2013) (treating a taxi driver's 911 call as an anonymous tip where the taxi driver did not give his name, even though "when an individual calls 911, the 911 operator can determine the phone number used to make the call" and "the 911 operator was later able to identify the taxicab driver"; the court noted that "the officers did not meet [the taxi driver] face-to-face" and found that the tip failed to provide reasonable suspicion to support a stop of the other driver), *and* State v. Coleman, 228 N.C. App. 76, 76 (2013) (treating a telephone tip as anonymous even though "the communications center obtained the caller's name . . . and phone number").

101. State v. Hess, 185 N.C. App. 530, 534 (2007). *See also* State v. Johnson, 204 N.C. App. 259, 265 (2010) ("[T]he officers did lawfully stop the vehicle after discovering that the registered owner's driver's license was suspended."). Courts in other states have generally reached the same conclusion. *See, e.g.*, State v. Weber, 139 So. 3d 519, 522 (La. 2014) (citation omitted) (stating that "it is objectively reasonable to assume, even to a fair probability that might support a finding of probable cause . . . [that] the owner of a vehicle is also the driver" and collecting cases); State v. Owens, 599 N.E.2d 859, 860 (Ohio Ct. App. 1991) ("Officer Kiser received information that the owner of the Volkswagen was a six-foot-one, one-hundred-ninety-pound, middle-aged black male, and that his driving privileges had been suspended. Kiser had the opportunity to observe the driver as the Volkswagen passed his cruiser and as he followed the car, and concluded that the driver

example, if the driver is a female while the registered owner is a male. Presumably, an officer would also be justified in stopping a vehicle if the officer were to determine that the registered owner was the subject of an outstanding arrest warrant or other criminal process and if the officer does not possess information suggesting that someone other than the owner of the vehicle was driving.[102]

---

matched the description of the unlicensed owner. It is reasonable to assume that the driver of a vehicle is most often the owner of the vehicle. In this situation the officer acted on specific and articulable facts which, together with their rational inferences, reasonably warranted him to stop the vehicle and question the driver concerning a possible violation of the law.").

102. In *State v. Watkins*, 220 N.C. App. 384, 386 (2012), the court of appeals upheld a stop based in part on the fact that the registered owner of a vehicle had outstanding warrants even though the officers involved in the case were "pretty sure" that the driver was *not* the owner. The court noted that the defendant "was driving a car registered to another person," that the registered owner had outstanding warrants, and that there was a passenger in the vehicle who could have been the registered owner. *Id.* at 390.

Chapter 2

Checkpoints

Chapter 2

Checkpoints

I. Introduction

Law enforcement officers may use checkpoints to detect violations of motor vehicle laws,[1] so long as the checkpoints satisfy certain constitutional and statutory requirements. A typical motor vehicle checkpoint involves a brief stop of a series of motorists who are traveling along a roadway, without any particularized suspicion of wrongdoing. Such stops are seizures for purposes of the Fourth Amendment,[2] but notwithstanding the rule that seizures are "ordinarily unreasonable in the absence of individualized suspicion of wrongdoing,"[3] courts have upheld the use of certain motor vehicle checkpoints.[4] This point is worthy of emphasis. While checkpoints may be unremarkable to a modern motorist, they do represent an exception to a general rule of the Fourth Amendment, and the United States Supreme Court has been careful to limit the bounds of the exception. In addition to the limitations on checkpoints imposed by constitutional law, North Carolina regulates the operation of checkpoints by statute.[5] This chapter discusses the constitutional and statutory law of motor vehicle checkpoints.

II. Constitutional Limits

A. *United States v. Martinez-Fuerte*: U.S. Supreme Court Authorizes Border Checkpoints

The first major checkpoint decision by the U.S. Supreme Court was *United States v. Martinez-Fuerte*,[6] where the Court ruled that permanent immigration checkpoints sixty-six miles from the border between the United States and Mexico did not violate the Fourth Amendment. In *Martinez-Fuerte*, it

---

1. It also is legal to use checkpoints for purposes other than detecting violations of motor vehicle laws in certain circumstances. *See, e.g.,* United States v. Martinez-Fuerte, 428 U.S. 543 (1976) (finding an immigration checkpoint lawful). However, except for incidental reference to the use of checkpoints for other purposes, the primary focus of this chapter is the use of checkpoints for the purpose of enforcing North Carolina motor vehicle laws.

2. Mich. Dep't of State Police v. Sitz, 496 U.S. 444, 450 (1990).

3. City of Indianapolis v. Edmond, 531 U.S. 32, 37 (2000).

4. *Id.*

5. *See* Chapter 20, Section 16.3A of the North Carolina General Statutes (hereinafter G.S.).

6. 428 U.S. 543 (1976).

was "agreed that checkpoint stops are 'seizures' within the meaning of the Fourth Amendment."[7] The Court, however, rejected the defendants' contention that some quantum of individualized suspicion was an irreducible prerequisite to a constitutionally valid seizure.[8] The Court reasoned that the importance and difficulty of enforcing the immigration laws meant that "the need to make routine checkpoint stops [was] great," while the brief detention of travelers occasioned by a checkpoint stop meant that "the consequent intrusion on Fourth Amendment interests [was] quite limited."[9] Balancing the government's interest in enforcing the immigration laws against the associated intrusion on individuals' Fourth Amendment interests, the Court found that the checkpoint stops at issue did not violate the Fourth Amendment.[10] Following *Martinez-Fuerte*, the use of a balancing analysis to test the reasonableness of a checkpoint stop under the Fourth Amendment was refined and became a hallmark of the Court's checkpoint jurisprudence.

B. *Delaware v. Prouse*: U.S. Supreme Court Rejects Roving Patrols

The next significant Supreme Court decision related to checkpoints arose in *Delaware v. Prouse*,[11] a case that did not involve checkpoints at all, but instead addressed suspicionless stops by roving officers. The *Prouse* Court held that roving, suspicionless stops by officers for the purpose of checking a driver's license and registration violate the Fourth Amendment. In evaluating the degree of intrusion of a roving stop upon an individual's Fourth Amendment interests and balancing this intrusion against the state's interest in promoting public safety upon the roads, the Court contrasted roving stops with checkpoints. The Court found "insufficient resemblance between sporadic and random stops of individual vehicles making their way through city traffic and those stops occasioned by roadblocks where all vehicles are brought to a halt or to a near halt, and all are subjected to a show of the police power of the community."[12] The Court viewed roving stops as creating more fear and anxiety among motorists than do the brief and regularized stops associated with checkpoints. Thus, the Court characterized roving stops as relatively greater intrusions upon motorists' Fourth Amendment rights and found that they failed the balancing test that checkpoints pass.

C. *Michigan v. Sitz*: Sobriety Checkpoints Are Constitutional

The Supreme Court considered the constitutionality of checkpoints to detect impaired driving in *Michigan Department of State Police v. Sitz*,[13] holding that properly administered "sobriety checkpoints" are constitutional. The Court stated that "the magnitude of the drunken driving problem" in the nation was beyond serious dispute and found that a brief checkpoint stop was merely a slight intrusion upon motorists.[14] Explicitly endorsing a three-prong balancing analysis derived

---

7. *Id.* at 556.
8. *Id.* at 561–62.
9. *Id.* at 557.
10. *Id.* at 562. The balancing analysis tests whether a checkpoint stop is a reasonable seizure under the Fourth Amendment. This point is implicit in the *Martinez-Fuerte* opinion and is explicit in the Court's subsequent opinions. *See, e.g.*, Mich. Dep't of State Police v. Sitz, 496 U.S. 444, 450 (1990) (given that checkpoint stops are Fourth Amendment seizures, "[t]he question thus becomes whether such seizures are 'reasonable' ").
11. 440 U.S. 648 (1979).
12. *Id.* at 657.
13. 496 U.S. 444.
14. *Id.* at 451.

from *Brown v. Texas*[15] as the test by which to evaluate the constitutionality of checkpoints,[16] the Court weighed the state's interest in preventing impaired driving, the extent to which checkpoints advance that interest, and the degree of intrusion on motorists' freedom associated with a brief stop. The Court concluded that the balance weighed in favor of the use of sobriety checkpoints, at least as a general matter,[17] and that they were constitutionally permissible.

D. *Indianapolis v. Edmond*: "Ordinary Criminal Activity" Checkpoints Are Unconstitutional

The Supreme Court's next checkpoint decision was *City of Indianapolis v. Edmond*,[18] where the Court ruled that checkpoints could not be used to detect drug offenses or other "ordinary criminal wrongdoing." Distinguishing *Martinez-Fuerte* as dependent on the "particular context" of border enforcement, and distinguishing *Sitz* as involving an "immediate, vehicle-bound threat to life and limb," the Court stated that its "checkpoint cases have recognized only limited exceptions to the general rule that a seizure must be accompanied by some measure of individualized suspicion."[19] Because allowing drug or crime checkpoints would cause the exceptions to swallow the rule, the Court declined to permit them.

E. *Illinois v. Lidster*: Certain Information-Gathering Checkpoints Are Constitutional

Finally, in *Illinois v. Lidster*,[20] the Supreme Court ruled that checkpoints designed to gather information regarding a recently committed crime are constitutional under certain circumstances. The Court viewed such checkpoints as an important tool in the law enforcement toolbox and as unlikely "to provoke anxiety or to prove intrusive," as they are likely to be brief and not focused on eliciting self-incriminating information from the subject of the stop. The checkpoint in *Lidster* was established one week after a fatal hit and run, at the location where the incident took place and at the same time of night. The Court did not attempt to set out general rules for when information-seeking checkpoints are permitted, but did signal that they should be used sparingly, stating that "the Fourth Amendment's normal insistence that the stop be reasonable in context will still provide an important legal limitation on police use of this kind of information-seeking checkpoint."[21]

F. Synthesizing the U.S. Supreme Court Cases

Together, the cases establish that motor vehicle checkpoints may constitutionally be used for several purposes. Because border enforcement is uncommon in North Carolina and because information-gathering checkpoints are not prevalent, this chapter will focus mainly on checkpoints that are

---

15. 443 U.S. 47 (1979).

16. *Sitz*, 496 U.S. at 450 (identifying *Brown* and *Martinez-Fuerte* as the "relevant authorities"). The *Brown* test is discussed in more detail *infra* section III.

17. *Id.* at 450, 450–51 (emphasizing that the issue before the Court was "only the use of sobriety check-points generally" and that the Court was addressing "only the initial stop of each motorist . . . and the associated preliminary questioning and observation by checkpoint officers").

18. 531 U.S. 32 (2000).

19. *Id.* at 38, 43, 41.

20. 540 U.S. 419 (2004).

21. *Id.* at 426.

established for the purpose of detecting violations of the motor vehicle laws, such as impaired driving, driving without a valid license, and the like.

III. Framework for Analyzing Whether a Checkpoint Is Constitutional

The Supreme Court cases discussed above have produced a generally accepted two-step framework for determining the constitutionality of a motor vehicle checkpoint:

> In evaluating the constitutionality of a checkpoint, a reviewing court must first determine the primary programmatic purpose of the checkpoint under *City of Indianapolis v. Edmond*, 531 U.S. 32 (2000), and if the purpose is valid, must consider whether the checkpoint was reasonable under the balancing test articulated in *Brown v. Texas*, 443 U.S. 47 (1979).[22]

The burden is on the state to establish the constitutionality of a challenged checkpoint.[23]

A. Primary Programmatic Purpose

1. Proper and Improper Purposes

The Supreme Court has carefully limited the scope of checkpoints in light of the exception they represent to the Fourth Amendment's general requirement that seizures be based on individualized suspicion.[24] The Court ruled in *Sitz* that officers may establish a checkpoint for the purpose of detecting impaired driving.[25] The Court suggested in *Prouse* that checkpoints also may be a proper method for detecting license and registration violations,[26] and the North Carolina Court of Appeals has confirmed the propriety of "checkpoints designed to uncover drivers' license and vehicle registration violations."[27] The Supreme Court ruled in *Lidster* that officers may establish a checkpoint to gather information about a recently committed crime that, as a fatal hit and run, itself implicated roadway safety. Additionally, the Court stated in *Edmond* that "the Fourth Amendment would almost certainly permit [a checkpoint] set up to thwart an imminent terrorist attack or to catch a dangerous criminal who is likely to flee by way of a particular route."[28] In the context of motor vehicle checkpoints, this is a comprehensive list of the proper primary purposes so far identified by either the U.S. Supreme Court

---

22. State v. Veazey, 201 N.C. App. 398, 402 (2009) (citations omitted).

23. State v. Tarlton, 146 N.C. App. 417, 420 (2001) (citation omitted) ("Defendant correctly asserts that in a suppression hearing, the State has the burden to demonstrate the admissibility of the challenged evidence. In the case *sub judice*, defendant challenged the admission of the evidence obtained pursuant to the checkpoint stop. The State had the burden to demonstrate that the checkpoint stop was valid. The trial court found that the State had met its burden and the checkpoint in the present case was constitutional.").

24. *See, e.g., Edmond*, 531 U.S. at 41 ("[O]ur checkpoint cases have recognized only limited exceptions to the general rule that a seizure must be accompanied by some measure of individualized suspicion.").

25. 496 U.S. 444, 455 (1990).

26. 440 U.S. 648, 663 (1979).

27. State v. Veazey, 191 N.C. App. 181, 189 (2008).

28. 531 U.S. at 44.

or a North Carolina appellate court. By contrast, the U.S. Supreme Court has ruled that checkpoints may not be established for the purpose of general crime control.[29]

The preceding discussion listing the proper primary purposes so far identified by the courts in the context of motor vehicle laws is not meant to suggest that those purposes are the only purposes for which a checkpoint may be properly established. The Supreme Court stated in *Edmond* that it did not mean to "limit the purposes that may justify a checkpoint program to any rigid set of categories."[30] The Court further stated that "there are circumstances that may justify a law enforcement checkpoint where the primary purpose would otherwise, but for some emergency, relate to ordinary crime control."[31] Thus, a court may be called upon to decide whether a novel primary purpose for a checkpoint is proper.[32]

In making a determination of whether a novel primary purpose is proper, it is useful to note that the Supreme Court has identified a "common thread of highway safety" running through its catalog of proper primary purposes[33] and also has expressed willingness to account for circumstantial exigencies when they arise.[34] As another guidepost on the issue of proper primary purposes, courts have recognized that checkpoints are particularly appropriate tools for detecting motor vehicle offenses that are difficult to discover "simply by observing a vehicle during normal road travel."[35] For example, in *Martinez-Fuerte* the Court in part justified its conclusion that the checkpoint at issue was constitutional on the basis that "[a] requirement that stops . . . always be based on reasonable suspicion would be impractical because the flow of traffic tends to be too heavy to allow the particularized study of a given car that would enable it to be identified as a possible carrier of illegal aliens."[36] While this latter category may be a helpful guidepost, courts have upheld checkpoint stops for violations such as impaired driving and expired registration, offenses which may be discovered by observation. Again, as the Court noted in *Edmond*, proper primary purposes do not necessarily fall into a rigid set of categories.

As a practical matter, many checkpoints are conducted for the purpose of detecting impaired driving or license and registration violations. Therefore, whether checkpoints conducted for a novel purpose are constitutional may be an academic question.

---

29. Technically, a court must determine the *primary programmatic purpose* of a contested checkpoint. The focus on the primary purpose is important because "a checkpoint with an unlawful primary purpose will not become constitutional when coupled with a lawful secondary purpose." State v. Gabriel, 192 N.C. App. 517, 520 (2008).

30. 531 U.S. at 44.

31. *Id.*

32. As an example of a novel primary purpose, the state court of appeals has stated that "it is unclear whether a primary purpose of finding any and all *motor vehicle* violations is a lawful primary purpose." *Veazey*, 191 N.C. App. at 189. G.S. 20-16.3A(a) authorizes law enforcement agencies to conduct checkpoints "to determine compliance with [G.S. Chapter 20]," and, thus, appears to permit checkpoints for the purpose of detecting any motor vehicle violation. It is theoretically possible that a court could find that the statute goes beyond what is constitutionally acceptable.

33. *Edmond*, 531 U.S. at 40. Indeed, the Court explicitly stated in *Edmond* that there is a "difference in the Fourth Amendment significance of highway safety interests and the general interest in crime control." *Id.*

34. *Id.* at 44.

35. *See, e.g., Veazey*, 191 N.C. App. at 189–90 (so stating).

36. 428 U.S. 543, 557 (1976).

2. Establishing the Primary Purpose of a Checkpoint

If there is no evidence to the contrary, the state may establish the purpose of the checkpoint simply by having an officer who participated in planning or operating the checkpoint testify about it.[37] If there is no evidence to contradict the officer's testimony, it is sufficient to show the checkpoint's purpose. The testifying officer does not have to be the officer who supervised or approved the checkpoint. In *Edmond*, the Supreme Court stated that "the purpose inquiry . . . is to be conducted only at the programmatic level and is not an invitation to probe the minds of individual officers acting at the scene."[38] Defendants challenging checkpoints sometimes rely on this language as supporting the notion that a supervisor must testify. However, the Court's statement does not mean that it is necessary that a supervisor, rather than a field officer, testify to the purpose of a checkpoint. Rather, the Court appears to have intended to simply reiterate its earlier holding in *Whren v. United States* that the subjective intentions of individual officers "play no role in ordinary . . . Fourth Amendment analysis."[39] An illustrative North Carolina case on this issue is *State v. Burroughs*.[40] In *Burroughs*, the trial court found the testimony of a non-supervisory officer insufficient to establish the primary programmatic purpose of a checkpoint. On review, the court of appeals stated that this was a misapplication of the court's precedent on the issue and ruled that the officer's testimony was sufficient to establish that the primary purpose of the checkpoint was lawful, given that there was no evidence to the contrary.[41] On this point, it may be appropriate to be mindful of the potential for distinction between a particular officer's subjective intentions at a checkpoint and the objective purpose of the checkpoint as revealed by the totality of the available evidence.

In cases "where there is evidence in the record that could support a finding of either a lawful or unlawful purpose, a trial court cannot rely solely on an officer's bare statements as to a checkpoint's purpose" but instead must carry out a close review of that purpose.[42] In such a case, the court must make findings regarding the actual purpose of the checkpoint and must reach a conclusion as to whether the purpose is lawful.[43] Evidence sufficient to trigger a searching review may consist, for

---

37. *See, e.g., Veazey*, 191 N.C. App. at 187 ("Our Court has previously held that where there is no evidence in the record to contradict the State's proffered purpose for a checkpoint, a trial court may rely on the testifying police officer's assertion of a legitimate primary purpose."); State v. Townsend, 236 N.C. App. 456, 468–69 (2014) (finding that a checkpoint had a proper purpose based on the testimony of a supervisory officer "that the main purpose of the checkpoint was to check for DWIs," that the location of the checkpoint was based on the number of impaired driving offenses in the area, and that the timing of the checkpoint was based on the availability of a mobile breath alcohol testing lab); State v. Kostick, 233 N.C. App. 62, 74–75, 75 (2014) (officers testified that two checkpoints were established "to check all vehicles leaving [an area] for potential DWI, driver's license, insurance, and unsafe driving violations," and "[a]s defendant presented no evidence in the record to contradict the State's proffered purpose for the roadblock, the trial court could rely on the testifying police officers' assertions of a legitimate primary purpose").

38. 531 U.S. at 48.

39. 517 U.S. 806, 813 (1996).

40. 185 N.C. App. 496 (2007).

41. *Id.* at 498–503. *Cf. Kostick*, 233 N.C. App. at 74–75 (determining the primary programmatic purpose of a checkpoint based on the testimony of officers with no supervisory responsibilities that is noted in the opinion).

42. *Veazey*, 191 N.C. App. at 187.

43. State v. Jarrett, 203 N.C. App. 675, 678 (2010) ("Because variations existed in [the officer's] testimony regarding the primary purpose of the checkpoint, the trial court was required to make findings regarding the actual primary purpose."); *Veazey*, 191 N.C. App. at 190 (given the conflicting evidence regarding the purpose of the checkpoint, "the trial court was required to make findings regarding the actual primary purpose of

example, of an officer's conflicting testimony about the purpose of a checkpoint,[44] or of evidence that the checkpoint was conducted in a manner suggestive of an improper purpose.[45] For example, in *State v. Nolan*,[46] the court of appeals concluded that the trial court properly conducted a searching review of the primary purpose of a checkpoint where an officer testified both that the purpose of the checkpoint was "to stop subjects from driving while impaired" and to check for license violations, but also that officers would be looking for weapons, drugs, and other criminal violations.[47] Testimony established that one officer would approach stopped vehicles to examine drivers for signs of impairment and to check licenses and registrations, while another officer would look for other violations of the law.[48] A narcotics K-9 officer also was present at the checkpoint.[49] The trial court found that the primary purpose of the checkpoint was to detect impaired drivers and concluded that this purpose was proper, a ruling upheld on appeal.

3. Factors Indicative of Purpose

Among the factors that courts have recognized as indicative of the primary programmatic purpose of a checkpoint are the following:

- Officers' testimony about the purpose of the checkpoint[50]
- Statements in the checkpoint plan regarding the purpose of the checkpoint[51]
- The manner in which the checkpoint was conducted[52]
- The presence of a mobile breath alcohol testing lab (BATmobile)[53]
- The duties normally assigned to the officers who participated in the checkpoint[54]

---

the checkpoint and it was required to reach a conclusion regarding whether this purpose was lawful"); State v. Gabriel, 192 N.C. App. 517, 521 (2008) (same); State v. Rose, 170 N.C. App. 284, 285 (2005) (same).

44. *Jarrett*, 203 N.C. App. at 678 (determination of purpose required "[b]ecause variations existed in [the officer's] testimony regarding the primary purpose of the checkpoint"); *Veazey*, 191 N.C. App. at 189 (officer testified both that the checkpoint was for the purpose of detecting motor vehicle violations and for the purpose of detecting all criminal violations); *Gabriel*, 192 N.C. App. at 521 (officer testified both that the checkpoint was established because of several recent robberies in the area and in order to detect motor vehicle violations).

45. *Rose*, 170 N.C. App. at 290–93 (questioning the purpose of a checkpoint because most of the officers operating the checkpoint were narcotics officers, and when a vehicle was stopped, one of the officers would walk around the vehicle and scan its interior).

46. 211 N.C. App. 109 (2011).

47. *Id.* at 117–18.

48. *Id.*

49. *Id.*

50. This factor is discussed above.

51. *See, e.g., Nolan*, 211 N.C. App. at 118 ("When the officers' testimony [regarding the purpose of a checkpoint] is supplemented by a written plan, then the evidence must be viewed in its entirety."). For a more extensive discussion of checkpoint plans, see *infra* section IV.A.

52. *Compare* State v. Jarrett, 203 N.C. App. 675, 678–79 (2010) (finding a proper purpose in part because the checkpoint was actually conducted in compliance with the checkpoint policy: every car was stopped, blue lights were activated, and a supervisor was present), *with* State v. Rose, 170 N.C. App. 284, 292 (2005) (questioning the constitutionality of a checkpoint where "one officer would . . . ask for the license and registration, while a second officer would scan the inside of the vehicle and walk around it," in an apparent effort to look for "possible criminal activity" unrelated to the motor vehicle laws).

53. State v. Townsend, 236 N.C. App. 456, 468 (2014) (noting, in discussing the purpose of a checkpoint, that "the date for the checkpoint had been selected almost a year prior to that date based on when the [Breath] Alcohol Testing mobile lab would be available").

54. *See, e.g., Rose*, 170 N.C. App. at 290 (noting, in the course of remanding to the trial court for findings regarding the primary purpose of a checkpoint, that "[f]our of the five officers conducting the checkpoint

The manner in which a checkpoint is conducted may bear upon the primary purpose of a checkpoint as well as the severity of the checkpoint's interference with individual liberty, an issue discussed in more detail below.

4. Secondary and Multiple Purposes

If the primary purpose of a checkpoint is unlawful, a lawful secondary purpose will not render it constitutional.[55] However, if the primary purpose of a checkpoint is lawful, the fact that officers remain alert for crimes unrelated to that purpose does not invalidate the checkpoint.[56]

Even in cases where there is some evidence of an impermissible purpose motivating a checkpoint, courts have often found that the primary purpose was a lawful one. For example, in *State v. McDonald*,[57] the court of appeals considered a checkpoint that was administered pursuant to a plan that listed the purpose of the checkpoint as "[t]o increase police presence in the targeted area while checking for Operator's License and Vehicle Registration violations." The court rejected the defendant's claim that the statement regarding increasing police presence showed that the true purpose of the checkpoint was general crime control, noting that the "reference to increasing police presence was linked to the permissible purpose of checking for driver's license and vehicle registration violations."[58] Similarly, in *State v. Nolan*,[59] several officers made somewhat conflicting statements regarding the primary purpose of a checkpoint, sometimes emphasizing detection of DWIs and license and registration violations, but other times stating that they would be looking for weapons, drugs, and other crimes. The court of appeals affirmed the trial court's conclusion that the primary purpose was the proper one of detecting impaired driving, relying in part on the written checkpoint plan, which emphasized motor vehicle violations, to resolve any ambiguity in the officers' testimony. The court of appeals stated that "[w]hen the officers' testimony is supplemented by a written plan, then the evidence must be viewed in its entirety."[60]

---

were detectives with the Narcotics Division," while the fifth was a patrol officer). *See also* Jeff Welty, *Drug Dogs and Checkpoints*, N.C. Crim. L., UNC Sch. of Gov't Blog (Mar. 30, 2015), http://nccriminallaw .sog.unc.edu/drug-dogs-and-checkpoints/ (indicating that presence of a drug dog at a checkpoint does not necessarily establish that the checkpoint has an improper purpose, but that using a drug dog on every car would strongly suggest an improper purpose).

55. State v. Veazey, 191 N.C. App. 181, 189 (2008) ("[I]t is also clear that a checkpoint whose primary purpose is to find any and all criminal violations is unlawful, even if police have secondary objectives related to highway safety.").

56. *Jarrett*, 203 N.C. App. at 678 (ruling that a checkpoint had a permissible primary purpose where an officer testified that the purpose was to detect license and registration violations, even though the officer acknowledged on cross-examination that officers were also looking for "evidence that's in plain view of other crimes"). *See also* City of Indianapolis v. Edmond, 531 U.S. 32, 48 (2000) ("[P]olice officers [may] act appropriately upon information that they properly learn during a checkpoint stop justified by a lawful primary purpose, even where such action may result in the arrest of a motorist for an offense unrelated to that purpose.").

57. 239 N.C. App. 559, 561 (2015).

58. *Id*. at 568.

59. 211 N.C. App. 109, 117–18 (2011).

60. *Id*. at 118.

B. Balancing Test

If the primary purpose of a checkpoint is permissible, a court considering the constitutionality of the checkpoint must then consider whether the checkpoint was conducted in a reasonable manner under the Fourth Amendment. That requires the court to "weigh the public's interest in the checkpoint against the individual's Fourth Amendment privacy interest,"[61] considering

   (1) the gravity of the public interest served by the checkpoint,
   (2) the extent to which the checkpoint advances that interest, and
   (3) the severity of the checkpoint's interference with individual liberty.

If these considerations weigh on balance in favor of the public interest, "the checkpoint is reasonable and therefore constitutional."[62] This three-part analysis is sometimes called the *Brown* test, after the U.S. Supreme Court decision *Brown v. Texas*,[63] in which the prongs were first enunciated.

1. The Gravity of the Public Interest Served by the Checkpoint

The first of the three prongs of the balancing test looks to the purpose of the checkpoint and assesses the importance of that purpose to the public. Courts have recognized that the public has a "strong interest" in the enforcement of the motor vehicle laws.[64] This prong typically plays a minor role in the three-part analysis for two reasons. First, courts have stated that each of the explicitly recognized proper primary purposes for which a checkpoint may be established implicate significant public interests.[65] Second, in cases involving a primary purpose not already declared proper by binding precedent, this prong potentially would be subsumed as an analytical matter by the initial determination of whether the checkpoint has a lawful primary purpose.[66] Though possible, it seems unlikely that a court working within the two-step framework for evaluating the constitutionality of a checkpoint would first conclude that a checkpoint has a lawful primary purpose but go on to determine that the public does not have a strong interest in that purpose.[67] More important to the

---

61. *McDonald*, 239 N.C. App. at 566 (quoting State v. Veazey, 191 N.C. App. 181, 185 (2008)).

62. State v. Ashworth, ___ N.C. App. ___, ___, 790 S.E.2d 173, 180 (2016).

63. 443 U.S. 47 (1979). In *Brown*, the Court considered whether an officer could stop a pedestrian based on a hunch that the individual was involved in illegal activity, then require the person to identify himself under Texas's stop-and-identify statute. In the course of answering the question in the negative, the Court stated that determining "[t]he reasonableness of seizures that are less intrusive than a traditional arrest . . . involves a weighing of the gravity of the public concerns served by the seizure, the degree to which the seizure advances the public interest, and the severity of the interference with individual liberty." *Id.* at 50–51.

64. *See, e.g., Veazey*, 191 N.C. App. at 191 (internal quotation marks, citations omitted) ("Both the United States Supreme Court as well as our Courts have suggested that license and registration checkpoints advance an important purpose. The United States Supreme Court has also noted that states have a vital interest in ensuring compliance with other types of motor vehicle laws that promote public safety on the roads.").

65. *See, e.g.*, Mich. Dep't of State Police v. Sitz, 496 U.S. 444, 451 (1990) ("No one can seriously dispute the . . . States' interest in eradicating [drunken driving]"); *Veazey*, 191 N.C. App. at 191 (internal quotation marks, citation omitted) ("Both the United States Supreme Court as well as our Courts have suggested that license and registration checkpoints advance an important purpose.); Illinois v. Lidster, 540 U.S. 419, 427 (2004) (public's interest in finding perpetrator of fatal hit and run was "grave").

66. *Cf.* State v. Rose, 170 N.C. App. 284, 294 (2005) (referencing City of Indianapolis v. Edmond, 531 U.S. 32 (2000)) ("This factor is addressed by first identifying the primary programmatic purpose as required by *Edmond* and then assessing the importance of the particular stop to the public.").

67. As discussed above, the Supreme Court has identified a common thread of highway safety running through the cases where it has found a proper primary purpose justifying a checkpoint and also has expressed a willingness to allow checkpoints in exigent circumstances. It seems reasonable that a court could determine relatively easily that there is a strong public interest in a checkpoint serving such purposes.

three-prong balancing analysis is the extent to which the checkpoint advances the public interest and the severity of the checkpoint's interference with individual liberty. Though typically a relatively minor point of analysis, a trial judge passing upon the reasonableness of a checkpoint nevertheless must make findings and conclusions regarding this prong.[68]

2. The Extent to Which the Checkpoint Advances the Public Interest

The second prong of the balancing test examines the extent to which the checkpoint advances the public interest. There is not a substantial amount of law from the U.S. Supreme Court regarding how this prong of the balancing test should be analyzed in the context of checkpoints.[69] *Martinez-Fuerte* and *Prouse* each were decided prior to the articulation of the three-prong test in *Brown*, and in *Edmond* the Court concluded that the primary purpose of the checkpoint at issue was improper and did not proceed to the balancing analysis. Thus, *Sitz* and *Lidster* are left as the only Supreme Court checkpoint cases to explicitly consider this prong.

In *Sitz*, the Court explained that evaluation of this prong should not be an evaluation of the effectiveness of a checkpoint as a means of detecting crime as compared to alternative law enforcement techniques[70] and that the lower court was wrong to engage in a "searching examination of [the] 'effectiveness'" of the DWI checkpoint at issue.[71] The Court noted, however, that the checkpoint did in fact result in the arrest of two drunken drivers, and appeared to find this fact relevant to the analysis of the extent to which the checkpoint advanced the public interest.

In *Lidster*, the Court found that the checkpoint at issue advanced the public interest to an appreciable degree because "[t]he police appropriately tailored their checkpoint stops to fit important criminal investigatory needs" related to the primary purpose of the checkpoint, which was investigation of an unsolved fatal hit and run.[72] The Court noted that the checkpoint was established within a week of the accident, on the highway near the accident, and at about the same time of night as the accident. The Court further noted that officers "used the stops to obtain information from drivers."[73] The Court's analysis on this point is somewhat oblique as the issue of tailoring a checkpoint to fit its purpose is an inquiry similar to that required under the third *Brown* factor (the severity of a checkpoint's interference with individual liberty), discussed below, and the fact that officers obtained information from drivers seems to be little more than an acknowledgment that officers took some action related to the purpose of the checkpoint.

With a lack of Supreme Court guidance, North Carolina courts have attempted to apply the limited analysis of *Lidster* to investigatory checkpoint stops.[74] Thus, a number of state appellate court opinions

---

68. In the recent case *State v. Ashworth*, ___ N.C. App. ___, 790 S.E.2d 173 (2016), the state court of appeals found that the trial court's findings and conclusions reflected "sufficient consideration" of this prong of the analysis where the court found that "ensuring [at a drivers' license checkpoint] that drivers are properly licensed . . . [was] of 'vital interest.'" ___ N.C. App. at ___, 790 S.E.2d at 181.

69. *Cf. Sitz*, 496 U.S. at 454 (describing the reference to this factor in *Brown* as "rather general").

70. 496 U.S. at 453.

71. *Id.* at 454.

72. 540 U.S. 419, 427 (2004).

73. *Id.*

74. Recall that *Lidster* is factually unique to the extent that it involves a checkpoint designed to elicit information from drivers as potential witnesses rather than one designed to detect criminal activity committed by drivers passing through the checkpoint. Also note that three justices dissented from the portion of the *Lidster* majority opinion conducting the *Brown* analysis based on their view that "the outcome of the multifactor test prescribed in [*Brown*] is by no means clear on the facts of this case." 540 U.S. at 429 (Stevens, J., dissenting in part).

analyze the extent to which a checkpoint advances the public interest by determining "whether the police appropriately tailored their checkpoint stops to fit their primary purpose."[75]

The North Carolina Court of Appeals had this to say about tailoring in *State v. Veazey*:

> Our Court has previously identified a number of non-exclusive factors that courts should consider when determining whether a checkpoint is appropriately tailored, including: whether police spontaneously decided to set up the checkpoint on a whim; whether police offered any reason why a particular road or stretch of road was chosen for the checkpoint; whether the checkpoint had a predetermined starting or ending time; and whether police offered any reason why that particular time span was selected.[76]

Of the listed factors, the reason why a particular location was chosen for the checkpoint and the reason why a particular time span was selected appear to be the factors most similar to those identified in *Lidster* as bearing upon the extent to which a checkpoint advances the public interest.[77] In *State v. Townsend*, the trial court applied the public interest advancement prong of the balancing test by finding, among other things, that a DWI checkpoint was located within a mile of businesses which served alcohol and that the location was based on impaired driving statistics.[78] The court of appeals also has considered whether a checkpoint actually detected the type of violations it was intended to detect,[79] a consideration supported by *Lidster* and *Sitz*.[80]

Some of the factors listed above involve the degree to which officers' discretion is limited in conducting a checkpoint. Other opinions from the court of appeals analyzing whether a checkpoint is tailored to fit its primary purpose also have considered factors bearing on officers' discretion, including whether the checkpoint was conducted pursuant to a written plan[81] and whether participating officers were briefed on the plan.[82] Factors related to officers' discretion also bear upon the severity of a checkpoint's interference with individual liberty,[83] the third prong under *Brown*, and a court may find some analytical overlap between the two prongs. Regardless, as discussed in more

---

75. State v. Nolan, 365 N.C. 337 (2011).

76. 191 N.C. App. 181, 191 (2008).

77. *See Lidster*, 540 U.S. at 427 (noting with respect to these factors that the checkpoint at issue was established within a week of the hit and run, on the highway near the incident, and at about the same time of night).

78. 236 N.C. App. 456, 470 (2014).

79. State v. Jarrett, 203 N.C. App. 675, 680 (2010) (citing the fact that a series of checkpoints "did result in charges for license violations as well as DWI arrests" as supporting a finding of proper tailoring under this *Brown* factor).

80. *See Lidster*, 540 U.S. at 427 (finding it relevant to this *Brown* factor that officers in fact "used the stops to obtain information from drivers" as was the stated purpose of the checkpoint); Mich. Dep't of State Police v. Sitz, 496 U.S. 444, 454–55 (1990) (noting that the DWI checkpoint at issue resulted in the arrest of two drunken drivers). Recall, however, that the Supreme Court has admonished lower courts that evaluation of this factor does not call for a "searching examination" of the effectiveness of a checkpoint for detecting offenses as compared to an alternative investigative technique. *See Sitz*, 496 U.S. at 454.

81. *Townsend*, 236 N.C. App. at 470.

82. State v. Kostick, 233 N.C. App. 62, 76 (2014).

83. *See* 5 Wayne R. LaFave, Search and Seizure § 10.8(d), at 437 (5th ed. 2012). *See also* Brown v. Texas, 443 U.S. 47, 51 (1979) ("A central concern in balancing the [three factors] . . . has been to assure that an individual's reasonable expectation of privacy is not subject to arbitrary invasions solely at the unfettered discretion of officers in the field.").

detail below, a trial judge need not "mechanically engage in a rote application" of the factors relevant to balancing so long as the judge meaningfully applies the three prongs of the test.[84]

Though there appears to be no North Carolina appellate case discussing the issue, commentators suggest that the value of the deterrent effect of a checkpoint may be a valid consideration in determining the degree to which a checkpoint advances the public interest.[85]

3. The Severity of the Checkpoint's Interference with Individual Liberty

The final factor in the balancing test is "the severity of the interference with individual liberty" occasioned by the checkpoint. Though not an exhaustive list, the U.S. Supreme Court has found that the degree to which a checkpoint creates fear or surprise for an approaching motorist, the degree to which officers' discretion is limited in conducting the checkpoint, the duration of a motorist's seizure during a checkpoint, and the intensity of the investigation during the seizure are relevant considerations with regard to this prong.[86] The North Carolina Court of Appeals likewise has observed:

> Courts have previously identified a number of non-exclusive factors relevant to officer discretion and individual privacy, including: the checkpoint's potential interference with legitimate traffic, whether police took steps to put drivers on notice of an approaching checkpoint, whether the location of the checkpoint was selected by a supervising official, rather than by officers in the field, whether police stopped every vehicle that passed through the checkpoint, or stopped vehicles pursuant to a set pattern, whether drivers could see visible signs of the officers' authority, whether police operated the checkpoint pursuant to any oral or written guidelines, whether the officers were subject to any form of supervision, and whether the officers received permission from their supervising officer to conduct the checkpoint.[87]

The presence or absence of any single factor alone is not dispositive. Rather, all must be considered in a totality of the circumstances analysis.[88]

Both federal and state courts have recognized that well-marked checkpoints that are operated with visible signs of officers' authority mitigate the level of fear and anxiety motorists experience. Thus, such checkpoints intrude upon individual liberty to a lesser degree than would be the case if the checkpoints were operated in some contrary fashion.[89] In *State v. Jarrett*,[90] for example, the state court of appeals found that the trial court "adequately considered . . . appropriate factors under the

---

84. State v. McDonald, 239 N.C. App. 559, 571 (2015).

85. *See* 5 LaFave, *supra* note 83, § 10.8(d), at 436 (favorably citing state appellate court cases that recognize the deterrent value of DWI checkpoints; specifically noting one case that measured the deterrent value by comparing the checkpoint's purpose to its location and timing); Shea Denning, *No Checkpoint Policy? No Checkpoint Evidence*, N.C. Crim. L., UNC Sch. of Gov't Blog (Feb. 10, 2014), http://nccriminallaw.sog.unc .edu/no-checkpoint-policy-no-checkpoint-evidence/ (noting the deterrent value of checkpoints).

86. *See, e.g.,* Mich. Dep't of State Police v. Sitz, 496 U.S. 444, 451–52 (1990) (identifying each of these as considerations relevant to "the measure of the intrusion on motorists stopped . . . at sobriety checkpoints").

87. State v. Veazey, 191 N.C. App. 181, 193 (2008) (citations omitted).

88. *Id.*

89. *See, e.g.,* United States v. Martinez-Fuerte, 428 U.S. 543, 558 (1976) (citation, internal quotation marks omitted) (observing that the intrusiveness of checkpoints is minimized in part because "the motorist can see that other vehicles are being stopped, [and] he can see visible signs of the officers' authority"); *Sitz*, 496 U.S. at 452–53 (same; noting that checkpoint at issue involved uniformed officers); *Veazey*, 191 N.C. App. at 193 (favorably citing *Martinez-Fuerte* and *Sitz* for same proposition).

90. 203 N.C. App. 675, 682 (2010).

third prong of *Brown*" in the process of determining that a checkpoint was reasonable where, among other things, the trial court found that law enforcement vehicles were required to have blue lights on, officers were wearing their uniforms, and officers had a visibility of about 200 feet.[91] As discussed in more detail below, North Carolina statutory law requires that at least one law enforcement vehicle have its blue light in operation while a checkpoint is conducted.[92] This requirement likely satisfies the courts' suggestion that a constitutional checkpoint be well-marked and operated with visible signs of authority. It is not necessary that a warning sign or similar notification be displayed,[93] nor is it necessary that an agency publicize in advance that a checkpoint will be operated.[94] Of course, while not strictly necessary, the presence or absence of warning signs or advance publicity can be taken into account in the balancing test.

The degree to which field officers' discretion is limited in conducting a checkpoint is a particularly important factor under this prong of the reasonableness analysis.[95] As the court of appeals has stated, "courts have consistently required restrictions on the discretion of the officers conducting the checkpoint to ensure that the intrusion on individual liberty is no greater than is necessary to achieve the checkpoint's objectives."[96] Many of the relevant factors described in *Veazey* and quoted above bear upon field officers' discretion. Whether the location of the checkpoint was selected by a supervisor, whether officers exercised discretion in choosing which vehicles to stop, whether operational guidelines were in place, whether officers were supervised, and whether officers received permission from a supervisor to conduct a checkpoint all are factors that North Carolina appellate courts have identified as relevant to this prong of the reasonableness inquiry.[97] Courts have considered the extent to which officers' discretion is limited with regard to when and where a checkpoint will be established, as well as with regard to how the checkpoint will be conducted once established. In other words, it is important to consider the degree of field officers' discretion in both the creation and the operation of a checkpoint. Reinforcing the importance of limited discretion for field officers, G.S. 20-16.3A contains various provisions intended to limit field officer discretion; these statutory requirements are discussed in more detail below.

With regard to discretion in the creation of a checkpoint, North Carolina courts have suggested that it is not necessary for field officers to obtain prior authorization from a supervisor before establishing

---

91. *Id.* at 681.

92. G.S. 20-16.3A(a)(3).

93. *See* State v. Sanders, 112 N.C. App. 477, 478 (1993) (finding no Fourth Amendment violation in the operation of a checkpoint, despite the fact that officers "posted no signs warning the public that a license check was being conducted").

94. There are no North Carolina cases on point, but this is the weight of authority in other jurisdictions. *See, e.g.*, Brouhard v. Lee, 125 F.3d 656, 660 (8th Cir. 1997) (rejecting argument that checkpoint was unreasonable because there was no advance publication of checkpoint locations); United States v. Dillon, 983 F. Supp. 1037, 1039 (D. Kan. 1997) ("No controlling authority has ever required that advance notice should be required as part of the balancing formula to determine the constitutionality of [a] checkpoint, and this court finds that advance notice is not required for a valid checkpoint.").

95. *See* Delaware v. Prouse, 440 U.S. 648, 661–62 (1979) (explaining that the Supreme Court had "insisted that the discretion of the official in the field be circumscribed" in order to protect individuals' Fourth Amendment rights in cases where no individualized suspicion exists for a seizure); *see also* 5 LaFave, *supra* note 83, § 10.8(d), at 437–39 (describing the minimization of officer discretion as a "very strong theme" in Supreme Court precedent; collecting national case law demonstrating that failure to minimize the discretion of field officers is a "factor stressed by courts" in finding certain checkpoints illegal).

96. State v. Veazey, 191 N.C. App. 181, 192 (2008).

97. *See, e.g., id.*

a checkpoint.[98] However, as previously noted, whether the location of a checkpoint was selected by a supervising official and whether officers received permission from a supervisor to conduct a checkpoint each are factors relevant to this prong of the analysis.

The period of time for which a motorist is detained without individualized suspicion also is a factor relevant to the severity of a checkpoint's intrusion upon individual liberty.[99] Indeed, the fact that checkpoint stops typically are brief has been a primary basis for the Supreme Court's view that checkpoints are a permissible exception to the Fourth Amendment's general requirement that individualized suspicion justify a seizure. As the Court recognized in the foundational cases, brief stops impinge upon Fourth Amendment interests to a lesser degree than prolonged stops.

A defendant's argument that a checkpoint stop is unconstitutional because the period of detention is unreasonable may take various forms. Sometimes, the constitutionality of the whole of a checkpoint as a law enforcement technique is attacked. This was the case in *Martinez-Fuerte*, *Sitz*, and *Edmond*.[100] Thus, in discussing the duration of the stops in those cases, the Supreme Court explained that the seizures associated with the checkpoints were brief as a general matter. An illustrative North Carolina case is *State v. Townsend*,[101] where the defendant argued that the checkpoint at which he was discovered driving while impaired was unconstitutional. In conducting the reasonableness analysis, the court of appeals noted that non-impaired drivers were delayed only for about fifteen seconds each.[102] At least one out-of-state case found that a lengthy traffic delay resulting from a checkpoint resulted in an unreasonable seizure.[103] Thus, in evaluating a checkpoint, a court should be mindful not only of the duration of motorists' interactions with officers, but also of the total duration of motorists' delay associated with the operation of a checkpoint. As discussed in more detail below, North Carolina statutory law permits law enforcement agencies to include a contingency provision in a checkpoint plan for dealing with situations where a checkpoint causes a lengthy traffic delay.[104]

Other times, based on the duration of the stop, a defendant specifically challenges the constitutionality of his or her seizure during a checkpoint, notwithstanding the constitutionality of the checkpoint as a whole. Often, this line of attack involves a defendant's allegation that his or her seizure was unjustifiably extended beyond the period of time necessary to accomplish the purpose of the checkpoint.[105] In such a case, the analysis of the constitutionality of the duration of the stop is controlled by *Rodriguez v. United States*,[106] and the fact that the stop was initiated as a checkpoint stop

---

98. *See* State v. Tarlton, 146 N.C. App. 417, 422 (2001) ("There is no constitutional mandate requiring officers to obtain permission from a supervising officer before conducting a driver's license checkpoint."); State v. Mitchell, 358 N.C. 63, 67–68 (2004) (upholding checkpoint conducted pursuant to "standing permission" from a supervisor).

99. *See, e.g.,* Mich. Dep't of State Police v. Sitz, 496 U.S. 444, 451–52 (1990) (intrusion on Fourth Amendment interests is slight because motorists are subjected to only brief stop); United States v. Martinez-Fuerte, 428 U.S. 543, 557–58 (1976) (same).

100. Note that *Sitz* and *Edmond* (531 U.S. 32 (2000)) were civil cases.

101. 236 N.C. App. 456 (2014).

102. *Id*. at 471.

103. *See, e.g.,* State v. Barcia, 562 A.2d 246, 250 (N.J. Super. Ct. App. Div. 1989) (roadblock that caused a "traffic morass of monumental proportions," leading more than a million vehicles to come to a complete stop, some for several hours, unreasonably inconvenienced motorists).

104. G.S. 20-16.3A(a)(2a).

105. *See, e.g.,* State v. Jarrett, 203 N.C. App. 675, 682 (2010).

106. 575 U.S. ___, ___, 135 S. Ct. 1609, 1612 (2015) (holding that "a police stop exceeding the time needed to handle the matter for which the stop was made violates the Constitution's shield against unreasonable seizures").

is merely an incidental circumstance that does not call for specialized analysis. An illustrative North Carolina case is *State v. Jarrett*,[107] where the court determined that the duration of the defendant's stop was not unreasonable even though it extended beyond the time necessary to accomplish the primary purpose of a driver's license checkpoint because the officer developed reasonable suspicion that the underage defendant was driving after consuming alcohol.

As mentioned above, the intensity of the investigation to which a person is subjected during a checkpoint stop bears upon this prong of the balancing analysis.[108] To a significant degree, the intensity of the investigation, the duration of the stop, and the limited purposes for which checkpoints may be established are intertwined considerations.[109] The Supreme Court's view that suspicionless stops at checkpoints are constitutionally permissible in large part because of their typical brevity and limited scope of purpose presupposes that exhaustive investigative techniques are not a component of checkpoint stops absent some form of individualized suspicion.[110] Generally, an officer's investigative action must be "reasonably related . . . to the circumstances which justified" the checkpoint.[111] Therefore, at a license and registration checkpoint, an officer may request to see a driver's license and the vehicle's registration.[112] Likewise, at a sobriety checkpoint, an officer may attempt to detect impaired drivers using nonintrusive techniques such as observing the driver and engaging him or her in conversation.[113]

As a practical matter, an officer normally can quickly determine whether a driver is properly licensed and whether he or she appears to be impaired. Absent reasonable suspicion, it is not appropriate for an officer to order a driver out of his or her vehicle,[114] order the driver to undergo field sobriety testing, or require the driver to submit to an alcohol screening test.[115] Officers conducting checkpoints generally must refrain from engaging in investigative activity designed to discover evidence of crimes that are unrelated to the primary purpose of the checkpoint. Thus, the court of appeals has questioned the constitutionality of a checkpoint where "one officer would . . . ask for the license and registration, while a second officer would scan the inside of the vehicle and walk around it," in an apparent effort

---

107. 203 N.C. App. at 682 (note that *Jarrett* was decided prior to *Rodriguez* but remains good law on this point).

108. *See* Mich. Dep't of State Police v. Sitz, 496 U.S. 444, 452 (1990) (stating that the lower court "accurately gauged" the intrusion of a checkpoint by measuring the intensity of the investigation).

109. *See id.* (addressing duration of the stop and intensity of the investigation simultaneously).

110. *Cf.* United States v. Martinez-Fuerte, 428 U.S. 543, 566–67 (1976) ("The principal protection of Fourth Amendment rights at checkpoints lies in appropriate limitations on the scope of the stop.").

111. Terry v. Ohio, 392 U.S. 1, 20 (1968).

112. It is unclear whether an officer may conduct a computer check regarding an apparently valid driver's license. The North Carolina case that bears most closely on this issue suggests that the answer is "no." State v. Branch, 162 N.C. App. 707, 713 (2004) (apparently requiring, and finding on the specific facts of the case, "reasonable suspicion to justify investigation of the validity of the license" presented by a driver at a checkpoint), *vacated and remanded on other grounds*, 546 U.S. 931 (2005). However, *Branch* does not discuss the issue in detail, and there is contrary authority from other jurisdictions. *See, e.g.*, Price v. Commonwealth, 483 S.E.2d 496, 504 (Va. Ct. App. 1997) (appearing to allow a computer license and warrant check of every driver); Mullinax v. State, 920 S.W.2d 503 (Ark. Ct. App. 1996) (approving checkpoint where, for every fifth vehicle, officers would call in the driver's license number and the radio operator would inform them if the license was valid). Certainly a computer check would be reasonable when a driver is unable to produce a facially valid license.

113. State v. Colbert, 146 N.C. App. 506, 510 (2001).

114. 5 LaFave, *supra* note 83, § 10.8(a), at 401.

115. *Colbert*, 146 N.C. App. at 514 (requiring every driver to take an Alcosensor test "would violate the third prong of the balancing test" because it would be unduly intrusive).

to look for "possible criminal activity."[116] The court's apparent disapproval of conduct that does not alone amount to a Fourth Amendment search suggests that similar activity, such as having a drug dog sniff a vehicle at a checkpoint, also may be improper.[117] That said, an officer is not required to ignore evidence of crimes that he or she happens to observe in plain view while attending to the primary purpose of the checkpoint.[118] And if while diligently pursuing the primary purpose of a checkpoint stop an officer develops individualized suspicion that a person has committed a crime, the officer may investigate the person to the same degree as would be permissible regardless of the checkpoint.

Note that appellate decisions allow some of the same factors to be considered in the second and third prongs of the balancing test, such as whether the checkpoint was conducted pursuant to a written plan, how the location for the checkpoint was selected, how the checkpoint was marked, and whether the checkpoint had designated starting and ending times. The courts may not have been extremely careful in assigning factors to the proper parts of the balancing test, but given that the balancing test is a totality of the circumstances analysis, it likely does not matter much how each factor enters the mix so long as the court meaningfully applies each of the three prongs of the test.

4. Findings of Fact and Conclusions of Law

The court of appeals has ruled that, at least in superior court, a judge ruling on whether a checkpoint survives the balancing test must make findings of fact and conclusions of law. Although judges need not "mechanically engage in a rote application" of the factors relevant to balancing, orders upholding the constitutionality of a checkpoint "must contain findings and conclusions sufficient to demonstrate that the trial court has meaningfully applied the three prongs of the test articulated in *Brown*."[119] Outside the checkpoint context, rulings on motions to suppress likewise normally must include findings of fact and conclusions of law.[120] However, case law provides that a judge need not make findings of fact when there is no conflict in the evidence, as findings consistent with the evidence will be implied.[121] The state supreme court has said that "[a] written determination setting forth the findings and conclusions is not necessary, but it is the better practice."[122]

---

116. State v. Rose, 170 N.C. App. 284, 292 (2005). *Rose* considered this activity to be evidence that an improper purpose potentially animated the checkpoint at issue. As noted, the intensity of the investigation and the limited purposes for which checkpoints may be established are intertwined considerations.

117. *See* Welty, *supra* note 54 (indicating that presence of a drug dog at a checkpoint does not necessarily establish that the checkpoint has an improper purpose, but that using a drug dog to sniff every car would strongly suggest an improper purpose). As discussed elsewhere in this chapter, the presence of a drug dog at a checkpoint bears upon the analysis of whether a checkpoint has a proper purpose. Again, a checkpoint's purpose and the nature of the investigatory activity undertaken at the checkpoint are intertwined considerations.

118. City of Indianapolis v. Edmond, 531 U.S. 32, 48 (2000).

119. State v. McDonald, 239 N.C. App. 559, 571 (2015).

120. G.S. 15A-977(f), which pertains to motions to suppress evidence in superior court, states that a judge ruling on such a motion must "set forth in the record his findings of facts and conclusions of law." *See also id.* § 15A-974(b) ("The court, in making a determination whether or not evidence shall be suppressed under this section, shall make findings of fact and conclusions of law which shall be included in the record.").

121. *See, e.g.*, State v. Bartlett, 368 N.C. 309, 312 (2015) ("[O]ur cases require findings of fact only when there is a material conflict in the evidence."); State v. Munsey, 342 N.C. 882 (1996). The brief statement in *McDonald* that an order concerning the constitutionality of a checkpoint "must contain findings [of fact]" (*see supra* note 119) probably should not be interpreted as requiring explicit factual findings when there is no material conflict in the evidence.

122. *Bartlett*, 368 N.C. at 312.

When checkpoint issues arise in district court, they should be handled in the same way as other motions to suppress are handled in district court: in non-DWI cases, they may be ruled on briefly as they arise, while in DWI cases, they are subject to the special procedural rules for motions to suppress in such cases.[123] These rules are addressed in detail in another School of Government publication.[124]

IV. Statutory Requirements

The North Carolina General Statutes (hereinafter G.S.) explicitly authorize law enforcement agencies to conduct motor vehicle checkpoints and impose specific requirements regarding the operation of certain checkpoints. G.S. 20-16.3A(a) imposes specific operational requirements on law enforcement agencies "[i]f the agency is conducting a [checkpoint] for the purposes of determining compliance with [G.S. Chapter 20]." G.S. 20-16.3A(c) provides that "[l]aw enforcement agencies may conduct any type of [checkpoint] or roadblock as long as it is established and operated in accordance with the provisions of the United States Constitution and the Constitution of North Carolina." Read together, these provisions suggest that law enforcement agencies have greater latitude with respect to conducting checkpoints that are operated for some purpose other than determining compliance with G.S. Chapter 20. As previously discussed, however, the only primary purpose unrelated to detection of motor vehicle offenses that has been explicitly held valid by the Supreme Court or a North Carolina appellate court is the information-gathering checkpoint approved of in *Illinois v. Lidster*.[125] Additionally, the majority of checkpoints operated in North Carolina in fact are designed to detect violations of Chapter 20, and, consequently, the greater latitude afforded to other types of checkpoints under the statute is not of central importance in the majority of cases as a practical matter.

In general, the operational requirements of G.S. 20-16.3A minimize field officers' discretion with regard to conducting a checkpoint and ensure that the public has some notice that a checkpoint is being conducted. Thus, a court may find analytical overlap when considering whether a checkpoint was conducted in compliance with the statute and when considering its degree of interference upon individual liberty. A checkpoint that is statutorily compliant is not, however, necessarily constitutional for that reason alone.[126] A court must apply the two-step analytical framework discussed above when passing on the constitutionality of a checkpoint, even if the court is satisfied that the checkpoint complies with the statute.[127]

---

123. G.S. 20-38.6; 20-38.7.

124. *See* Shea Riggsbee Denning, The Law of Impaired Driving and Related Implied Consent Offenses in North Carolina (UNC School of Government, 2014).

125. 540 U.S. 419 (2004). Recall that the fact that other types of checkpoints have not been explicitly held valid does not necessarily mean that other types of checkpoints are impermissible. Recall also that the Supreme Court strongly suggested in *Edmond* that a checkpoint justified by exigent circumstances likely would not violate the Fourth Amendment.

126. State v. McDonald, 239 N.C. App. 559 (2015) (stating that an earlier analysis employed by the court to the effect that a checkpoint that was in substantial compliance with the statute was accordingly constitutional had been superseded by intervening case law from the U.S. Supreme Court).

127. *Id.* (so stating).

A. Mandatory Requirements for G.S. Chapter 20 Checkpoints

As mentioned above, G.S. 20-16.3A(a) imposes certain operational requirements for checkpoints designed to determine compliance with G.S. Chapter 20. Broadly, the operational requirements speak to three primary issues: the patterns used to stop vehicles and request information from drivers, written policies regarding the patterns, and notification to the public of the operation of the checkpoint.[128] The operational requirements are mandatory.[129]

G.S. 20-16.3A(a)(2) provides that the agency conducting a checkpoint must "[d]esignate in advance the pattern both for stopping vehicles and for requesting drivers that are stopped to produce drivers license, registration, or insurance information." The statutory language suggests that it is not necessary that the pattern for stopping vehicles be precisely the same as the pattern for requesting the identified information from drivers.[130] For example, the statute appears to permit an agency to designate a pattern of stopping every vehicle that passes through a checkpoint and a pattern of alternating requests for drivers' licenses with requests for insurance information.[131] Individual officers do not have discretion to deviate from the designated patterns.[132] G.S. 20-16.3A(a1) states that "[a] pattern designated by a law enforcement agency pursuant to [G.S. 20-16.3A(a)] shall not be based on a particular vehicle type, except that the pattern may designate any type of commercial motor vehicle as defined in G.S. 20-4.01(3d)." Subsection (a1) reiterates that the prohibition on basing a pattern on a particular vehicle type applies only to checkpoints to determine compliance with the provisions of G.S. Chapter 20, and is "not to be construed to restrict any other type of [lawful] checkpoint or roadblock."[133] If, for example, an agency was conducting a checkpoint based on the exigent circumstance that the agency believed that a particular type of vehicle was carrying a bomb, the agency would not be prohibited by statute from stopping only the vehicle type under suspicion.

G.S. 20-16.3A(a)(2a) requires that a law enforcement agency conducting a checkpoint "[o]perate under a written policy that provides guidelines for the pattern, which need not be in writing." This language has been interpreted to mean that the pattern itself need not be in writing.[134] The written operational policy must not give any individual officer "discretion as to which vehicle is stopped or, of the vehicles stopped, which driver is requested to produce drivers license, registration, or insurance information."[135] An agency may operate under its own written policy or under the written policy of

---

128. *See* G.S. 20-16.3A(a)(1) through (3).

129. *See* G.S. 20-16.3A (introducing the requirements with the mandatory language "must"); State v. White, 232 N.C. App. 296, 304 (2014) ("We observe that the language used in [G.S. 20-16.3A] is mandatory.").

130. *See also* G.S. 20-16.3A(a)(2a) (referring to "contingency provisions for altering *either* pattern" (emphasis added)).

131. Though the statute appears to permit different patterns as discussed in the main text, the North Carolina State Highway Patrol policy on checking stations directs that the same information be requested of every driver stopped. *See* North Carolina State Highway Patrol, Policy Manual Revision 17, Directive K.4, at 2 (2008).

132. G.S. 20-16.3A(a)(2a) ("[N]o individual officer may be given discretion as to which vehicle is stopped or, of the vehicles stopped, which driver is requested to produce drivers license, registration, or insurance information.").

133. G.S. 20-16.3A(a1).

134. Robert L. Farb, Arrest, Search, and Investigation in North Carolina 53–54 (UNC School of Government, 5th ed. 2016). *See also* Jeffrey B. Welty, *Motor Vehicle Checkpoints*, Admin. of Just. Bull. No. 2010/04 (UNC School of Government, Sept. 2010), www.sog.unc.edu/sites/www.sog.unc.edu/files/reports/aojb1004.pdf (noting that this statutory language is unclear; interpreting it to mean that the pattern itself need not be in writing).

135. G.S. 20-16.3A(a)(2a).

another law enforcement agency.[136] If an agency is operating under another agency's policy, that fact must be stated in writing.[137] The written operational policy "may include contingency provisions for altering either pattern if actual traffic conditions are different from those anticipated."[138] As an example of a contingency provision, a policy may authorize an on-site supervisor to permit all vehicles to pass through a checkpoint when a high volume of traffic causes a hazardous delay along the roadway where the checkpoint is being operated.[139]

Circumstances other than traffic flow may make it practically difficult to enforce a strict pattern of stopping vehicles without causing unreasonable delay to motorists. For example, at a checkpoint operated by a small number of officers it may become necessary to let traffic flow freely when officers are busy writing citations and therefore are unavailable to screen vehicles. The statute does not explicitly contemplate this situation, at least so far as it may be termed a "deviation" from the designated pattern.[140] Thus, it may be advisable to provide for such a situation in the written guidelines for the pattern in order to minimize the discretion given to individual officers since an arbitrary deviation from the pattern may violate the Fourth Amendment.

G.S. 20-16.3A(a)(3) requires that an agency conducting a checkpoint "[a]dvise the public that a [checkpoint] is being operated by having, at a minimum, one law enforcement vehicle with its blue light in operation during the conducting of the [checkpoint]." Some North Carolina law enforcement agency policies additionally direct officers to wear official uniforms while participating in a checkpoint.[141]

G.S. 20-16.3A(b) provides that "[a]n officer who determines there is a reasonable suspicion that an occupant has violated a provision of [G.S. Chapter 20], or any other provision of law, may detain the driver to further investigate in accordance with law."[142] In general, once an officer develops reasonable suspicion that an occupant of a vehicle, including the driver, has committed an infraction or a criminal offense, the lawfulness of the officer's investigation is analyzed in the same manner as would be the case had the stop been premised on individualized suspicion in the first place; the fact that the seizure originated as a checkpoint stop does not have special significance. Thus, "[a]lthough G.S. 20-16.3A(b) refers to reasonable suspicion relating to an 'occupant' but then refers to detaining the 'driver,' it is appropriate only to detain the person for whom reasonable suspicion exists, unless all occupants are being detained for officer safety reasons."[143] Chapter 3 provides a more extensive discussion of the permitted scope of investigation during a stop.

---

136. *Id.*

137. G.S. 20-16.3A(a)(2a) provides as follows: "If officers of a law enforcement agency are operating under another agency's policy, it must be stated in writing."

138. G.S. 20-16.3A(a)(2a).

139. *See* North Carolina State Highway Patrol, *supra* note 131, at 1 (providing such a contingency provision).

140. *See* G.S. 20-16.3A(a)(2a) (identifying the situation where "actual traffic conditions are different from those anticipated" as the only justification for deviation from the designated pattern).

141. *See* North Carolina State Highway Patrol, *supra* note 131, at 1 ("No checking station shall be conducted without at least two uniformed members present. . . .").

142. G.S. 20-16.3A(b).

143. Farb, *supra* note 134, at 54 n.248. *Cf.* United States v. Slater, 411 F.3d 1003, 1005 (8th Cir. 2005) (noting that officer testified that passenger was free to leave checkpoint during time in which driver took field sobriety tests and that passengers of other vehicles in fact did leave).

Under G.S. 20-16.3A(b), if an officer determines during the course of a checkpoint stop that a driver has previously consumed alcohol or has an open container of an alcoholic beverage in the vehicle, the driver "may be requested to submit to an alcohol screening test under G.S. 20-16.3."[144]

G.S. 20-16.3A(d) directs that "[t]he placement of checkpoints should be random or statistically indicated, and agencies shall avoid placing checkpoints repeatedly in the same location or proximity." A violation of this statutory directive is not grounds for a motion to suppress or a defense to any offense arising out of the operation of a checkpoint.[145] While a violation of G.S. 20-16.3A(d) is not itself grounds for a motion to suppress under the terms of the statute, it is conceivable that repeatedly operating a checkpoint in the same location could be grounds for a motion to suppress alleging a constitutional violation[146] if a challenger was able to marshal evidence that checkpoints were being operated in a discriminatory manner.[147] Motions to suppress are discussed in more detail below.

V. Motions to Suppress

A defendant in a criminal case may challenge the legality of a checkpoint through a motion to suppress evidence obtained as a result of the checkpoint.[148] In district court, such motions typically are made during trial,[149] except in impaired driving cases when the special timing rules of G.S. 20-38.6 apply.[150] In superior court, such motions usually are, and often must be, made before trial.[151]

Evidence obtained as a result of investigative action that violates the Fourth Amendment often must be suppressed.[152] Thus, if a checkpoint is operated in an unconstitutional manner, evidence obtained

---

144. G.S. 20-16.3A(b).

145. G.S. 20-16.3A(d). Perhaps this is because the Supreme Court stated in *United States v. Martinez-Fuerte*, 428 U.S. 543, 559 (1976), that the fact that the checkpoint at issue had a fixed location was a factor that weighed in favor of its constitutionality. For example, the Court noted that the location of fixed checkpoints is not subject to the discretion of officers in the field. *Id.* Also, the public arguably may be expected to experience a lesser degree of fear or surprise when a checkpoint is repeatedly operated in the same location.

146. *Cf.* G.S. 15A-974 (providing that a motion to suppress may be based on either a constitutional violation or a substantial violation of G.S. Chapter 15A). Note that G.S. 15A-974 does not speak to whether a motion to suppress is appropriate where a defendant alleges a violation of a Chapter other than 15A, but the court of appeals concluded in *State v. White*, 232 N.C. App. 296, 304–05 (2014), that a violation of G.S. 20-16.3A is a proper basis for a motion to suppress.

147. *Cf.* United States v. Johnson, 122 F. Supp. 3d 272 (M.D.N.C. 2015) (U.S. government alleged that Alamance County sherriff violated Hispanics' Fourth Amendment rights by targeting them by locating vehicle checkpoints in predominantly Hispanic neighborhoods).

148. *See generally* G.S. Chapter 15A, Article 53 (general provisions regarding motions to suppress in criminal cases).

149. G.S. 15A-973 (providing that in misdemeanor prosecutions in district court, motions to suppress should ordinarily be made during trial but may be made prior to trial; a motion may be heard prior to trial with the consent of the prosecutor and the district court judge).

150. G.S. 20-38.6(a) ("The defendant may move to suppress evidence or dismiss charges only prior to trial, except the defendant may move to dismiss the charges for insufficient evidence at the close of the State's evidence and at the close of all of the evidence without prior notice. If, during the course of the trial, the defendant discovers facts not previously known, a motion to suppress or dismiss may be made during the trial."). *See generally* DENNING, *supra* note 124.

151. G.S. 15A-975 (requiring motions to suppress to be made prior to trial except in specified circumstances).

152. *See, e.g.*, FARB, *supra* note 134, at 407–09 (generally discussing consequences of an unlawful search or seizure, including exclusion of evidence from criminal proceeding); State v. Veazey, 191 N.C. App. 181 (2008) (analyzing a motion to suppress arguing that a checkpoint violated defendant's Fourth Amendment rights).

at the checkpoint will normally be subject to suppression.[153] A court considering whether suppression is required would apply the two-step framework for determining whether a checkpoint had a proper primary purpose and, if so, whether the checkpoint was conducted reasonably, as discussed above.

In certain circumstances, evidence obtained at a checkpoint that is operated in compliance with the Constitution yet in violation of G.S. 20-16.3A also is subject to suppression.[154] While G.S. 20-16.3A does not explicitly state that a violation of the statute is a basis for suppression, the court of appeals held in *State v. White* that "because the General Assembly specifically included language in subsection (d) that it shall not be a basis for a motion to suppress, meanwhile excluding the same language in subsection (a)(2a), [a violation of] subsection (a)(2a) is a proper basis for a motion to suppress."[155] The logic dictating the holding in *White* suggests that a violation of a subsection other than (a)(2a) also would be a basis for suppression, however, no North Carolina appellate case has addressed the issue.

The trial court in *White* made a finding of fact that "there was a substantial violation of G.S. 20-16.3A."[156] In the context of suppressing evidence obtained in violation of G.S. Chapter 15A, G.S. 15A-974(a)(2) requires that the evidence be obtained as a result of a "substantial violation" of the provisions of the chapter and lists factors that a court must consider in determining whether a violation is substantial.[157] In *White*, the court of appeals did not explicitly address whether a violation of G.S. 20-16.3A must be a substantial violation in order to warrant suppression.

The checkpoint policy itself often is introduced during a hearing on a motion to suppress arising from a checkpoint, but introduction of the policy is not required.[158] An officer with knowledge of the policy can testify to its particulars.[159]

---

153. G.S. 15A-974(a)(1) (providing suppression remedy when evidence is obtained in violation of the state or federal constitution).

154. As mentioned, a violation of the requirements in G.S. 20-16.3A(d) regarding the placement of checkpoints is not itself a basis for suppression under the terms of the statute. Recall, however, that discriminatory placement of a checkpoint could give rise to a constitutional challenge.

155. 232 N.C. App. 296, 304–05 (2014).

156. *Id.* at 300–01.

157. The factors are: the importance of the particular interest violated, the extent of the deviation from lawful conduct, the extent to which the violation was willful, and the extent to which exclusion will tend to deter future violations of Chapter 15A. The statute also provides that "[e]vidence shall not be suppressed . . . if the person committing the violation [of Chapter 15A] . . . acted under the objectively reasonable, good faith belief that the actions were lawful."

158. Absent a motion to suppress, it is obvious that the state need not introduce a copy of the policy, as it is not essential to establish the elements of any crime. When offered at trial, the checkpoint policy is not hearsay because it is not admitted for the truth of the matter asserted. This also obviates any Confrontation Clause issue.

159. Perhaps testimony about the contents of the policy would violate the best evidence rule, but the rules of evidence do not apply when a court is determining questions of fact preliminary to admissibility of evidence. The best evidence rule is N.C. R. Evid. 1002, G.S. 8C-1002 ("To prove the content of a writing, recording, or photograph, the original writing, recording, or photograph is required, except as otherwise provided in these rules or by statute."). Under N.C. R. Evid. 1101(b)(1), G.S. 8C-1101, however, the rules of evidence do not apply when determining "questions of fact preliminary to admissibility of evidence."

VI. Operating a Checkpoint

A. Officer Participation

Any officer with territorial and subject matter jurisdiction may participate in the operation of a checkpoint.[160] So may any officer acting pursuant to a mutual aid agreement.[161] Thus, officers from several agencies may participate in a single checkpoint.[162] All the officers need not come from the agency that established or adopted the checkpoint policy.[163]

However, for both legal and practical reasons, it is advisable to have a single agency in charge of the checkpoint. The checkpoint should operate under that agency's checkpoint policy, and a supervisory officer from that agency should be responsible for determining whether, for example, traffic is backed up so far that it is necessary to deviate from the pattern for stopping vehicles. Furthermore, if many of the officers involved in a checkpoint have primary responsibilities other than the enforcement of the motor vehicle laws, a court may consider that fact when determining the primary programmatic purpose of the checkpoint, as discussed above.[164]

Sometimes, a magistrate will also be present at a checkpoint, typically in a mobile unit that includes an instrument for conducting chemical analyses of drivers' breath and office space for a magistrate.[165] Such arrangements are permitted by statute,[166] though of course the magistrate must remain neutral and independent.

B. Pulling a Vehicle Out of Line for Further Investigation

If there is reasonable suspicion that a driver or vehicle occupant has committed a crime, that person may be detained for additional investigation.[167] The person for whom reasonable suspicion exists often is pulled out of the checkpoint line and directed to a secondary checking station where the additional investigation takes place.[168] At the point at which a person is detained based upon reasonable suspicion, an officer may investigate the person to the same extent as would be permissible had the stop been

---

160. For a discussion of territorial and subject matter jurisdiction, see FARB, *supra* note 134, at 14–19. If an officer participates in the operation of a checkpoint outside his or her territorial jurisdiction, the defendant may argue that evidence obtained at the checkpoint should be suppressed. There is little support for this position in the case law. *Id.* at 97–98 (collecting and summarizing cases).

161. Mutual aid agreements are authorized by G.S. 160A-288 *et seq. See also* FARB, *supra* note 134, at 24–25.

162. Thus, in *White v. Tippett*, 187 N.C. App. 285, 286 (2007), a State Trooper "saw several [Charlotte] police officers conducting a checkpoint, so he pulled over to assist them."

163. State v. Colbert, 146 N.C. App. 506, 515 (2001) (upholding checkpoint involving "eight organizations" and stating that "nothing in the . . . statute or case law" precludes the involvement of officers from agencies other than the one that established or adopted the checkpoint policy).

164. *See* State v. Rose, 170 N.C. App. 284, 290 (2005) (noting that four of the five officers involved in a checkpoint were narcotics officers and treating that as a relevant factor in determining the purpose of the checkpoint).

165. Such mobile units are commonly called "BATmobiles," a partial acronym for Breath Alcohol Testing Mobile Units.

166. G.S. 20-38.4(a)(1) (directing magistrates to conduct initial appearances in impaired driving cases "at locations other than the courthouse when it will expedite the initial appearance" and is practicable).

167. *See* Terry v. Ohio, 392 U.S. 1 (1968); State v. Veazey, 191 N.C. App. 181, 195 (2008) (driver's signs of impairment "provided a sufficient basis for reasonable suspicion permitting [an officer] to pursue further investigation and detention of [driver]"); *see also* 5 LaFave, *supra* note 83, § 10.8(d), at 455.

168. *See, e.g., Veazey*, 191 N.C. App at 195 (describing this practice).

based on individualized suspicion in the first place;[169] the fact that the stop originated as a checkpoint stop is not of special significance. The scope of permissible investigation during a stop based on individualized suspicion is discussed in more detail in chapter 3.

C. Drug Dogs at Checkpoints

As discussed above, courts consider how a checkpoint is conducted when determining both its primary purpose and the degree to which it intrudes on individual liberty. The use of drug dogs at a checkpoint potentially bears upon each of these determinations. If officers were to deploy a drug dog on every vehicle, a court may conclude that the primary purpose of the checkpoint was drug enforcement, or it may conclude that the checkpoint was conducted unreasonably because it intruded upon individual liberty to an impermissible degree. In contrast, deploying a drug dog at the point at which a person has been detained based upon reasonable suspicion likely would not call into question whether the primary purpose of the checkpoint was proper, and the dog sniff itself is not a Fourth Amendment concern under *Illinois v. Caballes*.[170] The court of appeals commented favorably on such a procedure in *State v. Branch*:

> [T]he officers' detention of defendant [at a checkpoint] to verify whether her driving privileges were valid was reasonable under the circumstances. And once the lawfulness of a person's detention is established, *Caballes* instructs us that officers need no additional assessment under the Fourth Amendment before walking a drug-sniffing dog around the exterior of that individual's vehicle. . . . Thus, based on *Caballes*, once [the defendant] was detained to verify her driving privileges, [officers] needed no heightened suspicion of criminal activity before walking [a drug dog] around her car.[171]

A dog also was used on vehicles that had been pulled out of line in *State v. Nolan*,[172] a case where the court found that a checkpoint had a proper purpose despite the presence of the drug dog and where the dog was used on the defendant's vehicle only after the defendant was detained for sobriety tests. However, even when a driver is detained based on individualized suspicion, a drug dog cannot be used if it would impermissibly extend the stop under *Rodriguez v. United States*.[173] If the reason that the driver is detained is reasonable suspicion of a drug offense, then a reasonable delay to obtain and deploy a drug dog would be permitted.

If a dog may be deployed on a car that is pulled out of line, it follows that the mere presence of a dog on the scene does not render a checkpoint unlawful.[174]

---

169. *See generally*, Jessica Smith, *Warrantless Stops, in* North Carolina Superior Court Judges' Benchbook (UNC School of Government, 2014) (Jessica Smith, ed.), http://benchbook.sog.unc.edu/sites/benchbook.sog.unc.edu/files/pdf/Warrantless Stops.pdf.

170. 543 U.S. 405 (2005).

171. 177 N.C. App. 104, 108 (2006).

172. 211 N.C. App. 109 (2011).

173. 575 U.S. ___, 135 S. Ct. 1609 (2015).

174. *See also* Welty, *supra* note 54 (indicating that presence of a drug dog at a checkpoint does not necessarily establish that the checkpoint has an improper purpose, but that using a drug dog to sniff every car would strongly suggest an improper purpose).

D. Investigation of a Passenger

Though it is possible to find out-of-state cases where officers engage in investigative activity targeting passengers,[175] the practice is highly questionable because it potentially both brings the primary purpose of the checkpoint into question and intrudes upon individual liberty to a greater degree than contemplated in Supreme Court precedent.[176] Of course, if without any active investigation an officer develops individualized suspicion that a passenger is engaged in criminal activity, perhaps based on a plain view observation, the officer may investigate the passenger to the same extent as would be otherwise lawful regardless of the checkpoint.

E. Turning Away from a Checkpoint

It is reasonable to assume that some drivers who approach a checkpoint may wish to avoid it in order to prevent officers from discovering that they are engaged in illegal activity.

In *State v. Foreman*, the North Carolina Supreme Court held as follows:

> [I]t is reasonable and permissible for an officer to monitor a checkpoint's entrance for vehicles whose drivers may be attempting to avoid the checkpoint, and it necessarily follows that an officer, in light of and pursuant to the totality of the circumstances or the checkpoint plan, may pursue and stop a vehicle which has turned away from a checkpoint within its perimeters for reasonable inquiry to determine why the vehicle turned away.[177]

In *State v. Griffin*,[178] the state supreme court reiterated that a legal turn away from a checkpoint may provide reasonable suspicion for a stop based on the totality of the circumstances. In *Griffin*, an officer observed as a vehicle approaching a checkpoint "stopped in the middle of the road and appeared to initiate a three-point turn."[179] "Given the place and manner of defendant's turn in conjunction with his proximity to the checkpoint," the supreme court held that there was reasonable suspicion that he was violating the law.[180] Reaching this conclusion, the court stated that "[i]t is clear that this Court and the Fourth Circuit have held that even a legal turn, when viewed in the totality of the circumstances, may give rise to reasonable suspicion."[181] As can be seen from *Griffin*, the fact that a checkpoint is being conducted itself informs the analysis of the totality of the circumstances, and the nature of the turn also is an important consideration.

The analysis in *Griffin* did not address the court's clear indication in *Foreman* that a checkpoint plan could provide an independent basis for an officer to stop a vehicle which has turned away from a checkpoint within its perimeters, regardless of whether this behavior gives rise to reasonable

---

175. *See, e.g.*, United States v. Slater, 411 F.3d 1003, 1004 (8th Cir. 2005) (officer ran computer check on passenger and determined he had outstanding warrant).

176. *Cf.* State v. Rose, 170 N.C. App. 284, 292 (2005) (questioning the constitutionality of a checkpoint where "one officer would . . . ask for the license and registration, while a second officer would scan the inside of the vehicle and walk around it," in an apparent effort to look for "possible criminal activity."). *Rose* considered this activity to be evidence that an improper purpose potentially animated the checkpoint at issue. As previously noted, the limited purposes for which checkpoints may be established and the degree of intrusion upon individual liberty are intertwined considerations.

177. 351 N.C. 627, 632–33 (2000).

178. 366 N.C. 473 (2013).

179. *Id.* at 474.

180. *Id.* at 477.

181. *Id.*

suspicion.[182] In *Foreman*, the court stated that the perimeters of a checkpoint "include the area within which drivers may become aware of its presence by observation of any sign marking or giving notice of the checkpoint."[183]

The state supreme court has stated that it is unnecessary to analyze the constitutionality of a checkpoint when a motorist is pursued and stopped based on reasonable suspicion after turning away.[184] In contrast, though there is no North Carolina case law on point, it seemingly would be necessary to analyze the constitutionality of a checkpoint in cases where the checkpoint plan directed officers to pursue and stop every vehicle that turns away and a stop was made on that basis rather than on the basis of reasonable suspicion.[185]

As a final point, it seems likely that in practice agencies would attempt to avoid locating a checkpoint in an area where there was a legitimate opportunity for a significant number of drivers to make legal turns that, regardless of the driver's intention, result in avoiding the checkpoint.

F. Ruse Checkpoints

The law enforcement tactic of using so-called "ruse checkpoints" has not been addressed in a published North Carolina case, and the most common implementation of the tactic does not actually involve a checkpoint stop. Nevertheless, a brief discussion of the issue is warranted.

The ruse checkpoint tactic typically involves officers deploying large, flashing temporary signs on a divided highway that advertise that a checkpoint is being operated ahead.[186] Quite often, it is advertised that the checkpoint is a drug checkpoint.[187] In fact, the checkpoint advertised by the signs does not exist—the signs are a ruse designed to trap travelers engaged in illegal activity. The mechanics of the trap typically take one of two forms. Some ruse checkpoints actually involve a motor vehicle checkpoint located not where indicated by the flashing signs but, rather, at the first exit ramp after the signs.[188] Other ruse checkpoints do not involve any checkpoint whatsoever. Instead, officers monitor the exit ramp after the signs and attempt to make either valid pretextual stops based upon observed traffic violations or valid stops based upon individualized suspicion of criminal activity.[189] Regardless of the form of the ruse checkpoint, the theory behind each is that the signs will cause people engaged in criminal activity to exit the highway in order to avoid the advertised checkpoint.

---

182. *See Foreman*, 351 N.C. at 632–33 (emphasis added) ("[A]n officer, in light of and pursuant to the totality of the circumstances *or* the checkpoint plan, may pursue and stop a vehicle which has turned away from a checkpoint within its perimeters for reasonable inquiry to determine why the vehicle turned away."); *id.* at 634 (Frye, C.J., concurring) ("[I]f a systematic plan for an impaired driving checkpoint pursuant to [G.S. 20-16.3A] provides for stopping every car that turns off the highway within the perimeters of the checkpoint, then it is unnecessary to justify such a stop on the basis of reasonable and articulable suspicion.").

183. *Id.* at 632.

184. *Griffin*, 366 N.C. at 477.

185. Essentially, such a stop is simply a checkpoint stop that is executed away from the checkpoint, and thus must comply with the constitutional requirements applicable to all suspicionless checkpoint stops.

186. *See* Jeff Welty, *Ruse Checkpoints*, N.C. Crim. L., UNC Sch. of Gov't Blog (June 1, 2011), http://nccriminallaw.sog.unc.edu/ruse-checkpoints/.

187. Recall that drug checkpoints are forbidden under *City of Indianapolis v. Edmond*, 531 U.S. 32 (2000).

188. *See generally* United States v. Neff, 681 F.3d 1134, 1139 (10th Cir. 2012) (describing such a design as "first generation" because ruse checkpoints of this type were the first to be used following *Edmond*).

189. *Id.*

Defendants sometimes argue that the use of a ruse checkpoint constitutes illegal police activity. Courts outside of North Carolina have rejected this argument.[190]

The version of the ruse checkpoint that actually involves a checkpoint at the exit ramp has a more direct connection to the content of this chapter, and it is easier to explain the legal analysis of such a ruse checkpoint, at least as typically deployed. As mentioned, it is often advertised that the non-existent checkpoint is a drug checkpoint. In such a case, courts have found that the checkpoint located at the exit ramp is constitutionally "problematic because [its] primary purpose is ultimately indistinguishable from the general interest in crime control."[191] Even if officer testimony and the checkpoint plan indicated that the purpose of the exit ramp checkpoint was proper, the fact that ruse signs were deployed would be strong evidence that the checkpoint was designed for drug interdiction, a purpose held improper in *Edmond*.[192]

The version of the ruse checkpoint that does not involve an actual checkpoint but, rather, is designed to allow officers to monitor the exit ramp and attempt to make valid pretextual stops or stops premised on individualized suspicion has no direct connection to checkpoint-specific legal analysis. Instead, any traffic stop arising from such a tactic must be analyzed under the rubric of individualized suspicion, a topic discussed in detail in chapter 1. A driver's use of an exit after passing a ruse checkpoint sign potentially may be used by a court as one factor in the individualized suspicion analysis. An illustrative recent case is *United States v. Neff*.[193] In *Neff*, the Tenth Circuit squarely confronted this type of ruse checkpoint for the first time.[194] Surveying the law in other jurisdictions, the court concluded, in agreement with the Eighth Circuit, that a driver's decision to use a highway exit[195] after seeing ruse checkpoint signs "may serve as a valid, and indeed persuasive, factor in . . . [a] reasonable suspicion analysis" but is insufficient standing alone to justify a traffic stop.[196]

---

190. *See, e.g.*, United States v. Flynn, 309 F.3d 736, 738 (10th Cir. 2002) ("The posting of signs to create a ruse does not constitute illegal police activity"); State v. Hedgcock, 765 N.W.2d 469, 481 (Neb. 2009) ("We determine that the use of a ruse checkpoint, without an unreasonable seizure for Fourth Amendment purposes, is not unconstitutional simply because it is a ruse.").

191. *Neff*, 681 F.3d at 1139 (citation, internal quotation marks omitted).

192. Of course, it is conceivable that the ruse signs could advertise a non-existent checkpoint having a proper purpose, to detect impaired driving for example. In such a case, the purpose of the exit ramp checkpoint may not be tainted, but it is not clear that deploying such a ruse would offer any advantage to law enforcement.

193. 681 F.3d 1134.

194. *Id.* at 1138.

195. The court specifically noted that the exit at issue was a "rural highway exit."

196. 681 F.3d at 1141.

Chapter 3

Scope and Duration of Traffic Stops

Chapter 3

Scope and Duration of Traffic Stops

This chapter discusses what an officer may and may not do during a traffic stop and how long the stop may last. It covers issues such as whether an officer may order occupants out of a vehicle, when an officer may use a drug-sniffing dog, and how courts view officers' requests for consent to search vehicles.

The focus throughout is on stops that begin based on suspected violations of the motor vehicle laws. Officers sometimes stop vehicles for other reasons, such as when an officer has reasonable suspicion that a vehicle is being used to transport drugs. Some, but not all, of the legal principles discussed in this chapter apply to that type of vehicle stop as well.

I. Ordering a Driver to Produce His or Her License

An officer may order a driver to produce his or her license during a traffic stop.[1] Whether this authority exists outside the context of a valid stop, as when an officer approaches a motorist who has just parked, is unclear.[2] If the driver does not or cannot produce a license, the officer may charge the driver with failing to produce his or her license or with driving without carrying a license.[3]

An officer has no similar authority to order a passenger to produce a license or other identification during a traffic stop. Although so-called "stop and identify" laws, which require persons stopped by police to identify themselves or to produce identification documents, generally are constitutional,[4] North Carolina has no such law. However, if an officer develops a basis for issuing a citation to a

---

1. Chapter 20, Section 29 of the North Carolina General Statutes (hereinafter G.S.) (making it a misdemeanor for "[a]ny person operating or in charge of a motor vehicle, when requested by an officer in uniform" to fail to "produce his [or her] license").

2. In *Keziah v. Bostic*, 452 F. Supp. 912, 915 (W.D.N.C. 1978), the court considered a situation in which an officer followed a motorist into the motorist's own driveway and demanded to see the motorist's license. The court found the demand improper: "It is not material that petitioner's refusal to display his license constituted an independent violation of [G.S.] 20-29. Since the initial stop and demand themselves were illegal, the officer could not invoke [G.S.] 20-29 to bootstrap himself into a legal arrest."

3. G.S. 20-7(a) ("To drive a motor vehicle on a highway, a person must be licensed . . . and must carry the license while driving the vehicle.").

4. Hiibel v. Sixth Jud. Dist. Ct. of Nev., 542 U.S. 177 (2004).

passenger, the passenger's failure to identify himself or herself may constitute the offense of resisting a public officer.[5]

II. Ordering Occupants Out of a Vehicle

Officers frequently prefer that occupants of a vehicle remain in the vehicle during a traffic stop, and officers generally have the authority to require occupants to do so.[6]

The United States Supreme Court has ruled that officers also generally have the authority to order the occupants of a vehicle out of the vehicle during a traffic stop.[7] This authority is based on courts' concern for officer safety, but courts historically have concluded that the authority may be exercised whether or not the circumstances of a particular stop give rise to a safety concern.[8]

At the time of this writing, however, some uncertainty has arisen regarding officers' authority to order occupants out of their vehicles. In *Rodriguez v. United States*, the U.S. Supreme Court stated that "safety precautions taken to facilitate" detours from the "mission" of a traffic stop improperly extend the stop.[9] Based on this reasoning, some courts have ruled that an officer may not order an occupant out of a vehicle if doing so would needlessly prolong a stop—for example, if the officer is ready to conclude the stop by issuing a warning or a citation to a motorist but instead orders the motorist out of his or her vehicle to allow the officer additional time to observe the motorist and attempt to develop reasonable suspicion of a crime other than the motor vehicle violation that prompted the stop.[10] Exactly how far courts will go in examining officers' orders to exit vehicles is not yet clear. The Court

---

5. State v. Friend, 237 N.C. App. 490, 493 (2014) (holding that "the failure to provide information about one's identity during a lawful stop can constitute resistance, delay, or obstruction within the meaning of [G.S.] 14-223," as where the defendant-passenger refused to identify himself, making it impossible for an officer to issue him a citation for failure to wear a seat belt).

6. State v. Shearin, 170 N.C. App. 222, 230 (2005); ROBERT L. FARB, ARREST, SEARCH, AND INVESTIGATION IN NORTH CAROLINA 49 (UNC School of Government, 5th ed. 2016) (discussing this point and collecting cases).

7. Pennsylvania v. Mimms, 434 U.S. 106, 111 (1977) (driver); Maryland v. Wilson, 519 U.S. 408, 415–16 (1997) (passengers).

8. The officer in *Mimms* stated that it was his standard practice to order all motorists out of their vehicles during traffic stops; the Court's approval of this practice suggests that the authority exists even when no indicia of a threat are present. *See also* United States v. Sakyi, 160 F.3d 164, 168 (4th Cir. 1998) (interpreting *Mimms* as allowing an officer to order occupants out of a stopped vehicle "as a matter of course" and without any "specific, articulable suspicion of danger").

9. 575 U.S. ___, ___, 135 S. Ct. 1609, 1616 (2015).

10. *See generally* State v. Kjolsrud, 371 P.3d 647, 651 (Ariz. Ct. App. 2016) (finding that where an officer could have concluded a stop but instead "asked [a motorist] to step out of the car and walk back to his vehicle, under *Rodriguez*, this further delay amounted to an additional seizure requiring independent reasonable suspicion").

of Appeals of North Carolina has recently issued several opinions that closely scrutinize this sort of command.[11] However, those opinions have been stayed pending review by the state supreme court.[12]

Whether, and under what circumstances, an officer can order a driver or passenger not just out of the person's own vehicle, but into the back seat of the officer's cruiser, is the subject of a split of authority nationally[13] and is not clearly resolved in North Carolina. One reported case apparently approved of putting a motorist in a law enforcement vehicle where "there was a considerable amount of traffic" on the roadway, seemingly making it unsafe to leave the motorist on the roadside.[14] A more recent case, relying on *Rodriguez*, stated that an officer "was required to have reasonable suspicion before asking defendant to go to his patrol vehicle to be questioned," but that opinion has been stayed pending further review.[15] A cautious officer may wish to avoid ordering a motorist into a law enforcement vehicle absent a specific safety justification or reasonable suspicion that the person has committed a crime. For one thing, such a maneuver will often require frisking the motorist in the interest of safety or to satisfy agency policy, which will itself require reasonable suspicion as discussed below. For another, ordering a motorist into a police vehicle is substantially more intrusive than merely ordering a motorist out of his or her own vehicle, and so is more likely to be viewed as implicating the Fourth Amendment. Even taking the time to request that a driver or a passenger voluntarily enter an officer's vehicle may improperly prolong a stop if the request is not justified by officer safety concerns.[16]

---

11. State v. Bullock, ___ N.C. App. ___, ___, 785 S.E.2d 746, 753 (questioning whether an officer may order an occupant out of a vehicle without a specific justification after *Rodriguez* but "assuming" that an officer may do so, ruling that an officer is "required to have reasonable suspicion before asking [a motorist] to go to [the officer's] patrol vehicle to be questioned"), *temp. stay allowed*, 369 N.C. 37, *writ of supersedeas allowed*, 369 N.C. 37 (2016); State v. Reed, ___ N.C. App. ___, ___, 791 S.E.2d 486, 492 (2016) (stating that "an officer may offend the Fourth Amendment if he unlawfully extends a traffic stop by asking a driver to step out of a vehicle" and finding that an officer unlawfully extended a stop in part by ordering a driver out of his vehicle), *temp. stay allowed*, ___ N.C. ___, 793 S.E.2d 247 (2016). *See also* State v. Miller, ___ N.C. App. ___, ___, 795 S.E.2d 374, 378 (2016) (ruling that an officer violated the Fourth Amendment when he effectively abandoned the original purpose of a traffic stop and "ordered [the occupants] out of [a] vehicle and began an investigation into the presence of weapons and drugs;" the court stated that this could "hardly be seen as a safety precaution to facilitate the mission of the stop" and that "the exit order and extraneous questioning cannot be justified as a de minimis intrusion outweighed by the government's interest in officer safety"), *temp. stay allowed*, ___ N.C. ___, 794 S.E.2d 534 (2017).

12. In attempting to forecast how the state supreme court may rule, it may be worth noting that *Rodriguez* discusses *Mimms* without ever suggesting that *Mimms* was incorrect. ___ U.S. at ___, 135 S. Ct. at 1615–16.

13. Jeff Welty, *Traffic Stops, Part II*, N.C. CRIM. L., UNC SCH. OF GOV'T BLOG (Oct. 28, 2009), http://nccriminallaw.sog.unc.edu/traffic-stops-part-ii/.

14. State v. Hudson, 103 N.C. App. 708, 716 (1991). However, the court in *Hudson* focused more on the officer's authority to order the motorist out of his own vehicle than into the officer's vehicle.

15. *Bullock*, ___ N.C. App. ___, ___, 785 S.E.2d 746, 753, *temp. stay allowed*, 369 N.C. 37, *writ of supersedeas allowed*, 369 N.C. 37 (2016).

16. In *Bullock*, the officer frisked the defendant before the defendant entered the officer's vehicle. The State argued, in part, that the frisk was consensual, but the court ruled that even if it was, the request for consent was an undue extension of the stop. ___ N.C. App. at ___, 785 S.E.2d at 753 ("The dissent argues that defendant consented to the pat down search. We need not decide, however, whether defendant consented, because the moment [an officer] asked if he could search defendant's person, without reasonable suspicion that defendant was armed and dangerous, he unlawfully prolonged the stop. Under *Rodriguez*, other than running permissive checks, any additional amount of time [the officer] took that was unrelated to the mission of the stop unlawfully prolonged it.") The same analysis could apply to a request to sit in the officer's vehicle, even absent a frisk. However, in some cases, such a request might be made without prolonging the stop, as when one officer makes the request while another prepares a citation. Prolonging the stop is discussed generally later in this chapter.

III. Frisking Occupants of a Vehicle

Particularly if an officer orders an occupant out of a vehicle—or if an occupant exits his or her vehicle unprompted—the officer may wish to "frisk" the occupant, or pat the occupant's outer clothing in order to detect weapons. Perhaps because the concept of "stop and frisk" was discussed in *Terry v. Ohio*,[17] participants in the criminal justice system sometimes assume that whenever an officer makes a valid stop, the officer has the authority to frisk the person stopped. But in fact, a frisk is a separate Fourth Amendment intrusion, and it is justified only if the officer reasonably suspects that the person or people to be frisked are armed and dangerous.[18] As the U.S. Supreme Court has put it, "To justify a patdown of the driver or a passenger during a traffic stop . . . just as in the case of a pedestrian reasonably suspected of criminal activity, the police must harbor reasonable suspicion that the person subjected to the frisk is armed and dangerous."[19]

Whether such reasonable suspicion exists in a particular case is determined in light of all the circumstances. For example, a frisk was justified when a vehicle occupant continually eyed an officer, was wearing clothing suggestive of gang membership, was carrying a radio scanner in his pocket, and had recently been released from prison.[20] Likewise, a frisk was permitted when a driver "had prior convictions for drug offenses, [an officer] observed [the driver's] nervous behavior inside his vehicle, and [the officer] saw him deliberately conceal his right hand and refuse to open it despite repeated requests."[21] By contrast, a frisk was improper where a passenger had unspecified "priors" for armed robbery and misrepresented the validity of his driver's license.[22]

Courts have recognized that a "host of factors can contribute to a basis for reasonable suspicion,"[23] and it would be impossible to catalog every factor that a court has considered in determining whether reasonable suspicion was present. Among those factors are a person's nervousness and evasiveness,[24] the presence of a visible bulge in a person's clothing,[25] furtive or suspicious movements by the person,[26] whether the person has a criminal record[27] or apparent gang ties,[28] whether the interaction takes place late at night,[29] the crime rate in the area where the interaction takes place,[30] whether a weapon is visible in the person's vehicle,[31] and many others.

When an officer has a basis to frisk an occupant of a vehicle, it does not matter whether the occupant is the driver or a passenger. That is, an officer may frisk a passenger based on reasonable suspicion that the passenger is armed and dangerous, even if the officer does not suspect the passenger

---

17. 392 U.S. 1 (1968).

18. *Id.* at 30–31.

19. Arizona v. Johnson, 555 U.S. 323, 327 (2009).

20. *Johnson*, 555 U.S. 323.

21. State v. Henry, 237 N.C. App. 311, 317 (2014).

22. United States v. Powell, 666 F.3d 180 (4th Cir. 2011).

23. United States v. George, 732 F.3d 296, 299 (4th Cir. 2013).

24. State v. Johnson, ___ N.C. App. ___, 783 S.E.2d 753 (2016).

25. *Id.*

26. *George*, 732 F.3d 296.

27. *Powell*, 666 F.3d at 188 (noting that "a person's possible involvement in prior criminal activity . . . can be relevant in establishing reasonable suspicion").

28. Arizona v. Johnson, 555 U.S. 323 (2009).

29. *See, e.g.*, State v. King, 206 N.C. App. 585 (2010).

30. *George*, 732 F.3d 296.

31. *King*, 206 N.C. App. 585.

of criminal activity and even though the passenger is not responsible for whatever motor vehicle concern prompted the stop.[32]

An officer who lacks reasonable suspicion to conduct a frisk may ask for consent to do so. The law regarding such requests is unsettled at the time of this writing, with at least some courts viewing at least some such requests as involving an improper extension of a stop.[33]

IV. "Car Frisks"

In *Michigan v. Long*, the U.S. Supreme Court held that "the search of the passenger compartment of an automobile, limited to those areas in which a weapon may be placed or hidden, is permissible if the police officer possesses [reasonable suspicion] that the suspect is dangerous and the suspect may gain immediate control of weapons."[34] Although *Long* was decided in the context of what might be described as a *Terry* stop rather than a typical traffic stop, the two types of stops are similar if not identical for Fourth Amendment purposes,[35] and the concept of a car frisk also applies to traffic stops.[36]

Whether there is reasonable suspicion that a person is dangerous is essentially the same determination that must be made when deciding whether a frisk of the person is justified. That issue is discussed immediately above. Factors that courts have mentioned in the car frisk context include furtive movements by the occupants of the vehicle, lack of compliance with police instructions, belligerence, reports that the suspect is armed, and visible indications that a weapon may be present in the car.[37] While the fact that a person is suspected of criminal activity may contribute to suspicion of dangerousness, the mere fact that a person has committed a traffic infraction probably does not.

Whether an officer's belief that a suspect may gain immediate control of a weapon is reasonable depends on all the circumstances of the stop. Courts have considered the suspect's location relative

---

32. *Johnson*, 555 U.S. at 326–27.

33. *See supra* note 16 and accompanying text. *But see* State v Floyd, 898 N.W.2d 560, 570 (Wis. 2017) (concluding that an officer's request to "perform a search for his safety" was "related to officer safety and . . . negligibly burdensome" and so was "part of the traffic stop's mission" and not an unjustified extension of the stop). Requests for consent frisks are generally similar to requests for consent searches, a topic discussed in section VI.C of this chapter.

34. 463 U.S. 1032, 1049 (1983) (footnote omitted).

35. Named after *Terry v. Ohio*, 392 U.S. 1 (1968), a *Terry* stop takes place when an officer briefly detains a person based on reasonable suspicion that the person is involved in criminal activity. Likewise, a traffic stop is a brief detention based on reasonable suspicion that a person has violated the motor vehicle laws. Berkemer v. McCarty, 468 U.S. 420, 439 (1984) (footnote, internal citation omitted) ("[T]he usual traffic stop is more analogous to a so-called 'Terry stop' than to a formal arrest."); State v. Styles, 362 N.C. 412, 414 (2008) (citation omitted) ("Traffic stops have 'been historically reviewed under the investigatory detention framework first articulated in [*Terry*].'").

36. State v. Hudson, 103 N.C. App. 708, 718–19 (1991) (upholding car frisk arising out of a traffic stop).

37. *See, e.g.,* State v. Edwards, 164 N.C. App. 130, 136 (2004) (finding a car frisk justified where a sexual assault suspect was reported to have a gun, was noncompliant, and appeared to have reached under the seat of his vehicle); State v. Minor, 132 N.C. App. 478, 481–82 (1999) (holding a car frisk not justified where a suspect appeared to access the center console of the vehicle and later rubbed his hand on his thigh near his pocket; these movements were not "clearly furtive"); State v. Clyburn, 120 N.C. App. 377, 381–82 (1995) (ruling a car frisk justified where officers suspected that the defendant was involved in the drug trade and the defendant was belligerent during the stop).

to the vehicle and whether the suspect has been handcuffed, though the fact that a suspect has been handcuffed does not automatically rule out a car frisk.[38]

A car frisk is not a search for evidence, and so must be limited to locations in the vehicle where a weapon could be located.[39] The search may extend to the glove compartment[40] and, presumably, to other containers in the passenger compartment that could contain a weapon. In *State v. Parker*, the court held that an officer properly searched "a drawstring bag located underneath a piece of newspaper that fell to the ground" as he assisted an occupant out of a vehicle.[41] The court noted that the bag was located near a firearm and "was at least large enough to contain methamphetamine and a 'smoking device.' "[42]

Whether a car frisk could be done pursuant to a motorist's consent is an issue similar to whether the occupant of a vehicle may be frisked by consent. That issue is discused in the preceeding section of this chapter.

A full search of a vehicle is different from a car frisk and cannot be justified based merely on officer safety concerns. Whether an officer may seek consent for a full vehicle search during a traffic stop is discussed later in this chapter. Other possible justifications for full vehicle searches, such as searches incident to the arrest of a vehicle's occupant and inventory searches, might arise after the conclusion of a traffic stop; they are discussed elsewhere.[43]

V. License, Warrant, and Record Checks

In *Rodriguez v. United States*, the U.S. Supreme Court recognized that "checking the driver's license" and "determining whether there are outstanding warrants against the driver" are "ordinary inquiries" that are a legitimate part of a traffic stop.[44] This is consistent with prior case law finding various types of computer checks, and the associated brief delays, permissible, even absent any particular reason to believe that a motorist's license is invalid or that he or she is the subject of an outstanding warrant.[45]

---

38. *Compare Edwards*, 164 N.C. App. at 137 (a defendant suspected of possessing a handgun was handcuffed and sitting on the curb but remained in sufficiently "close proximity to the interior of the vehicle" to gain access to a weapon), *and* State v. Parker, 183 N.C. App. 1, 12 (2007) (defendant was handcuffed in the backseat of his own car when he disclosed that there was a gun in the car; two other passengers were also in the car; "these circumstances were sufficient to create a reasonable belief that defendant was dangerous and had immediate access to a weapon"), *with* State v. Braxton, 90 N.C. App. 204, 208–09 (1988) (it was "uncontroverted that defendant [stopped for speeding] could not obtain any weapon . . . from the car" where he was not in the car and detective testified that defendant could not have reached the area searched).

39. *Long*, 463 U.S. at 1049. *See also Parker*, 183 N.C. App. at 9 ("The scope of a valid 'vehicle frisk' does not extend to searching for evidence.").

40. *See, e.g., Clyburn*, 120 N.C. App. 377 (search of glove compartment justified under car frisk doctrine).

41. 183 N.C. App. at 12.

42. *Id. See also* United States v. Shranklen, 315 F.3d 959 (8th Cir. 2003) (search of a "black pouch" that was large enough to contain a weapon was justified as part of a car frisk).

43. *See generally* FARB, *supra* note 6, at 252–53, 261–62.

44. 575 U.S. ___, ___, 135 S. Ct. 1609, 1615 (2015).

45. State v. Velazquez-Perez, 233 N.C. App. 585, 595 (2014) (finding "no . . . authority" for the defendant's claim that a document check exceeded the scope of a speeding stop and noting that "officers routinely check relevant documentation while conducting traffic stops"); State v. Hernandez, 170 N.C. App. 299, 307–08 (2005) (holding that "running checks on Defendant's license and registration" was "reasonably related to the stop based on the seat belt infraction"); State v. Castellon, 151 N.C. App. 675, 680 (2002) (twenty-five minute "detention for the purpose of determining the validity of defendant's license was not unreasonable" when

Whether an officer may take time to run checks that focus on a motorist's criminal history rather than his or her driving status and the existence of outstanding arrest warrants is less clearly settled. The *Rodriguez* Court briefly suggested that criminal record checks may be permissible as an officer safety measure.[46] However, the Court did not address the issue in detail, and the North Carolina Court of Appeals stated in a recent opinion—albeit one that has been stayed by the state supreme court—that an officer "extended [a] stop further when he had defendant get into his patrol vehicle and ran defendant's name through numerous databases while being questioned, *as this went beyond an authorized, routine check of a driver's license or for warrants.*"[47] Similarly, at least one federal circuit court has found running one variety of criminal record check to be improperly directed at detecting evidence of ordinary criminal wrongdoing.[48] By contrast, the Fourth Circuit has stated that "[a]n officer is entitled to conduct safety-related checks that do not bear directly on the reasons for the stop, such as requesting a driver's license and vehicle registration, or *checking for criminal records* and outstanding arrest warrants.*"[49]

VI. Investigation of Other Criminal Activity

An officer may conduct a traffic stop, then come to suspect that one or more occupants of the vehicle are involved in criminal activity beyond the motor vehicle violation that prompted the stop. Sometimes substantial evidence of criminal activity is immediately apparent, as when an officer sees rolling papers or other indicators of drug activity inside the vehicle. In such a case, the interaction may become a *Terry* stop for investigation of the criminal activity. The officer is then entitled to take a reasonable amount of time to investigate the criminal activity through questioning and other measures.[50]

---

officer's computer was working slowly). *See also, e.g.,* United States v. Villa, 589 F.3d 1334, 1339 (10th Cir. 2009) (citation omitted) ("It is well-established that [a] law enforcement officer conducting a routine traffic stop may request a driver's license and vehicle registration, run a computer check, and issue a citation."). *See generally* Wayne R. LaFave, *The "Routine Traffic Stop" from Start to Finish: Too Much "Routine," Not Enough Fourth Amendment,* 102 MICH. L. REV. 1843, 1874–85 (2004) (noting that most courts have permitted license, warrant, and record checks incident to traffic stops, though criticizing some of those conclusions).

46. 575 U.S. at ___, 135 S. Ct. at 1616 (citing United States v. Holt, 264 F.3d 1215 (10th Cir. 2001) (en banc), for the proposition that running a motorist's criminal record is justified by officer safety).

47. State v. Bullock, ___ N.C. App. ___, ___, 785 S.E.2d 746, 753 (emphasis supplied), *temp. stay allowed,* 369 N.C. 37, *writ of supersedeas allowed,* 369 N.C. 37 (2016).

48. United States v. Evans, 786 F.3d 779 (9th Cir. 2015) (ruling that an officer improperly extended a traffic stop to conduct an "ex-felon registration check," a procedure that inquired into a subject's criminal history and determined whether he had registered his address with the sheriff as required for certain offenders in the state in which the stop took place).

49. United States v. Palmer, 820 F.3d 640, 649 (4th Cir. 2016) (emphasis supplied). The court also stated that "[a] police officer is entitled to inquire into a motorist's criminal record after initiating a traffic stop." *Id.* at 651. *See also* United States v. Hill, 852 F.3d 377, 383 (4th Cir. 2017) (finding no unjustified delay when an officer checked multiple computer databases, including one that tracked every person who had contact with the local police department: "In our view, an officer reasonably may search a computer database during a traffic stop to determine an individual's prior contact with local law enforcement, just as an officer may engage in the indisputably proper action of searching computer databases for an individual's outstanding warrants").

50. For a recent example of a case of this kind, see *State v. Castillo,* ___ N.C. App. ___, ___, 787 S.E.2d 48, 55–56 (2016) ("Based on defendant's bizarre travel plans, his extreme nervousness, the use of masking odors, the smell of marijuana on his person, and the third-party registration of the vehicle, it is reasonable that

The situation is more complex when the officer lacks reasonable suspicion that the occupants of a vehicle are involved in criminal activity but nonetheless has a hunch that the officer wishes to pursue while continuing the traffic stop. For many years, courts generally allowed officers the leeway to undertake a modicum of additional investigation, so long as the investigative techniques used did not themselves constitute searches or seizures, on the theory that a few minutes of additional investigation were an inconsequential addition to the intrusion inherent in the traffic stop itself. So an officer could ask a few questions about the presence of weapons in a vehicle or could detain a driver for a few minutes while deploying a drug dog on a vehicle. Neither asking questions nor deploying a drug dog is itself a search, and any additional time consumed in these activities was seen as de minimis.[51]

The U.S. Supreme Court flatly rejected this approach in its recent ruling in *Rodriguez v. United States*.[52] The case arose when, after midnight, a Nebraska law enforcement officer saw a vehicle veer onto the shoulder of a state highway, then pull back onto the road. Nebraska law prohibits driving on the shoulder, so the officer stopped the vehicle. The driver provided the officer with his license, registration, and proof of insurance. The passenger provided his license as well. License and warrant checks on both men apparently came back clean, and the officer issued a warning ticket to the driver.

The officer suspected that the driver might be involved in drug activity, so he asked the driver for permission to run the officer's drug dog around the vehicle. The driver said no. The officer then called for backup and detained the driver for a few minutes until another officer arrived. At that point, the officer walked his dog around the vehicle twice and the dog alerted. The alert led to a search and the discovery of methamphetamine. The total delay to allow the drug dog to sniff the car was seven or eight minutes.

The Supreme Court ultimately ruled that a stop may not be extended beyond the time necessary to complete the "mission" of the stop, which is "to address the traffic violation that warranted the stop, and attend to related safety concerns." In other words, "[a]uthority for the seizure thus ends when tasks tied to the traffic infraction are—or reasonably should have been—completed."[53]

---

even an untrained person would doubt defendant's story, much less a fifteen-year veteran with interdiction training. Thus, we hold that Officer Green had reasonable suspicion to extend the stop and could run such ancillary records checks as he believed reasonable until his investigation was complete.").

51. North Carolina cases in this vein include *State v. Sellars*, 222 N.C. App. 245, 252 (2012) (holding that a delay of four minutes thirty-seven seconds to allow a drug dog to search a car was de minimis), and *State v. Brimmer*, 187 N.C. App. 451, 457 (2007) (similar holding, four-minute delay). *But see* State v. Cottrell, 234 N.C. App. 736, 748 (2014) (stating that the court does "not believe that the *de minimis* analysis applied in *Brimmer* and *Sellars* should be extended to situations when, as here, a drug dog was not already on the scene"). Federal cases generally followed the de minimis analysis described in the text. *See, e.g.*, United States v. Green, 740 F.3d 275, 281 (4th Cir. 2014) (running a "criminal history check added just four minutes to the traffic stop" and "at most, amounted to a de minimis intrusion . . . [that] did not constitute a violation of [the defendant's] Fourth Amendment rights"); United States v. Mason, 628 F.3d 123, 132 (4th Cir. 2010) ("The one to two of the 11 minutes [that the stop took] devoted to questioning on matters not directly related to the traffic stop constituted only a slight delay that raises no Fourth Amendment concern."); United States v. Harrison, 606 F.3d 42, 45 (2d Cir. 2010) (per curiam) (five to six minutes of questioning unrelated to the purpose of the traffic stop "did not prolong the stop so as to render it unconstitutional"); United States v. Turvin, 517 F.3d 1097, 1101 (9th Cir. 2008) (asking a "few questions" unrelated to the stop that prolonged the stop by a "few moments" was not unreasonable, and collecting cases). Of course, courts recognized some outer limit to what could be viewed as de minimis. *See* United States v. Digiovanni, 650 F.3d 498, 510 (4th Cir. 2011) (unreasonable to spend ten minutes of a fifteen-minute traffic stop asking drug-related questions); United States v. Peralez, 526 F.3d 1115, 1121 (8th Cir. 2008) (extending a traffic stop by ten minutes to ask drug-related questions was unreasonable).

52. 575 U.S. ___, 135 S. Ct. 1609 (2015).

53. *Id.* at ___, 135 S. Ct. at 1614 (citation omitted).

Applying this reasoning to the case at bar, the Court stated that a dog sniff is not a task "tied to the traffic infraction," as it is "aimed at detecting . . . ordinary criminal wrongdoing."[54] Therefore, if such a sniff prologs a stop at all, as it did in the case before the Court, it violates the Fourth Amendment. The Court allowed no exception for "de minimis" delays.

Rodriguez does not prohibit officers from investigative activity that is not directed at the traffic violation that motivated the stop. It merely provides that *if* such activity prolongs the stop, it is unreasonable. Thus, an officer—or a team of officers working together—may be able to comply with *Rodriguez* by multitasking: deploying a drug dog while waiting for a response on a license check, or asking investigative questions of the driver while filling out a citation.[55] Defendants may argue that such multitasking inherently slows an officer down, and it is easy to imagine difficult factual disputes on this point.[56]

One issue that seems especially likely to arise is whether waiting for a backup officer to arrive is an activity that is a necessary and appropriate part of a particular traffic stop. If so, an officer might be able to observe a vehicle's occupants, question them, or undertake other investigation of non-traffic related matters while waiting for backup without running afoul of *Rodriguez*. The Court in *Rodriguez* acknowledged that "attend[ing] to . . . safety concerns" is a part of the "mission" of a stop,[57] but whether a given stop presents safety concerns sufficient to justify waiting for a backup officer may be debatable, with courts likely to consider factors such as the number of occupants in the vehicle, whether any occupants have criminal records, the time of day or night, and the location of the stop.[58]

---

54. *Id.* at ___, ___, 135 S. Ct. at 1614, 1620.

55. *See, e.g.,* United States v. Collazo, 818 F.3d 247, 258 (6th Cir. 2016) (finding that an officer's questions to the occupant of a vehicle about her prior criminal record did not violate the Fourth Amendment, in part because the officer "was waiting on the completion of the license check while he spoke to" the occupant).

56. The Oregon courts essentially adopted the rule of *Rodriguez* years before *Rodriguez* was decided, and a robust body of case law has developed around the rule. A frequently-litigated issue is whether an officer's investigative activity came during an "unavoidable lull" in the stop. *Compare, e.g.,* State v. Dennis, 282 P.3d 955 (Or. Ct. App. 2012) (an officer's request that the defendant remove an item from his pants did not occur during an "unavoidable lull" in a jaywalking stop), *with, e.g.,* State v. Jones, 245 P.3d 148 (Or. Ct. App. 2010) (an officer's request to search the defendant took place during an "unavoidable lull" in a stop as the officer sought to confirm the defendant's identity).

57. 575 U.S. at ___, 135 S. Ct. at 1614.

58. *Compare, e.g.,* United States v. Frierson, 611 F. App'x 82, 84 (3d Cir. 2015) (ruling that it was appropriate for an officer to wait twenty-six minutes for a backup officer where the first officer had stopped a vehicle with two occupants, one of whom "had an extensive criminal history, including convictions for voluntary manslaughter, possession of an assault weapon and body armor, and cocaine possession, transportation, or sale"), *and* United States v. Crawley, 526 F. App'x 551, 556–57 (6th Cir. 2013) (waiting for backup was "a short and reasonable delay to ensure the officer's safety" where the officer stopped a vehicle containing multiple occupants with criminal records), *with, e.g.,* State v. Bravo-Zamora, 340 P.3d 1236 (Kan. Ct. App. 2015) (noting that an officer "extended the normal amount of time to process this traffic stop by speaking with [a] DEA agent and waiting for [a] backup officer to arrive"), *and* State v. Hoefler, 306 P.3d 337 (Kan. Ct. App. 2013) ("[W]e find the stop was unnecessarily extended under the pretense of waiting for another officer to arrive. . . . The State failed to come forward with evidence or a persuasive argument as to why there was a need to legally extend the stop for a highway trooper to arrive."). If an officer develops reasonable suspicion that a motorist is involved in criminal activity beyond whatever motor vehicle violation led to the stop, and the stop becomes a *Terry* stop, a brief delay associated with waiting for backup is more likely to be permissible. *See, e.g.,* United States v. Castro, 647 F. App'x 388, 392 (5th Cir. 2016) ("Officer Guerra's reasonable suspicion of a drug crime justified the time taken to process the initial traffic infraction, wait for the arrival of backup, and question Castro."); United States v. Lester, 477 F. App'x 697, 701 (11th Cir. 2012) ("[T]he only delay in the investigation was the five to ten minutes that it took for backup to arrive. Under the circumstances [where an officer had detained a person, carrying a "manufactured piece of wood," who the officer thought may have

The remainder of this section explores how *Rodriguez* applies to specific investigative techniques that an officer might use during a traffic stop.

A. Questioning Occupants of a Vehicle

When an officer questions a person, the officer conducts neither a search nor a seizure. The U.S. Supreme Court so held in *Muehler v. Mena*,[59] and although *Muehler* involved a person who was detained during the execution of a search warrant, not the subject of a traffic stop, the Court has since recognized that its reasoning applies equally in the traffic stop setting.[60] Thus, an officer may question a person who has been stopped about a matter unrelated to the justification for the stop without any individualized suspicion supporting the questions. *Rodriguez* teaches, however, that if the questioning prolongs the detention, the detention itself becomes unreasonable.[61]

In many cases involving an officer's questions, the first issue that a court should address is whether the officer's questions are or are not pertinent to the traffic stop. If they are pertinent to the stop, then

---

been involved in a robbery], this wait was reasonable to ensure the officer's safety."); United States v. Luginbyhl, 321 F. App'x 780, 787 (10th Cir. 2009) (reasonable for an officer to "prolong[] the encounter waiting for backup to arrive so that he would not have to perform the protective frisk [of the suspect] alone"); United States v. Martin, 422 F.3d 597, 602 (7th Cir. 2005) (citation omitted) ("In light of the developing information, it was not unreasonable for Trooper Wood to suspect that Mr. Martin was trafficking narcotics. Nor was it unreasonable to detain Mr. Martin [twenty minutes] for the canine unit to arrive and confirm or deny the troopers' suspicions. . . . There was no unreasonable delay waiting for backup and the canine unit."); United States v. Scheets, 189 F.3d 829 (7th Cir. 1999) (ruling that a *Terry* stop was reasonable even though it involved a fifteen-minute wait for a second officer to arrive); State v. Williams, 87 N.C. App. 261, 265 (1987) (ruling that the duration of a *Terry* stop was reasonable where it involved a delay of "no more than six or seven minutes to await [another officer's] arrival"). A related issue is whether, when multiple officers are present, both must work on addressing the traffic violation that prompted the stop or whether one may address the traffic violation while the other undertakes other duties. In *United States v. Hill*, 852 F.3d 377, 383, 384 (4th Cir. 2017), the Fourth Circuit found that it was reasonable for one officer to "stand next to the car during most of the stop, rather than to assist [another officer] in completing" tasks related to the mission of the stop; the court noted that "the NCIC database returned an alert that the two men were 'likely armed'" and ruled that "given the inherent risks involved in such traffic stops, we conclude that the decision here by the two officers to allocate duties at the scene of the traffic stop, so that one remained in the immediate proximity of the vehicle's occupants at all times, was not unreasonable."

59. 544 U.S. 93, 101–02 (2005).

60. Arizona v. Johnson, 555 U.S. 323, 333 (2009) ("An officer's inquiries into matters unrelated to the justification for the traffic stop, this Court has made plain, do not convert the encounter into something other than a lawful seizure, so long as those inquiries do not measurably extend the duration of the stop."). *See also, e.g.*, United States v. Olivera-Mendez, 484 F.3d 505, 510–11 (8th Cir. 2007); United States v. Stewart, 473 F.3d 1265, 1268–69 (10th Cir. 2007).

61. The state court of appeals prefigured *Rodriguez* as it pertains to questioning in *State v. Jackson*, 199 N.C. App. 236, 243 (2009) (ruling that an officer's decision to ask a handful of drug-related questions "was indeed an extension of the detention beyond the scope of the original traffic stop as the interrogation was not necessary to confirm or dispel [the officer's] suspicion that [the driver] was operating without a valid driver's license . . . . Accordingly, for this extended detention to have been constitutional, [the officer] must have had grounds which provided a reasonable and articulable suspicion or the encounter must have become consensual."). It subsequently applied *Rodriguez* to questioning unrelated to the mission of a traffic stop in *State v. Bedient*, ___ N.C. App. ___, ___, 786 S.E.2d 319, 324 (2016) (reasoning that "after [an officer] verbally warned defendant about her failure to dim her high beams and failure to maintain the proper address on her license, the two purposes—the two missions—of the traffic stop were addressed" so that the officer "needed reasonable, articulable suspicion that criminal activity was afoot before he prolonged the detention by asking additional questions;" because he did not have reasonable suspicion, the further questioning violated the Fourth Amendment).

any time required to ask the questions is reasonable. If they are not, then it becomes necessary to ask whether the questions prolonged the stop. Whether questions are relevant to the mission of the stop will not always be obvious: Is initial chit-chat about the weather permissible rapport-building that is appropriately a part of a traffic stop? If the conversation turns to travel plans, is that still acceptable even though reasonable suspicion of criminal activity might be predicated in part upon uncertain travel plans or travel plans involving drug-source cities? What about questions concerning who owns the vehicle or the relationship between the vehicle's occupants?

Courts are just beginning to address these issues. One early case is *United States v. Iturbe-Gonzalez*, where the court ruled that an officer may make "traffic safety-related inquiries of a general nature[, including about the driver's] travel plans and travel objectives," and said that "any suggestion to the contrary would ask that officers issuing traffic violations temporarily become traffic ticket automatons while processing a traffic violation, as opposed to human beings."[62] Of course, even if a question or two about travel plans is sufficiently related to the purpose of a traffic stop, a court might take a different view of an officer's extended discussion of itineraries with multiple vehicle occupants.[63]

If the questioning is not connected to the mission of the stop but instead is an effort to investigate another offense, a court then must determine whether the questioning extended the stop. Again, courts are just beginning to tackle this question. Early decisions on point generally focus on whether the officer was working diligently on the stop at the same time or whether the questioning was a stand-alone activity that lengthened the stop.[64]

---

62. 100 F. Supp. 3d 1030, 1037–38 (D. Mont. 2015).

63. For additional cases on this issue, see *United States v. Cone*, ___ F.3d ___, No. 16-5125, 2017 WL 3623921 (10th. Cir. Aug. 24, 2017) (ruling that questions about a driver's criminal history were pertinent to officer safety and therefore permissible), *United States v. Moore*, 795 F.3d 1224, 1229 (10th Cir. 2015) (stating, in a discussion of post-*Rodriguez* traffic stop principles, that "[a]n officer may also generally inquire about the driver's travel plans"), and *Fisher v. State*, 481 S.W.3d 403, 407, 411 (Tex. App. 2015) (discussing the issue extensively; stating that "[i]n the course of a routine traffic stop, the detaining officer may . . . question the vehicle's occupants regarding their travel plans;" noting that "cases from the federal courts demonstrate that questions about a driver's origination, destination, and travel purpose are related to the general purposes for a traffic stop because of their potential to determine the existence of an extenuating circumstance [e.g., that the driver was speeding to take a pregnant woman to the hospital] or driver impairment;" and concluding that such questions are permissible of both drivers and passengers, whether the basis for the stop is a moving violation or an equipment malfunction).

64. United States v. Collazo, 818 F.3d 247, 258 (6th Cir. 2016) (finding that an officer's questions to the occupant of a vehicle about her prior criminal record did not violate the Fourth Amendment, in part because the officer "was waiting on the completion of the license check while he spoke to" the occupant); State v. Bullock, ___ N.C. App. ___, 785 S.E.2d 746 (emphasis supplied) ("By requiring defendant to submit to a pat-down search *and questioning in the patrol car unrelated to the purpose of the traffic stop*, the officer prolonged the traffic stop beyond the time necessary to complete the stop's mission and the routine checks authorized by *Rodriguez*."), *temp. stay allowed*, 369 N.C. 37, *writ of supersedeas allowed*, 369 N.C. 37 (2016); United States v. Ramos, 194 F. Supp. 3d 1134, 1170 (D.N.M. 2016) (finding officer's questions about driver's travel plans permissible in part because "[t]here is no evidence that this questioning increased the amount of time it took [the officer] to write the citation"); United States v. Archuleta, 619 F. App'x 683, 691 (10th Cir. 2015) (unpublished) (citing *Rodriguez* and ruling that a bicycle stop was improperly prolonged "in order to ask a few additional questions" unrelated to the bicycle law violations that prompted the stop).

B. Use of Drug-Sniffing Dogs

Like asking questions, having a dog sniff a car is not a search and so requires no individualized suspicion.[65] The U.S. Supreme Court has ruled that a drug dog "discloses only the presence or absence of narcotics" and that there is no legitimate privacy interest in the possession of narcotics.[66] Therefore, a dog sniff is permitted during any traffic stop, so long as the sniff does not extend the stop. Any extension of the stop would need to be supported by reasonable suspicion of drug activity.

Presumably, it would be difficult for a single officer to deploy a drug dog and monitor its behavior while simultaneously moving diligently towards the completion of a traffic stop. However, in several recent cases, courts have found no Fourth Amendment violation when two officers worked together on a stop, with one deploying the drug dog while the other attended to the traffic violation.[67] These holdings seem sound only if there was nothing that the second officer could have done to move the traffic stop towards completion. Otherwise, if the second officer chooses to deploy a drug dog rather than to assist with the processing of the traffic stop, the effect of the officer's decision would be to prolong the stop.[68]

C. Asking for Consent to Search

Requests for consent to search made during a traffic stop probably should be analyzed just like any other inquiry about matters unrelated to the purpose of the stop. Such a request is not, in itself, a search or a seizure, so making a request requires no justification. However, if making the request extends the duration of a traffic stop—even momentarily—it violates the Fourth Amendment unless an officer has developed reasonable suspicion of criminal activity that supports the extension of the

---

65. Illinois v. Caballes, 543 U.S. 405, 408–09 (2005).

66. *Id.* at 409, 408.

67. *See* State v. Jackson, 38 N.E.3d 407 (Ohio Ct. App. 2015) (a traffic stop was not impermissibly extended by a dog sniff where the sniff was conducted by a different trooper while the trooper who initiated the stop was in the process of investigating the defendant's background and producing a traffic citation); Lewis v. State, 773 S.E.2d 423 (Ga. Ct. App. 2015) (similar).

68. The analysis may be different if a second officer, instead of deploying a drug dog, attends to safety and security concerns rather than assisting the primary officer in the processing of the traffic stop. *See* United States v. Hill, 852 F.3d 377, 383, 384 (4th Cir. 2017) (finding no unreasonable extension of the stop where one officer elected to "stand next to the car during most of the stop, rather than to assist [another officer] in completing" tasks related to the mission of the stop; the court noted that "the NCIC database returned an alert that the two men were 'likely armed' " and ruled that "given the inherent risks involved in such traffic stops . . . the decision here by the two officers to allocate duties at the scene of the traffic stop, so that one remained in the immediate proximity of the vehicle's occupants at all times, was not unreasonable").

stop. Pre-*Rodriguez* cases routinely upheld requests for consent to search made during traffic stops,[69] but several post-*Rodriguez* cases have found that such requests entailed impermissible delays.[70]

If an officer obtains a valid consent to search without delaying a traffic stop—perhaps where an officer asks for consent to search while waiting for the driver to locate his or her license—the time spent conducting the search is probably justified by the consent and should not count as an improper extension of the stop.

Requests for consent to search may also be made after a traffic stop is complete. Such requests are discussed briefly in connection with the termination of traffic stops, later in this chapter.

VII. Total Duration

In *Rodriguez*, the U.S. Supreme Court did not attempt to define the permissible total duration of a traffic stop. Nor have lower courts attempted to create a bright-line rule regarding the length of traffic stops, because the duration of a stop inevitably depends on "a multitude of factors."[71] Among the

---

69. 4 Wayne R. LaFave, Search and Seizure § 9.3(e) (5th ed. 2012). *See also* United States v. Turvin, 517 F.3d 1097, 1103–04 (9th Cir. 2008) (because "officers do not need reasonable suspicion to ask questions unrelated to the purpose of an initially lawful stop," a request for consent to search that did not substantially prolong a traffic stop was permissible). Arguably contrary to this view is *State v. Parker*, 183 N.C. App. 1, 9 (2007), where the court stated that "[i]f the officer's request for consent to search is unrelated to the initial purpose for the stop, then the request must be supported by reasonable articulable suspicion of additional criminal activity." However, the court's reasoning appears to have been that such a request inherently involves at least a minimal extension of the stop, not that asking for consent is itself a search or seizure. More typical is *State v. Jacobs*, 162 N.C. App. 251, 258 (2004), where the court stated: "Defendant argues alternatively that the State failed to establish that Officer Smith had sufficient reasonable suspicion to request defendant's consent for the search [during an investigative stop]. No such showing is required."

70. *See, e.g.*, State v. Bullock, ___ N.C. App. ___, ___, 785 S.E.2d 746, 752–53 ("We need not decide, however, whether defendant consented [to a frisk of his person], because the moment [an officer] asked if he could search defendant's person, without reasonable suspicion that defendant was armed and dangerous, he unlawfully prolonged the stop."), *temp. stay allowed*, 369 N.C. 37, *writ of supersedeas allowed*, 369 N.C. 37 (2016); State v. Kimmons, 352 P.3d 68, 73–74 (Or. Ct. App. 2015) (applying Oregon law similar to the holding of *Rodriguez*, the court "conclude[d] that the police unlawfully extended [a] stop" where officers sought consent to search a vehicle for weapons during a stop for parking the vehicle in a private lot without paying for parking; "[r]ather than proceeding with [the parking] matters, through pertinent inquiries or issuance of citations (or possible arrest for criminal trespass), the police, instead, sought consent to search for items unrelated to those matters;" "[b]ecause—and this is undisputed—the request did not occur during an 'unavoidable lull' as to the investigation and processing of defendant's possible criminal trespass, or any insurance related violation—that conduct effected an unconstitutional seizure" by extending the stop); Villanueva v. State, 189 So. 3d 982, 985 (Fla. Dist. Ct. App. 2016) (ruling that an officer's request for consent to search involved an improper extension of a stop where "at the time of the request for consent to search . . . the only thing [the officer] had left to do was issue the citation"). *Cf.* State v. Bedient, ___ N.C. App. ___, 786 S.E.2d 319 (2016) (asking "additional questions," such as "[d]o you have anything in the vehicle," improperly prolonged a traffic stop). An extreme example is *United States v. Hight*, 127 F. Supp. 3d 1126 (D. Colo. 2015). In that case, an officer stopped a truck for a traffic violation, ran standard checks on the driver and spoke briefly with him, and decided that he wanted to ask for consent to search. The officer called for backup and spent at least nine minutes waiting for another officer and working on a consent form. When backup arrived, the officer terminated the stop, then asked for and obtained consent; the court ruled that the nine-minute extension of the stop was improper and that it required suppression even if consent to search was obtained voluntarily after the stop ended.

71. United States v. Digiovanni, 650 F.3d 498, 511 (4th Cir. 2011) (concluding that the proper duration of a traffic stop "cannot be stated with mathematical precision," *id.* (internal quotation marks, citations omitted)).

factors that may influence the duration of the stop are considerations like the number of occupants in the vehicle, whether a language barrier exists between the officer and the occupants, the nature and severity of the violation that prompted the stop, whether the driver has an in-state or an out-of-state identification, whether the driver responds promptly and accurately to the officer's queries, whether heavy traffic or inclement weather conditions are present, how quickly the officer's computer system works, and many more.

Some have suggested that "routine" stops that exceed twenty minutes may deserve closer scrutiny.[72] However, both shorter and longer stops have been upheld by the courts.[73]

VIII. Termination of the Stop

A. When Termination Takes Place

"Generally, an initial traffic stop concludes . . . after an officer returns the detainee's license and registration."[74] When an officer takes other documents from the driver, such as insurance documents, these, too, must be returned before the stop ends.[75] As the Fourth Circuit has explained, when an officer returns a driver's documents, it "indicate[s] that all business with [the driver is] completed and that he [is] free to leave."[76] The U.S. Supreme Court has rejected the idea that drivers must be told expressly that they are free to go before a stop terminates.[77]

However, while returning the driver's paperwork is a strong signal that a stop has terminated, it is not always dispositive. Some commentators have argued that many motorists will not, in fact, feel free to depart until they are expressly permitted to do so.[78] And the Court of Appeals of North Carolina has held, in at least one case, that under the totality of the circumstances, the occupants of a vehicle remained seized even after the return of the driver's paperwork, in part because the officer "never told [the driver] he was free to leave."[79] Thus, a cautious officer may choose to inform a driver that he or she is free to leave in order to establish the conclusion of a stop, though doing so is not necessarily legally required.

---

72. *See* FARB, *supra* note 6, at 46 & n.187 (proposing the twenty-minute rule of thumb and noting that others have advanced it as well).

73. *See, e.g.*, State v. Heien, 226 N.C. App. 280, 287 (thirteen minutes was "not unduly prolonged"), *aff'd per curiam*, 367 N.C. 163 (2013), *aff'd on other grounds*, ___ U.S. ___, 135 S. Ct. 530 (2014); United States v. Rivera, 570 F.3d 1009, 1013–14 (8th Cir. 2009) (seventeen minutes); United States v. Eckhart, 569 F.3d 1263, 1273–74 (10th Cir. 2009) (twenty-seven minutes); United States v. Muriel, 418 F.3d 720, 725 (7th Cir. 2005) (thirteen minutes).

74. State v. Jackson, 199 N.C. App. 236, 243 (2009); *Heien*, 226 N.C. App. at 287 ("Generally, the return of the driver's license or other documents to those who have been detained indicates the investigatory detention has ended."), *aff'd per curiam*, 367 N.C. 163 (2013), *aff'd on other grounds*, ___ U.S. ___, 135 S. Ct. 530 (2014).

75. State v. Velazquez-Perez, 233 N.C. App. 585, 595 (2014) (even though an officer had returned a driver's license and issued a warning citation, "[t]he purpose of the stop was not completed until [the officer] finished a proper document check [of registration, insurance, and other documents the officer had taken] and returned the documents").

76. United States v. Lattimore, 87 F.3d 647, 653 (4th Cir. 1996).

77. Ohio v. Robinette, 519 U.S. 33, 42 (1996) (adopting a totality of the circumstances approach).

78. LaFave, *supra* note 45, at 1899–1902.

79. State v. Myles, 188 N.C. App. 42, 45–46, *aff'd per curiam*, 362 N.C. 344 (2008). *See also* State v. Kincaid, 147 N.C. App. 94, 98–100 (2001) (suggesting that the return of a driver's license and registration is a necessary, but not invariably a sufficient, condition for the termination of a stop).

B. Effect of Termination

Once a stop has ended, the driver and any other occupants of the vehicle may depart. Any further interaction between the officer and the occupants of the vehicle is, therefore, consensual. The officer may ask questions about any subject at all, for as long as the occupants are willing to entertain the conversation; may request consent to search; and so on. In other words, the "time and scope limitations" that apply to a traffic stop cease to be relevant.[80] A typical case of this type is *United States v. Meikle*,[81] where an officer issued a warning citation to a driver, "returned [the driver's] license and registration and shook [the driver's] hand," then asked the driver if he could talk to him further. When the driver agreed, the officer proceeded to inquire whether there were any drugs in the vehicle and whether the officer could search the vehicle. The driver allowed the search, which turned up contraband. The Fourth Circuit found no Fourth Amendment problem: "It was clear that [the driver] was free to go. A reasonable person would have felt free to decline [the officer's] request to speak to [him] further. Therefore, a consensual encounter commenced the moment the officer asked if he could speak to [the driver] again and [the driver] agreed."[82]

---

80. LaFave, *supra* note 45, at 1898.
81. 407 F.3d 670 (4th Cir. 2005).
82. *Id.* at 673.

Chapter 4

Driver's License and Vehicle Registration Laws

Chapter 4

Driver's License and Vehicle Registration Laws

To determine whether an officer had reasonable suspicion to stop a person for a suspected traffic violation, one must be familiar with the laws defining such offenses. This chapter covers the statutory scheme that governs the driving of vehicles in North Carolina, including the state's driver's license and vehicle registration, inspection, and financial responsibility requirements, and reviews the elements of several of the most commonly charged motor vehicle offenses. The offense of impaired driving and other alcohol-related motor vehicle offenses are discussed in a separate School of Government publication.[1]

I. Key Definitions

The definitions of several terms are critical to understanding North Carolina's driver's license and motor vehicle laws.

A. Drive

The term "driver" is defined in Chapter 20, Section 4.01(7) of the North Carolina General Statutes (hereinafter G.S.) as being synonymous with the term "operator," defined in G.S. 20.4.01(25). Cognates of both words (such as drive, driving, operate, operating) also share the same meaning. An operator is "[a] person in actual physical control of a vehicle which is in motion or which has the engine running."[2]

A defendant's purpose for taking actual physical control of a car is not relevant to consideration of whether he or she was driving.[3] Thus, in the criminal prosecution of defendants for offenses of which driving is an element, there is no requirement that the State establish that the vehicle was in motion with the defendant behind the wheel or that the defendant started the car for purposes of driving it.[4] In *State v. Fields*,[5] for example, a law enforcement officer came upon a vehicle sitting in the right-hand lane of the road. The vehicle was motionless and the defendant was seated behind the

---

1. Shea Riggsbee Denning, The Law of Impaired Driving and Related Implied Consent Offenses in North Carolina (UNC School of Government, 2014).
2. Chapter 20, Section 4.01(25) of the North Carolina General Statutes (hereinafter G.S.).
3. State v. Fields, 77 N.C. App. 404 (1985).
4. *Id.*
5. *Id.*

wheel. The vehicle's owner was seated on the passenger side. Both the defendant and the passenger testified at trial that the passenger had been driving and stopped the vehicle on the street so that they could use the bathroom. The defendant got back into the driver's seat of the car and started it because he was cold. The court found that this constituted sufficient evidence of driving in the prosecution of the defendant for the offense of driving while impaired.

Driving can be established by circumstantial as well as direct evidence. In *State v. Dula*,[6] the court found sufficient evidence to justify the inference that the defendant was driving where the driver of another car saw black tire marks on the highway, dust in the air, and a car, with its headlights on, lying on its top in a field near the highway. The driver of the other car stopped at the scene and found the defendant in the overturned car, the doors of which were closed and the windows rolled up. He did not see anyone else in the area. The investigating officer saw tire marks leading from the black marks on the highway across the highway shoulder and into the field where the overturned car was located. The officer could not open the car doors. Testimony from a witness for the defendant that the witness was driving the car and fled the scene did not render the State's evidence insufficient. Likewise, in *State v. Riddle*,[7] the court found circumstantial evidence of driving sufficient to warrant submission of the case to the jury where the defendant was seen getting out of a car immediately after a collision and no one else was seen in or near the car. The defendant said that his friend had been driving and left the scene of the accident, running through the woods. A witness and law enforcement officers checked the woods and discovered no evidence to support the defendant's claim. The defendant in *Riddle* claimed that the driver of the car left through the driver's side door, but an investigating law enforcement officer was unable to open the door because of the damage it sustained during the collision. When a wrecker driver arrived, the defendant pulled the keys to the car out of his pocket and handed them to the wrecker driver.[8]

The court reached a different conclusion in *State v. Ray*,[9] finding insufficient evidence to support an impaired driving charge where the only evidence that the defendant was driving was that he was sitting "halfway [in] the front seat."[10] In *Ray*, an officer responded to an accident call and saw the defendant seated in a car that had hit two parked cars. There was no evidence that the car had been operated recently or that the motor was running.

B. Vehicle

The term "vehicle" is defined in G.S. 20-4.01(49) as "[e]very device in, upon, or by which any person or property is or may be transported or drawn upon a highway, excepting devices moved by human power or used exclusively upon fixed rails or tracks." There are several exceptions to this general definition. First, despite the exclusion from the definition for devices moved by human power, bicycles

---

6. 77 N.C. App. 473 (1985).

7. 56 N.C. App. 701 (1982).

8. *See also* State v. Mack, 81 N.C. App. 578, 579, 583 (1986) (the defendant's admission that he fell asleep driving and "ran over there to the fence," combined with an officer's observation of the defendant's car sitting on top of a chain link fence approximately forty-five feet from the road with the headlights on, the "key in the ignition, the warm hood, the defendant asleep in the driver's seat, and the near-empty bottle of Canadian Mist on the floorboard" were "sufficient to allow a reasonable jury to infer that defendant drove the vehicle on a public street").

9. 54 N.C. App. 473 (1981).

10. *Id.* at 475.

are deemed vehicles for purposes of G.S. Chapter 20.[11] Second, several other devices that would satisfy the general definition are excepted and thus are not vehicles for purposes of Chapter 20. The term "vehicle" does not include certain devices used as a means of transportation by a person with a mobility impairment. To qualify for the exception, the device must be "designed for and intended to be used as a means of transportation for a person with a mobility impairment, or who uses the device for mobility enhancement, [be] suitable for use both inside and outside a building, including on sidewalks, and [be] limited by design to 15 miles per hour when the device is being operated by a person with a mobility impairment, or who uses the device for mobility enhancement."[12] The state court of appeals in *State v. Crow*[13] rejected an argument by the defendant, a healthy 25-year-old man who had no mobility impairment, that the motorized scooter he was driving was not a "vehicle" in that it was a device used for mobility enhancement. The scooter the defendant was driving "was powered by an electric motor and was likened at trial to a skateboard with handlebars on the front."[14] It had two wheels, six to eight inches in diameter, that were arranged in tandem. The court held that the device did not qualify for the mobility impairment exception, explaining that the legislature's addition in 2001 of the term "mobility enhancement" to the sentence in G.S. 20-4.01(49) concerning "mobility impairment" "was a technical change that did not substantively expand the existing mobility impairment exception to the term 'vehicle'. "[15] Thus, the court concluded that the defendant's use of the scooter solely for "recreational purposes" did not except the device from the definition of vehicle.[16]

Electric personal assistive mobility devices also are excluded from the definition of vehicle.[17] These are self-balancing, non-tandem, two-wheeled devices that are designed to transport one person and have a propulsion system that limits their maximum speed to 15 miles per hour or less.[18] The "Segway Human Transporter"[19] is an example of such a device. The court in *Crow* concluded that the defendant's scooter did not qualify for this exception, as it was not self-balancing and its wheels were arranged in tandem.[20]

Animals that are ridden or that pull a vehicle also are considered vehicles for purposes of G.S. Chapter 20.[21] Horses, however, are specifically excluded from the definition of vehicle for purposes of the statute prohibiting driving while impaired.[22]

---

11. G.S. 20-4.01(49) further provides that "every rider of a bicycle . . . upon a highway shall be subject to the provisions of this Chapter applicable to the driver of a vehicle except those which by their nature can have no application."

12. *Id.*

13. 175 N.C. App. 119 (2005).

14. *Id.* at 121.

15. *Id.* at 124.

16. *Id.* at 124–25.

17. G.S. 20-4.01(49).

18. G.S. 20-4.01(7b).

19. *Crow*, 175 N.C. App. at 124.

20. *Id.*

21. G.S. 20-171 (stating that "[e]very person riding an animal or driving any animal drawing a vehicle upon a highway shall be subject to the provisions of this Article applicable to the driver of a vehicle, except those provisions of the Article which by their nature can have no application"); *see also* State v. Dellinger, 73 N.C. App. 685 (1985) (upholding conviction for impaired driving under former version of G.S. 20-138.1 based upon defendant's riding of a horse on a street with an alcohol concentration of 0.18).

22. G.S. 20-138.1(e).

C. Motor Vehicle

The term "motor vehicle" is defined as "[e]very vehicle which is self-propelled and every vehicle designed to run upon the highways which is pulled by a self-propelled vehicle."[23] Thus, bicycles, which are vehicles, are not "motor vehicles" because they are not self-propelled but instead are propelled by human power. Trailers that are pulled by self-propelled vehicles are, however, defined as motor vehicles.

Even though they are self-propelled, mopeds are not considered motor vehicles so long as they satisfy the definition of moped set forth in G.S. 20-4.01(27)d1. That provision defines a moped as "[a] vehicle, other than a motor-driven bicycle or electric assisted bicycle, that has two or three wheels, no external shifting device, a motor that does not exceed 50 cubic centimeters piston displacement and cannot propel the vehicle at a speed greater than 30 miles per hour on a level surface."[24] A moped's motor may be powered by electricity, alternative fuel, motor fuel, or a combination of each.[25]

D. Street, Highway

G.S. 20-4.01(13) defines the term "highway" as "[t]he entire width between property or right-of-way lines of every way or place of whatever nature, when any part thereof is open to the use of the public as a matter or right for the purposes of vehicular traffic." The provision further specifies that "[t]he terms 'highway' and 'street' and their cognates are synonymous."[26] There is no requirement that the street be part of the state highway system.[27]

E. Public Vehicular Area

"Public vehicular areas" (or PVAs) are defined to include four broad types of areas: (1) areas "used by the public for vehicular traffic at any time;" (2) beach areas used by the public for vehicular traffic; (3) roads used by vehicular traffic within or leading to a gated or non-gated subdivision or community, whether or not the subdivision or community roads have been offered for dedication to the public; and (4) portions of private property used by vehicular traffic and designated by the private property owner as a public vehicular area in accordance with G.S. 20-219.4.[28] G.S. 20-4.01(32)a. sets forth several examples of areas satisfying the first type. Under this provision, public vehicular areas include drives, driveways, roads, roadways, streets, alleys, or parking lots upon the grounds or premises of any of the following:

---

23. G.S. 20-4.01(23).

24. G.S. 20-4.01(27)d1.

25. *Id.*

26. G.S. 20-4.01(13); *see also id.* § 20-4.01(46) (similarly providing that the "terms 'highway' and 'street' and their cognates are synonymous").

27. *Cf.* State v. Hopper, 205 N.C. App. 175, 181 (2010) (rejecting defendant's argument that the provisions of G.S. 20-129 requiring lighted headlamps and rear lamps during certain conditions did not apply to his driving because the street on which he was driving was not part of the state highway system; concluding that officer's testimony that the street on which the defendant drove was within an apartment complex owned by the City of Winston-Salem that the officer was assigned to patrol and that there were parking spots on the street with cars parked in them at the time of the stop was sufficient to support the trial court's finding that the defendant was traveling on a street "open to the use of the public as a matter of right for the purposes of vehicular traffic" per G.S. 20-4.01(13)).

28. G.S. 20-4.01(32).

1. Any public or private hospital, college, university, school, orphanage, church, or any of the institutions, parks, or other facilities maintained and supported by the State of North Carolina or any of its subdivisions
2. Any service station, drive-in theater, supermarket, store, restaurant, or office building, or any other business, residential, or municipal establishment providing parking space whether the business establishment is open or closed
3. Any property owned by the United States and subject to the jurisdiction of the State of North Carolina[29]

North Carolina's appellate courts have adopted a broad view of the term "public vehicular area."[30] The court of appeals has deemed the following locations to be public vehicular areas:

- the parking lot of a car wash, notwithstanding a town ordinance prohibiting parking on the premises unless the facilities were being used;[31]
- a privately maintained paved road in a privately owned mobile home park;[32]
- a wheelchair ramp in the parking lot of a hotel;[33]
- an area of a public park occasionally used for public parking;[34] and
- the parking lot of a private nightclub.[35]

Though the term "public vehicular area" has been broadly construed, it is not limitless in application. The court of appeals in *State v. Ricks*[36] held that the State failed to establish that a dirt drive on a vacant lot on which a law enforcement officer had seen people walk and ride bicycles and that was wide enough to drive on was a public vehicular area. The court explained that although the examples in G.S. 20-4.01(32)a. of areas used by the public for vehicular traffic are listed "by way of illustration and not limitation[,]" they are "a component of the relevant definition" that "cannot be ignored."[37] *Ricks* explained that the examples reveal that public vehicular areas are "areas generally open to and used by the public for vehicular traffic as a matter of right or areas used for vehicular traffic that are associated with places generally open to and used by the public, such as driveways and parking lots to institutions and businesses open to the public."[38] Furthermore, the court noted that a separate subsection of the public vehicular area definition incorporates "'private property used by vehicular

---

29. G.S. 20-4.01(32)a.

30. *See* State v. Robinette, 124 N.C. App. 212 (1996); State v. Turner, 117 N.C. App. 457 (1994); State v. Mabe, 85 N.C. App. 500 (1987); State v. Carawan, 80 N.C. App. 151 (1986).

31. *Robinette*, 124 N.C. App. 212.

32. *Turner*, 117 N.C. App. 457.

33. *Mabe*, 85 N.C. App. 500.

34. *Carawan*, 80 N.C. App. 151.

35. State v. Snyder, 343 N.C. 61 (1996). The definition of public vehicular area in effect at the time of the offense in *Snyder* was significantly narrower than the current one and consisted of areas "generally open to and used by the public for vehicular traffic," including parking lots upon the grounds of a business establishment "providing parking space for customers, patrons, *or* the public." *Id.* at 67 (referencing former G.S. 20-4.01(32)). *Snyder* explained that "even if an establishment is cloaked in the robe of being a private club, it is still a 'business establishment providing parking space for its customers, patrons, *or* the public' and cannot escape liability simply because a membership fee is required." *Id.* at 69.

36. 237 N.C. App. 359 (2014).

37. *Id.* at 365.

38. *Id.* at 365–66.

traffic and designated by the private property owner as a public vehicular area.'"[39] If every area used by the public for vehicular traffic at any time is a public vehicular area, this separate subsection would be "superfluous," the court reasoned.

II. Driver's License Requirements in North Carolina

A. General Introduction

The laws governing the licensing of drivers are contained in the Uniform Driver's License Act, Article 2 of G.S. Chapter 20.[40] G.S. 20-7 requires that a person be licensed by the North Carolina Division of Motor Vehicles (hereinafter NCDMV or DMV) to drive a motor vehicle on a highway.

1. Rules for Nonresidents

Nonresidents who are at least 16 years old and are licensed by their home states or countries are excepted from the requirement that a person be licensed by NCDMV to drive on a highway in this state.[41] To meet the exception, the nonresident must have in his or her immediate possession a valid driver's license issued to him or her in his or her home state or country.[42]

A "nonresident" is defined in the General Statutes as "[a]ny person whose legal residence is in some state, territory, or jurisdiction other than North Carolina or in a foreign country."[43] Any person who has resided in North Carolina for "other than a temporary or transitory purpose for more than six months" is presumed to be a resident of the state, and "absence from the State for more than six months shall raise no presumption that the person is not a resident of this State."[44] An exemption from license requirements for nonresidents "specifically applies to nonresident military spouses,

---

39. *Id.* at 366 (quoting G.S. 20-4.01(32)d.).

40. Article 2B of G.S. Chapter 20 governs the issuance of identification cards for North Carolina residents who do not drive.

41. G.S. 20-8(3).

42. An international driver's permit (sometimes called an international driver's license or an international driving privilege) does not satisfy this requirement. The United States is a party to a United Nations treaty that gives residents of one country the right to drive in other countries using the driver's license issued by the government of the jurisdiction in which they live. Convention on Road Traffic art. 24, annex 10, Apr. 16, 1952, 3.3 U.S.T. 3008, 3016, 3048. *See also Why Carry an IDP?* AAA.com, www.aaa.com/vacation/idpf.html (explaining benefits of international driver's permit); Office of Consumer & Bus. Educ., Bureau of Consumer Prot., Fed. Trade Comm'n, FTC Consumer Alert, Ads for International Drivers' Licenses or Permits Could Be a Dead End (Jan. 2003), https://permanent.access.gpo.gov/lps29210/driveralrt.pdf (cautioning consumers that although international driver's permit is real document when issued by proper authorities, it is not legal alternative to state-issued license). International drivers' permits were created under this treaty to facilitate local officials' determination of whether a person is validly licensed by his or her home country. FTC Consumer Alert, *supra.* These permits translate government-issued drivers' licenses into ten languages to assist officials in interpreting a foreign driver's license. International drivers' permits issued to residents of the United States have no use, purpose, or effect within the United States. *Id.* They do not replace state-issued driver's licenses or restore revoked driving privileges, and they are not proof of identity. *Id.* (noting that U.S. Department of State has authorized only two organizations, the American Automobile Association (AAA) and the American Automobile Touring Alliance (AATA), to issue international driver's permits to U.S. residents). The AAA and the AATA may sell international drivers' permits only to people who are at least 18 years old and have a valid driver's license issued by a U.S. state or territory. *Id.*

43. G.S. 20-4.01(24).

44. G.S. 20-4.01(34).

regardless of their employment status, who are temporarily residing in North Carolina due to the active duty military orders of a spouse."[45]

A person whose legal residence under G.S. Chapter 20 is North Carolina must obtain a North Carolina driver's license to drive on the highways of this state lawfully and may not rely on a license issued by his or her former state or jurisdiction of residence.[46] A new resident of the state who has a *regular* driver's license issued by another jurisdiction must obtain a license from DMV within sixty days after becoming a resident.[47]

In addition to nonresidents who are licensed in their home states or countries, three more categories of people are exempted from otherwise applicable driver's license requirements. First, a person may lawfully operate a motor vehicle owned by and in the service of the U.S. armed forces without a North Carolina driver's license.[48] This exemption does not extend to people who operate vehicles of the U.S. Civil Conservation Corps.

Second, a person may lawfully drive a road machine, a farm tractor, or an implement of husbandry temporarily on a highway without a North Carolina driver's license.[49] Finally, a person who is at least 16 years old may lawfully operate a moped on a highway without being licensed.[50]

B. Application for an Original License

To obtain an original (as distinguished from a renewed) North Carolina driver's license, an applicant must appear in person at a DMV office.[51] The applicant must provide the following information about himself or herself:

- full name
- mailing address and residence address
- a physical description, including sex, height, eye color, and hair color
- date of birth
- a valid Social Security number
- a signature

The only statutory exception to the requirement that an applicant present a Social Security number applies to an applicant who presents valid documentation issued by, or under the authority of, the U.S. government that proves his or her legal presence of limited duration in the United States.[52] DMV must

---

45. G.S. 20-8(3).

46. G.S. 20-7(a).

47. *Id.* A "regular" driver's license is a license to drive a noncommercial motor vehicle or a commercial motor vehicle that is exempt from the commercial driver's license requirements. *Id.* Special provisions apply to holders of commercial drivers' licenses, the issuance of which, and the qualifications and the requirements for which, are set forth in the Commercial Driver License Act, Article 2C of G.S. Chapter 20.

48. G.S. 20-8(1).

49. G.S. 20-8(2). The term "road machine" is not defined in G.S. Chapter 20. The court of appeals held in *State v. Ellison*, 122 N.C. App. 638, 641 (1996), that an automobile was not a "road machine" and that "a road machine differs from an automobile in that it involves only temporary operation for purposes other than travel." A "farm tractor" is a motor vehicle designed and used primarily as a farm implement for pulling plows and agricultural vehicles. G.S. 20-4.01(11). An "implement of husbandry" is a vehicle designed for agricultural purposes and used exclusively to carry out agricultural operations. *Id.* § 20-4.01(15).

50. G.S. 20-8(7).

51. A person may also acquire an identification card from DMV to use for identification purposes only. It confers no driving privileges.

52. G.S. 20-7(s).

issue to an applicant who presents such valid documentation and meets other licensing requirements a license of limited duration, which may not expire later than the expiration of the authorization of the applicant's legal presence in the United States.[53]

Licenses issued to noncitizens have the wording "Legal Presence Expiration Date [xx/xx/xxxx]" printed on the back.[54] The legal presence expiration date, which may differ from the license expiration date, is based on the expiration date of the document submitted to establish legal presence. Moreover, the expiration date of the document does not always coincide with the expiration of the authorization of the applicant's legal presence in the United States. Licenses issued to certain refugees and people granted asylum, as well as to lawful permanent residents whose I-551 Permanent Resident cards have no expiration date but who have Social Security numbers, will not bear the "legal presence" notation.[55]

In addition to completing an application, an applicant for an original license in North Carolina must present at least two forms of identification of the type approved by the commissioner of motor vehicles.[56]

1. Proof of Residency

Only North Carolina residents are eligible to obtain a North Carolina driver's license. Therefore, applicants must submit verified or verifiable residency and address information contained in documents of the type specified by NCDMV.[57]

An applicant who cannot produce any approved documentation of residency or, in the case of a minor applicant, a parent or a legal guardian of the applicant who cannot produce such documentation, may complete an affidavit on a form provided by NCDMV and sworn to before an NCDMV official indicating the applicant's current residence address.[58]

2. Proof of Age and Identity

To obtain a regular driver's license, a person must have reached the minimum age required by the class of license sought: Class A: 18 years old; Class B: 18 years old; Class C: 16 years old.[59] License (and vehicle) classes are discussed in more detail in section II.D, below.

---

53. G.S. 20-7(f)(3). G.S. 20-7 groups driver's license applicants into two categories: those who have Social Security numbers and those who have legal presence of limited duration. There is, however, a third group of applicants who may not be included in either statutory category. Some immigrants, such as lawful permanent residents and refugees, are authorized to remain in the United States permanently but may not have Social Security numbers. Although NCDMV includes documents establishing permanent legal status among the documents that it accepts as establishing a legal presence of *limited* duration, immigrants with permanent legal status are issued drivers' licenses of regular duration (that is, five or eight years, depending on their age) regardless of whether they also have a Social Security number.

54. *See* Memorandum from Tony W. Spence, Acting Dir., Driver & Vehicle Servs., N.C. Div. of Motor Vehicles (NCDMV), to NCDMV Driver and Vehicle Services staff 4 (Mar. 27, 2009).

55. *Id.* at 10–12.

56. "Acceptable identity documents" include drivers' licenses, birth certificates, certain school documents (e.g., a diploma or GED), U.S. military IDs, passports, and certified marriage certificates. *See* N.C. DEP'T OF TRANSP., NCDMV, GETTING A LICENSE OR LEARNER PERMIT, STEPS, www.ncdot.gov/dmv/driver/license/#documents.

57. G.S. 20-7(b3), (b4); N.C. DEP'T OF TRANSP., NCDMV, NORTH CAROLINA DRIVER'S HANDBOOK 18 (2016), www.ncdot.gov/download/dmv/handbooks_NCDL_English.pdf.

58. G.S. 20-7(b5).

59. G.S. 20-9.

A first-time applicant may prove his or her age and identity by presenting two forms of identification of a type accepted by NCDMV.[60]

3. Physical and Mental Requirements

To obtain a driver's license, a person must demonstrate his or her physical or mental ability to drive safely a motor vehicle included in the class of license for which the person has applied.[61] A person seeking only an identification card does not have to make such a showing.

4. License Restrictions

DMV is authorized to "impose any restriction it finds advisable on a drivers license."[62] A commonly imposed restriction is that a person operate a motor vehicle only while wearing corrective lenses.[63] Another type of restriction is an alcohol concentration restriction, which limits the concentration of alcohol that may be present in a driver's body at the time of driving. This type of restriction is required for a person whose driving privileges are restored following a conviction for impaired driving or driving after consuming by a person under 21 years old.[64] It is unlawful for the holder of a restricted license to operate a motor vehicle without complying with the restriction and is the equivalent of operating a motor vehicle without a license.[65]

5. Proof of Financial Responsibility

NCDMV may not issue a driver's license to a person until he or she has furnished proof of financial responsibility in a prescribed format.[66] This requirement does not apply to a person who seeks to renew his or her driver's license or to an applicant for a learner's permit or an identification card.

6. Additional Limitations

Additional restrictions on NCDMV's authority to issue licenses, but not identification cards, exist. They are based on an applicant's driving and criminal history, as well as on substance abuse and mental health issues.[67] Among the restrictions is a prohibition against issuance of a driver's license to a person whose license or driving privilege has been cancelled, suspended, or revoked in any jurisdiction if the basis for the action would be grounds for like action in North Carolina.[68] Any such cancellation, suspension, or revocation does not prohibit issuance for a period in excess of eighteen months. In addition, NCDMV may not license an applicant who currently holds a license to drive in another state unless the applicant surrenders the out-of-state license.[69]

---

60. The *North Carolina Driver's Handbook* lists identification documents that NCDMV will accept as proof of age and identity. *See* NCDMV, *supra* note 56, at 16–17.

61. G.S. 20-7(b1).

62. G.S. 20-7(e).

63. Administrative regulations require that a driver's license applicant's visual acuity be 20/40 or better in either eye or both eyes together to receive an unrestricted license. Title 19A, Chapter 03B, Section .0201(a)(3) of the North Carolina Administrative Code (hereinafter N.C.A.C.). A license is restricted to require corrective lenses if acuity is less than 20/40 in either eye or in both eyes together. *Id.*

64. G.S. 20-19(c3).

65. G.S. 20-7(e).

66. G.S. 20-7(c1). This requirement does not apply to certain applicants who do not own currently registered motor vehicles but who meet other requirements. *Id.*

67. G.S. 20-9.

68. G.S. 20-9(f).

69. G.S. 20-9(h).

7. Duration of Licenses

A person between the ages of 16 and 18 may, on meeting statutory requirements, be issued a full provisional license, which grants all the privileges of a regular driver's license other than the privilege to use a mobile telephone while driving.[70] A full provisional license issued to a person under the age of 18 expires on the person's 21st birthday.[71]

An original regular driver's license issued to a person at least 18 years old but less than 66 years old expires on the birthday of the licensee in the eighth year after issuance.[72] An original driver's license issued to a person who is at least 66 years old expires on the birthday of the licensee in the fifth year after issuance.[73]

A renewed driver's license issued to a person aged 18 to 65 expires eight years after the expiration date of the license that is renewed.[74] A renewed driver's license issued to a person at least 66 years old expires five years after the expiration date of the license that is renewed.[75]

NCDMV may determine that a license of shorter duration should be issued for applicants who have legal presence of limited duration in the United States. A license of limited duration may not expire later than the expiration of the authorization for the applicant's legal presence in the United States.[76]

8. Renewal Procedure

A person may apply to NCDMV to renew a license during the 180-day period before the license expires.[77] Historically, most people were required to appear in person to renew a driver's license. Only two groups of people were permitted renew a driver's license by mail: (1) people serving on activity duty in the U.S. armed forces and stationed outside the state and (2) North Carolina residents who have been residing outside the state for at least thirty continuous days.[78] Licenses renewed by mail pursuant to G.S. 20-7(b)(4) are temporary licenses that expire sixty days after the licensee returns to North Carolina.[79] In 2014, however, the legislature authorized NCDMV to offer remote renewal of driver's licenses.[80]

People seeking to renew their licenses who do not meet the criteria for remote renewal must appear at an NCDMV driver's license office, provide necessary documentation, have their photograph taken,

---

70. G.S. 20-11(a), (g); *id.* § 20-137.3(b).

71. G.S. 20-7(f)(1).

72. G.S. 20-7(f)(2).

73. *Id.*

74. G.S. 20-7(f)(2a).

75. *Id.*

76. G.S. 20-7(f)(3).

77. G.S. 20-7(f)(3a). NCDMV may renew a driver's license, without limitation on the period of time before the license expires, if the person applying for renewal is a member of the U.S. armed forces or of a reserve component of the U.S. armed forces and provides orders that place the member on activity duty and duty station outside North Carolina. G.S. 20-7(f)(3b)a.

78. G.S. 20-7(f)(4).

79. *Id.*

80. G.S. 20-7(f)(6). S.L. 2014-100, § 34.8(b) made G.S. 20-7(f)(6) effective August 7, 2014, and applicable to driver's licenses renewed on or after NCDMV adopts rules as required by G.S. 20-7(f)(6)d. The rules adopted by NCDMV are codified in Title 19 of the North Carolina Administrative Code. 19A N.C.A.C. 03B, § .0201. Instructions for remote renewal are available on the NCDMV website at www.ncdot.gov/dmv.

A person may renew online if he or she has a valid, unexpired Class C North Carolina driver's license that was issued when the person was at least 18 years old and that has no restriction other than a restriction for corrective lenses. The person's most recent renewal must have been an in-person renewal and the person must otherwise be eligible to renew his or her license.

and pay the fee for renewal. The fee due on license renewal is $5.00 for each year in the renewal period. The fee for a motorcycle endorsement is $2.30 per year for the period for which the endorsement is issued.[81] The person must pay the fee before the endorsement may be issued.

Before 2008, a person seeking an original or a renewed driver's license could visit any NCDMV office, provide the appropriate documentation, have his or her photograph taken, pay the applicable fee, and leave with a newly minted driver's license in hand. Now, however, drivers' licenses, learners' permits, and identification cards are produced and issued from a central location and are mailed to license holders, permit holders, and cardholders at their home addresses. NCDMV provides temporary driving certificates at its driver's license offices. The temporary driving certificate is valid for sixty days.[82] These certificates establish a person's privilege to drive but are not identification documents.

Newly issued drivers' licenses are mailed to applicants' residences by first-class mail. Licenses may be mailed to a post office box only if the licensee is ineligible for postal service delivery at his or her home or if the applicant's only mailing address before July 1, 2009, was a post office box in North Carolina, provided that NCDMV has verified the applicant's residential address.

9. Notice of Change of Address or Name

Under G.S. 20-7.1, a person whose address changes from the address stated on his or her driver's license must notify NCDMV of the change within sixty days after the change occurs.[83] If the person's address changed because he or she moved, the person must obtain a duplicate license within sixty days stating the new address.[84] Violation of these provisions is an infraction.[85] A person whose address changes because of a governmental address change rather than a move may not be charged with violating this statute.[86]

A person whose name changes from the name stated on a driver's license must notify NCDMV of the change within sixty days after the change occurs and obtain a duplicate driver's license stating the new name.[87]

A person may obtain a duplicate of a license issued by NCDMV by paying a fee of $13 and giving NCDMV satisfactory proof that (1) the person's license has been lost or destroyed; (2) it is necessary to change the name or the address on the license; (3) because of age, the person is entitled to a license with a different-color photographic background or a different-color border; or (4) NCDMV revoked the person's license, the revocation period has expired, and the period for which the license was issued has not expired.[88]

---

81. G.S. 20-7(i).
82. G.S. 20-7(f)(5).
83. G.S. 20-7.1(a).
84. *Id.*
85. G.S. 20-35(a2)(3).
86. G.S. 20-7.1(a).
87. G.S. 20-7.1(b).
88. G.S. 20-14. Since October 1, 2008, drivers' licenses, learners' permits, and special identification cards issued to applicants under the age of 21 have been printed in vertical format, whereas drivers' licenses issued to applicants at least 21 years of age are printed horizontally. The contrasting format is designed to help sales clerks who sell age-restricted products such as alcoholic beverages and tobacco distinguish underage persons from those who are at least 21. Licenses issued to applicants who are less than 21 years old also feature a red border around the licensee's photo.

10. Application-Related License Offenses

G.S. 20-30 defines two Class 1 misdemeanors that are related to the application for a driver's license: (1) using a false name or address in applying for an original or renewed driver's license, learner's permit, or special identification card or (2) knowingly making a false statement, concealing a material fact, or otherwise committing fraud in such an application or procuring or permitting another to do so.[89] Any license, permit, or identification card procured as the result of such a false statement is void.

a. Felony Violations

The sale or offering for sale of a facsimile driver's license, learner's permit, or special identification card by anyone other than a DMV agent or employee in the course and scope of his or her employment is a Class I felony.[90] It also is a Class I felony to display or use a driver's license, learner's permit, or special identification card that contains a false name in the commission or attempted commission of a felony.[91]

C. Graduated Licensing

North Carolina was among the pioneers of graduated licensing for young drivers, adopting, along with Georgia and Michigan, a full three-tier stage licensing system in 1997.[92] Under a graduated licensing system, a state grants driving privileges to drivers under the age of 18 only after they have been driving under a permit with supervision for a lengthy period of time and, even then, only by degrees. Drivers' licenses issued to such teenagers typically restrict nighttime driving and/or the number of minors who may be present in the vehicle for some period of time after initial licensure. North Carolina's graduated licensing system has been associated with a reduced crash risk for 16-year-old drivers in the years following initial licensure.[93]

1. Limited Learner's Permit

To obtain a driver's license in North Carolina, a 16-year-old must meet several requirements. The first is that he or she must have held a limited learner's permit issued by NCDMV for at least twelve months.

To obtain a limited learner's permit, a person must be at least 15 but less than 18 years old.[94] He or she must pass a driver education course offered through a public high school[95] or at a licensed

---

89. G.S. 20-30(5).

90. G.S. 20-30(7).

91. G.S. 20-30(9).

92. *See* Arthur Goodwin, Robert Foss, Jamie Sohn, & Daniel Mayhew, Transp. Research Bd., Nat'l Coop. Highway Research Program, NCHRP Report 500, Guidance for Implementation of the AASHTO Strategic Highway Safety Plan, Volume 19: A Guide for Reducing Collisions Involving Young Drivers III-4 (2007), *download available at* http://onlinepubs.trb.org/onlinepubs/nchrp/nchrp_rpt_500v19.pdf.

93. See Scott Masten & Robert Foss, *Long-Term Effect of the North Carolina Graduated Driver Licensing System on Licensed Driver Crash Incidence: A 5-Year Survival Analysis*, 42 Accident Analysis & Prevention, 1647–52, 1651 (stating that the findings "provide further evidence that crashing among young drivers is more commonly the result of what they have not yet learned than it is the result of the 'foolishness of youth.'")

94. G.S. 20-11(b).

95. G.S. 115C-215(a) requires the State Superintendent of Public Instruction to organize and administer a standardized program of driver education to be offered at public high schools for physically and mentally qualified persons who (1) are older than 14 years and 6 months; (2) are approved by the principal of the

commercial driver training school.[96] The person must pass a written test administered by DMV and must have a driving eligibility certificate or a high school diploma or its equivalent.[97]

a. Driving Eligibility Certificate

A driving eligibility certificate establishes that (1) the person is currently enrolled in school and is making progress toward obtaining a high school diploma or its equivalent, (2) a substantial hardship would be placed on the person or the person's family if the person does not receive a certificate, or (3) the person cannot make progress toward obtaining a high school diploma or its equivalent.[98] The certificate must be signed by the school principal if the person is in public school or by the corresponding official if the person is enrolled in a nonpublic school, a charter school, or a community college or if he or she is home-schooled.[99]

b. Lose Control, Lose License

The driving eligibility certificate must also establish (1) that the person has not been subject to disciplinary action by the school in which he or she is enrolled for certain conduct or (2) that, notwithstanding the disciplinary action, the person is eligible for a certificate.[100]

c. Covered Disciplinary Actions

A disciplinary action is an expulsion, a suspension for more than ten consecutive days, or an assignment to an alternative educational setting for more than ten consecutive days.[101] The conduct covered by the driving eligibility certificate is (1) the possession or sale of an alcoholic beverage or an illegal controlled substance on school property; (2) the bringing, possession, or use on school property of a weapon or firearm that resulted in disciplinary action under the federal Gun Free Schools Act (or that could have resulted in that disciplinary action if it had occurred in a public school); or (3) the physical assault on a teacher or other school personnel on school property.[102] To be covered by the provisions of G.S. 20-11(n1), the disciplinary action must have occurred after the earlier of the first

---

school, pursuant to rules adopted by the State Board of Education; (3) are enrolled in a public or private high school within the state or are receiving instruction through a home school; and (4) have not previously enrolled in the program.

The driver education curriculum must include (1) instruction on the rights and privileges of the handicapped and the signs and symbols used to assist the handicapped relative to motor vehicles, (2) at least six hours of instruction on the offense of driving while impaired and related subjects, (3) at least six hours of actual driving experience, and (4) at least one hour of motorcycle safety awareness training. G.S. 115C-215(b).

   96. G.S. 20-11(b)(1).
   97. G.S. 20-11(b)(2), (3).
   98. G.S. 20-11(n).
   99. G.S. 20-11(n)(4).
  100. G.S. 20-11(n)(1a), (n1).
  101. G.S. 20-11(n1)(1)c.
  102. G.S. 20-11(n1)(1)d. G.S. 115C-390.10(a) requires local boards of education to develop and implement written policies and procedures, as required by the federal Gun Free Schools Act, 20 U.S.C. § 7151, requiring suspension for 365 calendar days of any student who is determined to have brought or been in possession of a firearm or destructive device on educational property or to have brought/been in possession of a firearm or destructive device at a school-sponsored event off of educational property.

For purposes of the disqualifying conduct of assaulting a teacher or other school personnel on school property, "school property" is defined as "[t]he physical premises of the school, school buses or other vehicles under the school's control or contract and that are used to transport students, and school-sponsored curricular or extracurricular activities that occur on or off the premises of the school." G.S. 20-11(n1)(1)g.

day of July before the school year in which the student enrolled in the eighth grade or the student's 14th birthday.[103]

d. Eligibility Following Covered Disciplinary Action

A student who is subject to disciplinary action for enumerated student conduct is eligible for a driving eligibility certificate when the school administrator at the school in which the student is enrolled determines that the student has exhausted all administrative appeals connected to the disciplinary action and one of the following conditions is met:

- The enumerated student conduct occurred before the student was 15 years old and the student is now at least 16 years old.
- The enumerated student conduct occurred after the student reached the age of 15 and it is at least one year after the date the student exhausted all administrative appeals connected to the disciplinary action.
- The student needs the certificate to drive to and from school, a drug or alcohol treatment counseling program, or a mental health treatment program and no other transportation is available.[104]

In addition, a student whose permit or license is denied or revoked due to ineligibility for a driving eligibility certificate may be eligible for such a certificate if, after six months from the date of ineligibility, the school administrator at the school in which the student is enrolled determines that one of the following conditions is met:

- The student has returned to school or has been placed in an alternative educational setting and has displayed exemplary student behavior.
- The disciplinary action was for the possession or sale of an alcoholic beverage or an illegal controlled substance on school property and the student subsequently attended and successfully completed a drug or alcohol treatment counseling program.[105]

e. Level 1

A limited learner's permit is classified as "Level 1" of the graduated licensing process. The permit authorizes the holder to drive a specified type or class of motor vehicle under the following conditions:[106]

1. The limited learner's permit holder must be in possession of the permit.
2. A "supervising driver"[107] must be seated beside the permit holder in the front seat of the vehicle while it is in motion. No person other than the supervising driver can be in the front seat.
3. For the first six months after issuance of a limited learner's permit, the permit holder may drive only between the hours of 5 a.m. and 9 p.m.

---

103. G.S. 20-11(n1)(2).

104. G.S. 20-11(n1)(3).

105. G.S. 20-11(n1)(4).

106. G.S. 20-11(c) (setting forth Level 1 restrictions).

107. To qualify as a supervising driver, a person must be a parent, grandparent, or guardian of the limited learner's permit holder or of the license holder or must be a responsible person approved by the parent or guardian or DMV. G.S. 20-11(k). A supervising driver must be a licensed driver who has been licensed for at least five years. *Id.* At least one supervising driver must sign the application for a permit or license. *Id.*

4. After the first six months of issuance, the permit holder may drive at any time.
5. Every person inside the vehicle driven by the limited learner's permit holder must be wearing a properly fastened safety belt or must be restrained by a child passenger restraint system as provided in G.S. 20-137.1 when the vehicle is in motion.
6. The limited learner's permit holder may not use a mobile telephone or associated technology while operating the motor vehicle on a public street or highway or public vehicular area.[108]

The fee for a limited learner's permit is $20.[109] Under G.S. 20-11(m), "[t]he holder of a limited learner's permit is not considered a licensed driver for the purpose of determining the inexperienced operator premium surcharge under automobile insurance policies."

A limited learner's permit expires on the permit holder's 18th birthday.[110] If that date falls on a weekend or state holiday, the permit remains valid through the fifth regular state business day following the expiration date.[111]

2. Limited Provisional License

A person who is at least 16 but less than 18 years old may obtain a limited provisional license—"Level 2" of the graduated licensing process—if the person meets all of the following requirements:[112]

1. The person must have held a limited learner's permit issued by DMV for at least twelve months.
2. The person must not have been convicted of a motor vehicle moving violation, a seat belt infraction, or a violation of the law prohibiting use of a mobile phone by drivers under 18 in the preceding six months.
3. The person must pass a road test administered by DMV.
4. The person must have a driving eligibility certificate or a high school diploma or its equivalent.
5. The person must have completed a driving log detailing a minimum of sixty hours of driving, at least ten of them at night.[113]

A limited provisional license authorizes the holder to drive a specified type or class of motor vehicle only under the following conditions:[114]

1. The limited provisional license holder must be in possession of the license.
2. The license holder may drive without supervision in the following circumstances: (a) between the hours of 5 a.m. and 9 p.m.; (b) when he or she is driving directly to and from work; (c) when he or she is driving directly to or from an activity of a volunteer

---

108. *See also* G.S. 20-137.3 (generally prohibiting persons under the age of 18 from operating a motor vehicle on a street, highway, or public vehicular area while using a mobile telephone or associated technology and providing for limited exceptions).

109. G.S. 20-11(j).

110. *Id.*

111. *Id.*

112. G.S. 20-11(d).

113. No more than ten hours of driving per week may be counted toward the sixty-hour requirement. The driving log must be signed by the supervising driver and submitted to the DMV. If DMV has cause to believe that a driving log has been falsified, the applicant will be required to complete a new driving log and will be ineligible to obtain a limited provisional license for six months.

114. G.S. 20-11(e).

fire department, a volunteer rescue squad, or a volunteer emergency medical service, provided the driver is a member of the organization sponsoring the activity.

3. The limited provisional license holder may drive with supervision at any time.[115]

4. Whenever the license holder is driving the vehicle without the supervising driver, there may be no more than one passenger under the age of 21 in the vehicle.[116]

5. Every person in the vehicle must be wearing a properly fastened safety belt or must be restrained by a child restraint system as required by G.S. 20-137.1 when the vehicle is in motion.

6. The limited provisional license holder may not use a mobile telephone or associated technology while operating the vehicle on a street, highway, or public vehicular area.

The fee for a limited provisional license is $20.[117]

Failure to comply with the time-of-driving restriction constitutes operating a motor vehicle without a license, a Class 3 misdemeanor.[118] Failure to comply with the limitations on the number of passengers is an infraction, punishable by a fine of up to $100.[119]

A limited provisional license expires on the license holder's 18th birthday.[120] If that date falls on a weekend or state holiday, the license remains valid through the fifth regular state business day following the expiration date.[121]

3. Full Provisional License

A 16-year-old who has held a limited provisional license for six months may obtain a full provisional license—Level 3 of the graduated licensing process—if he or she meets all of the following requirements:[122]

1. The person must not have been convicted of a motor vehicle moving violation, a seat belt infraction, or a violation of the law prohibiting use of a mobile phone by drivers under 18 in the preceding six months.

2. The person must have a driving eligibility certificate, a high school diploma, or a GED.

3. The person must complete and submit to DMV a driving log documenting at least twelve hours of driving, six of them at night.[123]

---

115. When the limited provisional license holder is driving with supervision, the supervising driver must "be seated beside the license holder in the front seat of the vehicle when it is in motion." G.S. 20-11(e)(3). The supervising driver need not be the only other occupant of the front seat, but he or she must be seated beside the license holder.

116. This limitation does not apply to passengers who are members of the limited provisional license holder's immediate family or those whose primary residence is the same household as the license holder. G.S. 20-11(e)(4). If a family member or member of the same household as the limited provisional license holder who is younger than 21 years of age is a passenger in the vehicle, no other passengers under the age of 21 who are not members of the license holder's immediate family or members of the license holder's household may be in the vehicle. *Id.*

117. G.S. 20-11(j).

118. G.S. 20-11(l).

119. *Id. See also id.* § 20-176(b) (setting out maximum penalty for infractions under G.S. Chapter 20, Article 3).

120. G.S. 20-11(j).

121. *Id.*

122. G.S. 20-11(f).

123. The driving log must be signed by the supervising driver for any hours for which supervision was required. G.S. 20-11(f)(4). If DMV has cause to believe that the log has been falsified, the limited provisional licensee must complete a new driving log and is ineligible for a full provisional license for six months. *Id.*

The fee for a full provisional license is $5 for each year the license is effective—the same as that for a regular driver's license.[124]

A full provisional license expires on the license holder's twenty-first birthday.[125]

The restrictions on time of driving, supervision, and passengers do not apply to a full provisional licensee. Such drivers are, however, prohibited from using mobile phones while driving, subject to limited exceptions.[126]

a. Minors with Out-of-State or Federal Driving Privileges

Several provisions of North Carolina's driver's license law address the situation faced by minors between the ages of 15 and 18 who move to North Carolina after obtaining driving privileges in their former states or from the federal government.[127] Such minors may be eligible to obtain driving privileges in North Carolina after submitting appropriate documentation.

b. Suspension of Provisional Licenses

DMV is authorized under G.S. 20-13 to suspend the license of a provisional licensee upon receiving notice of the person's conviction of multiple *motor vehicle moving violations* for offenses committed while he or she was a provisional licensee.

While the term "motor vehicle moving violation" is not defined by statute, G.S. 20-13(a) specifies that the term—as used in this statute—does not include the following offenses:

- overloads
- over length
- over width
- over height
- illegal parking
- carrying concealed weapon
- improper plates
- improper registration
- improper muffler
- improper display of license plates or dealers' tags
- unlawful display of emblems and insignia
- failure to display current inspection certificate
- equipment violations set forth in Part 9 of Article 3 of G.S. Chapter 20 (G.S. 20-115 through -137.5)

---

124. G.S. 20-11(j) (providing that the fee for a full provisional license is the amount set under G.S. 20-7(i)).

125. G.S. 20-7(f)(1); 20-11(j) (providing that a full provisional license expires on the date set under G.S. 20-7(f)).

126. *See* G.S. 20-11(g) (providing that the prohibition against operating a motor vehicle while using a mobile telephone under G.S. 20-137.3(b) applies to a full provisional license).

127. *See* G.S. 20-11(h) (setting forth requirements for persons aged 16 to 18 who have unrestricted out-of-state licenses); 20-11(h1) (setting forth requirements for persons 16 to 18 who have out-of-state restricted licenses); 20-11(h2) (setting forth requirements for 15-year-olds who have licenses from other states); 20-11(h3) (setting forth requirements for persons under 18 who have federal licenses).

DMV is authorized to suspend a provisional license as follows:

- For the conviction of a second motor vehicle moving violation committed within twelve months of the first offense, DMV may suspend the license for up to thirty days.
- For the conviction of a third motor vehicle moving violation committed within twelve months of the first offense, DMV may suspend the license for up to ninety days.
- For the conviction of a fourth motor vehicle moving violation committed within twelve months of the first offense, DMV may suspend the license for six months.[128]

DMV may, in lieu of suspension and with the written consent of the licensee, place the licensee on probation for a maximum of twelve months.[129]

DMV may not suspend a provisional license for the first motor vehicle moving violation.[130] Two or more motor vehicle moving offenses committed on a single occasion count as a single offense for purposes of G.S. 20-13.[131]

D. Classes of Licenses

DMV issues two types of driver's licenses: regular and commercial.[132] There are three classes of regular drivers' licenses: Class A, Class B, and Class C.[133] A license authorizes the holder to drive any vehicle included in the class of the license sought and any vehicle included in a lesser class of license, except a vehicle for which an endorsement is required.[134] To drive a vehicle for which an endorsement is required, a person must obtain both a license and an endorsement for the vehicle.[135] A regular driver's license is considered a lesser class of license than its commercial counterpart.[136]

1. Vehicle Classifications

Because a driver's license authorizes its holder to drive vehicles placed within a certain classification, it is necessary to review vehicle classifications before turning to license classifications.

a. Class A: Combination Motor Vehicles

A Class A motor vehicle is a combination of motor vehicles that meets either of the following descriptions: (1) vehicle has a combined gross vehicle weight rating (GVWR)[137] of at least 26,001 pounds and includes as part of the combination a towed unit that has a GVWR of at least 10,001 pounds or (2) vehicle has a combined GVWR of less than 26,001 pounds and includes as part of the combination a towed unit that has a GVWR of at least 10,001 pounds.[138]

---

128. G.S. 20-13(b)(2)–(4).
129. G.S. 20-13(b).
130. G.S. 20-13(b)(1).
131. G.S. 20-13(c).
132. G.S. 20-7(a).
133. *Id.*
134. *Id.*
135. *Id.*
136. *Id.*
137. A GVWR is the value specified by a vehicle's manufacturer as the maximum loaded weight a vehicle is capable of safely hauling. G.S. 20-4.01(12f). The GVWR of a combination vehicle is the GVWR of the power unit plus the GVWR of the towed unit or units. *Id.*
138. G.S. 20-4.01(2a).

b. Class B

A Class B motor vehicle is a single motor vehicle that has a GVWR of at least 26,001 pounds or a combination of motor vehicles that includes a towing unit with a GVWR of at least 26,001 pounds and a towed unit that has a GVWR of less than 10,001 pounds.[139]

c. Class C

A Class C motor vehicle is a single motor vehicle not included in Class B or a combination of motor vehicles not included in Class A or Class B.[140]

d. Commercial Motor Vehicles

A commercial motor vehicle is any of the following motor vehicles that are designed or used to transport persons or property:[141]

- a Class A motor vehicle that has a combined GVWR of at least 26,001 pounds and includes as part of the combination a towed unit that has a GVWR of at least 10,001 pounds;
- a Class B motor vehicle; or
- a Class C motor vehicle that (a) is designed to transport sixteen or more passengers, including the driver, or (b) is transporting hazardous materials and is required by federal regulations to be placarded.

2. Regular Driver's License

There are three types of regular drivers' licenses: Class A, Class B, and Class C.

a. Class A License

A Class A driver's license authorizes the holder to drive any of the following types of vehicles: (1) a Class A motor vehicle that is exempt under G.S. 20-37.16 from the commercial driver's license requirements and (2) a Class A motor vehicle that has a combined GVWR of less than 26,001 pounds and includes as part of the combination a towed unit that has a GVWR of at least 10,001 pounds.[142]

i. Vehicles Exempt under G.S. 20-37.16

The classifications for commercial drivers' licenses are prescribed by G.S. 20-37.16. Certain vehicles for which a commercial driver's license otherwise would be required are exempted from that requirement. They are

- vehicles used for personal use, such as recreational vehicles;
- vehicles owned or operated by the U.S. Department of Defense, including the National Guard, while they are driven by activity duty military personnel or members of the National Guard while on active duty, in the pursuit of military purposes;
- vehicles used as firefighting or emergency equipment to preserve life or property or to carry out emergency governmental functions; and

---

139. G.S. 20-4.01(2b).
140. G.S. 20-4.01(2c).
141. G.S. 20-4.01(3d).
142. G.S. 20-7(a)(1).

- farm vehicles that (1) are controlled and operated by a farmer or the farmer's employee and are used exclusively for farm use; (2) are used to transport agricultural products, farm machinery, or farm supplies to or from a farm; (3) are not used in the operations of a for-hire motor carrier; and (4) are used within 150 miles of a farmer's farm. A farm vehicle includes a forestry vehicle that meets the listed criteria when applied to forestry operations.

A person must be at least 18 years old to obtain a Class A driver's license.[143]

b. Class B License

A Class B license authorizes the holder to drive any Class B motor vehicle that is exempt under G.S. 20-37.16 from the commercial driver's license requirements. A person must be at least 18 years old to obtain a Class B driver's license.[144]

c. Class C License

A Class C license authorizes the holder to drive any of the following:

- any Class C vehicle that is not a commercial motor vehicle;
- a Class A or Class B firefighting, rescue, or EMS motor vehicle, or a combination of these vehicles, when such vehicle is operated by a volunteer member of a fire department, a rescue squad, or an emergency medical service (EMS) in the performance of a duty; or
- a combination of noncommercial motor vehicles that have a gross vehicle weight rating (GVWR) of more than 10,000 pounds but less than 26,001 pounds, provided the license holder is at least 18 years old.[145]

A person must be at least 16 years old to obtain a Class C driver's license.[146]

d. Motorcycle Endorsement

To drive a motorcycle,[147] a person must have one of the following:

- a full provisional license with a motorcycle learner's permit,
- a regular driver's license with a motorcycle learner's permit,
- a full provisional license with a motorcycle endorsement, or
- a regular driver's license with a motorcycle endorsement.[148]

---

143. G.S. 20-9(a).

144. *Id.*

145. G.S. 20-7(a)(3).

146. G.S. 20-9(a).

147. Motorcycles are defined in G.S. 20-4.01(27)d. as "[v]ehicles having a saddle for the use of the rider and designed to travel on not more than three wheels in contact with the ground, including autocycles, motor scooters, and motor-driven bicycles." Notwithstanding this definition, the following types of vehicles are not considered to be motorcycles:

- Tractors and utility vehicles equipped with an additional form of device designed to transport property,
- Three-wheeled vehicles used by law enforcement agencies, and
- Mopeds.

148. G.S. 20-7(a1).

Even though autocycles[149] are a type of three-wheeled motorcycle, no motorcycle endorsement is required to drive an autocycle.[150]

In addition, to obtain a motorcycle endorsement, a person who is at least 18 years old must pass a knowledge test about motorcycles and *either* pass a road test or successfully complete the North Carolina Motorcycle Safety Education Program Basic Rider or Experienced Rider Course or any course approved by DMV that is consistent with the instruction provided through the Motorcycle Safety Instruction Program at participating community colleges.[151]

A person who is under 18 can obtain a motorcycle endorsement only by passing a knowledge test and completing one of the courses mentioned above. A road test may not substitute for such a course.[152] A person younger than 18 with a motorcycle endorsement may not drive a motorcycle with a passenger.[153]

Neither a driver's license nor a motorcycle endorsement is required to drive a moped.[154]

e. Motorcycle Learner's Permit

To obtain a motorcycle learner's permit, a person who is at least 16 but less than 18 years old must have a full provisional license issued by DMV. The person must also successfully complete the North Carolina Motorcycle Safety Education Program Basic Rider Course or any course approved by DMV that is consistent with the instruction provided through the community college Motorcycle Safety Instruction Program.[155]

A person seeking a motorcycle learner's permit who is 18 or older must have a license issued by DMV. All applicants, regardless of age, must pass vision, road sign, and knowledge tests.[156]

A motorcycle learner's permit expires twelve months after it is issued and may be renewed for one additional six-month period. The holder of a motorcycle learner's permit may not drive a motorcycle with a passenger.[157]

3. Commercial Driver's License

The Commercial Driver's License Act is codified in Article 2C of G.S. Chapter 20. The Act implements federal law governing the issuance of commercial drivers' licenses[158] and aims to "reduce or prevent commercial motor vehicle accidents, fatalities, and injuries" by

- permitting commercial drivers to hold one license,
- disqualifying commercial drivers who have committed specified offenses, and
- strengthening commercial driver licensing and testing standards.[159]

---

149. Under G.S. 20-4.01(27)a., an autocycle is a "three-wheeled motorcycle that has a steering wheel, pedals, seat safety belts for each occupant, antilock brakes, completely or partially enclosed seating that does not require the operator to straddle or sit astride, and is otherwise manufactured to comply with federal safety requirements for motorcycles."

150. A person with a regular driver's license may drive an autocycle. G.S. 20-7(a3).

151. G.S. 20-7(a1).

152. *Id.*

153. *Id.*

154. *Id.*

155. G.S. 20-7(a2).

156. *Id.*

157. *Id.*

158. *See generally* 49 U.S.C. Chs. 311, 313.

159. G.S. 20-37.11.

A commercial driver's license (commonly referred to as a CDL) is required to operate a commercial motor vehicle on streets and highways in North Carolina.[160]

a. Commercial Motor Vehicles

The following types of vehicles are commercial motor vehicles:

- a Class A motor vehicle that has a combined gross vehicle weight rating (GVWR) of at least 26,001 pounds and includes as part of the combination a towed unit that has a GVWR of at least 10,001 pounds;
- a Class B motor vehicle; and
- a Class C motor vehicle that is designed to transport sixteen or more people, including the driver, or that is transporting hazardous materials and is required under federal regulations to be placarded.[161]

A CDL must be in the driver's immediate possession and must authorize the person to drive the type of vehicle he or she is driving.[162] A person who has a commercial driver's learner's permit may operate a commercial motor vehicle on state roadways while accompanied by the holder of a CDL valid for the vehicle being driven.[163]

A person may operate a commercial motor vehicle in North Carolina if he or she (1) has a valid commercial driver's license issued by the state where he or she resides or by the federal government and (2) has that license in his or her possession.[164]

b. Requirements for Issuance

Under G.S. 20-37.13(a), to be issued a commercial driver's license by NCDMV, a person must

- be a resident of North Carolina,[165]
- be at least 21 years old,[166]
- have passed a knowledge test and a skills test[167] for driving a commercial motor vehicle that comply with minimum standards set by federal regulations,
- have satisfied all other requirements of federal law, and
- have held a commercial learner's permit for a minimum of fourteen days.[168]

No commercial driver's license or learner's permit may be issued to a person while the person is disqualified from driving a commercial motor vehicle or while the person's driver's license is suspended

---

160. G.S. 20-37.12(a).

161. G.S. 20-4.01(3d).

162. G.S. 20-37.12(a).

163. *Id.*

164. G.S. 20-37.12(d).

165. DMV may issue a nonresident commercial driver's license (NRCDL) to a resident of a foreign jurisdiction if the U.S. Secretary of Transportation has determined that the commercial motor vehicle testing and licensing standards in the foreign jurisdiction do not meet federal standards. G.S. 20-37.14.

166. An exemption applies for a person who is at least 18 years old who is not subject to the age requirements of federal motor carrier safety regulations. G.S. 20-37.13(a).

167. DMV may waive the skills test for qualified military applicants who meet the requirements in G.S. 20-37.13(c1).

168. The issuance of a commercial driver learner's permit is a precondition to the initial issuance of a commercial driver's license. It is also a precondition to the upgrade of a commercial driver's license if the upgrade requires a skills test. G.S. 20-37.13(g).

in any state.[169] In addition, an applicant must surrender all other drivers' licenses issued by DMV or by another state before he or she may be issued a CDL.[170]

A commercial driver learner's permit may be issued to a person who holds a regular Class C driver's license and has passed the knowledge test for the class and type of commercial motor vehicle the person will be driving.[171] The permit is valid for up to six months and may be renewed or reissued once within a two-year period.

c. Classifications of CDLs

There are three classes of commercial drivers' licenses just as there are three classes of regular drivers' licenses: Class A, Class B, and Class C.[172]

A Class A CDL authorizes the holder to drive any Class A motor vehicle.[173]
A Class B CDL authorizes the holder to drive any Class B motor vehicle.[174]
A Class C CDL authorizes the holder to drive any Class C motor vehicle.[175]

4. Special Endorsements

There are seven types of endorsements that are required in North Carolina to drive certain motor vehicles.[176] Below is a chart listing each endorsement and the type of vehicle that may be driven by an individual holding the endorsement.[177]

Endorsement	Vehicles That Can Be Driven
H	Vehicles, regardless of size or class, except tank vehicles, when transporting hazardous materials, when transporting hazardous materials that require the vehicle to be placarded
M	Motorcycles
N	Tank vehicles not carrying hazardous materials
P	Vehicles carrying passengers
S	School buses
T	Double trailers
X	Tank vehicles carrying hazardous materials

---

169. G.S. 20-37.13(d).
170. *Id.*
171. G.S. 20-37.13(e).
172. G.S. 20-37.16(b).
173. G.S. 20-37.16(b)(1).
174. G.S. 20-37.16(b)(2).
175. G.S. 20-37.16(b)(3).
176. G.S. 20-37.16(c).
177. *Id.*

E. Commonly Charged Driver's License Offenses

1. No Operator's License

As previously noted, a person must be licensed by DMV (or be exempt from licensing requirements) to drive a motor vehicle on a highway and must carry his or her driver's license while driving the vehicle.[178] The person also must comply with any restriction placed on the driver's license by DMV.[179]

A person violates the provisions of G.S. 20-7(a) and commits the offense commonly referred to as "no operator's license" if he or she

(1) drives
(2) a motor vehicle
(3) on a highway
(4) without being licensed by DMV or being exempt from licensing requirements.

a. Punishment

Driving without an operator's license is classified as a Class 3 misdemeanor.[180]

2. Failure to Comply with License Restrictions

A person fails to comply with a license restriction in violation of G.S. 20-7(e) if he or she

(1) drives
(2) a motor vehicle
(3) on a highway
(4) in violation of a driver's license restriction.

As mentioned earlier in this chapter, DMV is authorized to impose restrictions on drivers' licenses. One common restriction is that a person must wear corrective lenses while operating a vehicle.[181] Thus, a person with a corrective lens restriction who operates a motor vehicle on a highway without wearing corrective lenses commits the offense of failure to comply with a license restriction.

a. Punishment

This offense is classified as a Class 3 misdemeanor.[182]

b. Violation of Alcohol-Concentration Restrictions

When NCDMV restores a person's North Carolina driver's license after it has been revoked for impaired driving or driving by a person under 21 after consuming, the license is restored subject to certain restrictions.[183]

---

178. G.S. 20-7(a).

179. G.S. 20-7(e).

180. G.S. 20-35(a1)(1).

181. *See* 19A N.C.A.C. 03B, § .0201(a)(3) (administrative regulation stating that a license is restricted to require corrective lenses if acuity is less than 20/40 in either eye or in both eyes together).

182. G.S. 20-35(a1)(2).

183. G.S. 20-19(c3). The restriction codes are set forth on side two of form AOC-CVR-1A, available at www.nccourts.org/Forms/Documents/1049.pdf.

- If the person's driver's license was revoked for impaired driving[184] and this is the first time the person's license has been restored, the license is restored subject to the condition that "the person not operate a vehicle with an alcohol concentration of 0.04 at any relevant time after the driving."[185] This restriction is denoted on the person's physical license card as Restriction 19.
- If the person's driver's license was revoked for driving after consuming by a person under 21,[186] the license is restored subject to the condition that "the person not operate a vehicle with an alcohol concentration of 0.00 at any relevant time after the driving."[187] This restriction is denoted on the person's physical license card as Restriction 21. Restriction 21 also applies to a person whose license is restored for a second or subsequent time following a conviction of impaired driving.
- The licensee must agree to submit to a chemical analysis (breath, blood, or urine test) at the request of a law enforcement officer who has reasonable grounds to believe that the licensee is operating a motor vehicle on a highway or public vehicular area in violation of the license restrictions. The person must also agree to be transported by the law enforcement officer upon the officer's request to the place where chemical analysis is to be administered.[188]

Because G.S. 20-7(e) makes it unlawful for the holder of a restricted license to operate a motor vehicle without complying with the applicable restriction and provides that this conduct "is the equivalent of operating a motor vehicle without a license," a person who operates a motor vehicle in violation of an alcohol concentration restriction or who refuses to be transported for chemical testing commits the offense of failure to comply with a license restriction, a Class 3 misdemeanor.[189]

3. Allowing Unlicensed Person to Drive

A person allows an unlicensed person to drive in violation of G.S. 20-34 if he or she

(1) authorizes or knowingly permits
(2) a motor vehicle that he/she owns or controls
(3) to be driven on a highway
(4) by a person who is not licensed to drive the motor vehicle.

a. Punishment

This offense is classified as a Class 3 misdemeanor.[190]

---

184. G.S. 20-138.1.
185. G.S. 20-19(c3)(1).
186. G.S. 20-138.3.
187. G.S. 20-19(c3)(3).
188. G.S. 20-19(c3).
189. A law enforcement officer who has probable cause to believe that a person has violated a restriction imposed pursuant to G.S. 20-19(c3) must complete an affidavit indicating the restriction violated and must mail the affidavit to DMV. The form affidavit (AOC-CVR-1A) used to report such a violation is the same form used to report a person's refusal to submit to a test of his or her breath, blood, or urine. Upon receipt of a properly executed affidavit, DMV must notify the person that his or her driver's license is revoked for one year.
190. G.S. 20-35(a1)(3).

4. Other Driver's License Offenses

The following license-related acts are prohibited by G.S. 20-30 and are classified as Class 2 misdemeanors:

- displaying or possessing a driver's license, learner's permit, or special identification card known to be fictitious, canceled, revoked, or altered
- counterfeiting, selling, or lending a driver's license, learner's permit, or special identification card to a person who is not entitled to use the license, permit, or card
- knowingly permitting the use of a driver's license, learner's permit, or special identification card by a person who is not entitled to use the license, permit, or card
- displaying or representing as one's own a driver's license, learner's permit, or special identification card that was not issued to the person
- failing or refusing to surrender to NCDMV upon demand any driver's license, learner's permit, or special identification card that has been canceled or revoked
- making a color photocopy or color reproduction of a driver's license, learner's permit, or special identification card without authorization from NCDMV[191]
- possessing more than one commercial driver's license or possessing a commercial driver's license and a regular driver's license[192]

The violations of the state's driver's license law discussed in the following three paragraphs are classified as infractions. An infraction is "a noncriminal violation of law not punishable by imprisonment."[193] While an officer may detain a person for a reasonable period to issue and serve a citation charging an infraction, a person may not be arrested for commission of an infraction.[194]

Failure to carry a valid license while driving a motor vehicle on a highway is a violation of G.S. 20-7(a) and is an infraction.[195] A person may not be found responsible for failure to carry a regular driver's license if he or she produces in court at the time of trial a regular driver's license that was valid when he or she was charged with the offense.[196]

Driving a motor vehicle on a highway with an expired license also is an infraction.[197] A person may not be found responsible for this offense if, at trial, he or she shows the following: (1) at the time of the offense, he or she had an expired license; (2) he or she renewed the license within thirty days after it expired and now has a current, valid license; and (3) he or she could not have been charged with driving without a license had he or she renewed the license when charged with the offense.[198]

---

191. G.S. 20-30(6) expressly provides that it is permissible to make a black and white photocopy or reproduction of a driver's license, learner's permit, or special identification card.

192. G.S. 20-30(8) provides that "[a]ny commercial drivers license other than the one most recently issued is subject to immediate seizure by any law enforcement officer or judicial official." In addition, "[a]ny regular drivers license possessed at the same time as a commercial drivers license is subject to immediate seizure by any law enforcement officer or judicial official."

193. G.S. 14-3.1(a).

194. Robert L. Farb, Arrest, Search, and Investigation in North Carolina 88 (UNC School of Government, 5th ed. 2016).

195. G.S. 20-35(a2)(1).

196. G.S. 20-35(c). G.S. 20-37.12(a) similarly requires that a person be in immediate possession of a commercial driver's license when operating a commercial motor vehicle. A similar defense likewise applies. *Id.* § 20-37.12(f) (a person may not be convicted of failing to carry a commercial driver's license if he or she produces in court a commercial driver's license issued to him or her that was valid on the date of the offense).

197. G.S. 20-35(a2)(2).

198. G.S. 20-35(c).

Finally, failing to notify DMV of an address change for a driver's license within sixty days after the change occurs in violation of G.S. 20-7.1 is an infraction.[199]

5. Driving While License Revoked

A person commits the offense of driving while license revoked (DWLR) under G.S. 20-28(a), a Class 3 misdemeanor, if he or she

(1) drives
(2) a motor vehicle
(3) on a highway
(4) while his or her driver's license or driving privileges are revoked and
(5) he or she has knowledge of the revocation.

a. While His or Her Driver's License Is Revoked

The offense of DWLR has historically been interpreted to require that the State of North Carolina, through its courts or through DMV, have taken action to revoke the defendant's driver's license or driving privileges,[200] though it is possible to read the language more broadly to encompass revocations by other jurisdictions.

The terms "revocation" and "suspension" are synonymous for purposes of G.S. Chapter 20 and are defined as the "[t]ermination of a licensee's or permittee's privilege to drive . . . for a period of time stated in an order of revocation or suspension."[201] The requirement that the termination be stated in an order of revocation or suspension corresponds to the requirement that the State prove that a defendant had actual or constructive knowledge of the revocation, as discussed below.

An order by a North Carolina court or by DMV revoking a person's driver's license clearly is one type of order contemplated by this statutory definition. Just as DMV may suspend or revoke the driving privileges of a North Carolina resident, it may also suspend or revoke the privileges of nonresidents and may prohibit a person from operating under a foreign license while subject to such a revocation order.[202] Thus, there is no question that a nonresident's driving privileges are revoked for purposes of G.S. 20-28(a) when DMV or a North Carolina court revokes the person's privilege to drive.

It is unclear whether a revocation imposed by another state is a revocation for purposes of the offense of DWLR. As noted earlier in this chapter, a nonresident who is at least 16 years old who has in his or her immediate possession a valid driver's license issued in his or her home state or country may lawfully drive in North Carolina if he or she operates the motor vehicle in accordance with the license restrictions and vehicle classifications that would apply in his or her home state or country.[203] The revocation of the nonresident's valid license in his or her home state "terminat[es]" the nonresident's "privilege to drive" in North Carolina, thereby arguably satisfying the definition of

---

199. G.S. 20-35(a2)(3).
200. *See* BEN F. LOEB, JR. & JAMES C. DRENNAN, MOTOR VEHICLE LAW AND THE LAW OF IMPAIRED DRIVING IN NORTH CAROLINA 84 (UNC Institute of Government, 2000); *see also* N.C.P.I.—CRIM. 271.10 (stating that for a jury to find that notice of the revocation was given, of which the defendant had knowledge, the State must prove beyond a reasonable doubt that (1) notice was personally delivered, (2) the defendant surrendered his or her license to an official of the court, or (3) that DMV provided notice by mail in accordance with G.S. 20-48).
201. G.S. 20-4.01(36), (47).
202. G.S. 20-21; 20-22; *see also id.* §§ 20-16.5(a)(5), (e), (f) (requiring surrender of a driver's license from any jurisdiction pursuant to civil license revocation in an implied consent case).
203. G.S. 20-8(3).

"revocation" in G.S. 20-4.01(36). No appellate court case addresses whether revocations imposed by other states with no corresponding action by NCDMV are revocations for purposes of G.S. 20-28.

b. With Knowledge of the Revocation

The statute defining DWLR does not specify that the defendant must have knowledge of the revocation.[204] Nevertheless, the state supreme court has held that the legislature intended that a defendant have actual or constructive knowledge that his or her license had been suspended or revoked before the defendant may be convicted of violating G.S. 20-28(a).[205] While the mailing of a notice by DMV in accordance with G.S. 20-48 raises a prima facie presumption that a defendant received the notice and thereby acquired knowledge of the suspension or revocation, a defendant may rebut this presumption.[206] G.S. 20-48 permits DMV to provide notice by U.S. mail to the address contained in its records. Notice provided by mail is complete four days after the mailing. Proof of notice may be made by a notation in DMV records; there is no requirement that the actual notice be produced.

Proof that DMV complied with the notice provisions of G.S. 20-48 creates a presumption that a defendant received notice of license revocation and therefore had the requisite knowledge. "When there is some evidence to rebut this presumption, the issue of guilty knowledge . . . must be determined by the jury [in superior court] under appropriate instruction from the trial court."[207] If there is no evidence to rebut the presumption (in other words, no evidence that the defendant was not notified), the trial court is not required to instruct the jury regarding guilty knowledge.[208] Presumably, the State also can prove actual knowledge based upon a defendant's admission that he or she knew his or her license was revoked or by a defendant's act of surrendering his or her license to the court upon conviction of an offense that requires revocation pursuant to G.S. 20-24(a).

---

204. G.S. 20-28(a).

205. State v. Atwood, 290 N.C. 266 (1976). The *Atwood* court based this determination on the requirement in G.S. 20-16(d) that DMV notify a person that his or her license is suspended or revoked and provide an opportunity for a hearing on the matter. Atwood's license was suspended based upon her conviction within twelve months of two offenses of speeding over 55 miles per hour. Then, as now, G.S. 20-16 afforded DMV discretion regarding whether to revoke a person's license for this reason and required that DMV provide an opportunity for a hearing in the event it elected to do so. While some license revocations are discretionary, like that in *Atwood*, many are not. G.S. 20-17(a) sets forth offenses for which conviction requires that DMV revoke a person's driver's license. Among these are impaired driving and manslaughter resulting from the operation of a motor vehicle. Upon receiving notice of conviction of such an offense (which the clerk of court must provide pursuant to G.S. 20-24(b)), DMV must revoke the defendant's license. Unlike G.S. 20-16, G.S. 20-17 does not require that DMV provide a defendant notice or an opportunity to be heard, though DMV nevertheless provides notice of mandatory revocations. Had the holding in *Atwood* been based solely on the notice and hearing requirements applicable to discretionary revocations, the knowledge requirement for conviction under G.S. 20-28(a) might be limited only to circumstances in which the revocation was ordered pursuant to G.S. 20-16. But the *Atwood* court went on to state that the "lack of actual notice and resulting knowledge removes the criminal character from the defendant's conduct," 290 N.C. at 272–73, thereby indicating that its interpretation of G.S. 20-28(a) also was founded upon the traditional criminal law requirement that a defendant act with guilty knowledge. Justice Exum embraced this implied mens rea argument in his concurrence in *Atwood*. 290 N.C. at 276. Subsequent cases make clear that knowledge is an element of DWLR regardless of the reason for the underlying revocation. *See, e.g.,* State v. Curtis, 73 N.C. App. 248 (1985).

206. *Atwood*, 290 N.C. at 271 (citations omitted) ("For purposes of a Conviction for driving while license is suspended or revoked, mailing of the notice under G.S. 20-48 raises only a Prima facie presumption that defendant received the notice and thereby acquired knowledge of the suspension or revocation. Thus, defendant is not by this statute denied the right to rebut this presumption.").

207. *See* State v. Chester, 30 N.C. App. 224, 227 (1976).

208. *Id.*

c. Relationship to Offense of No Operator's License

A person may not be prosecuted for DWLR and no operator's license based on the same conduct, as each of the elements of driving with no operator's license are included within the offense of DWLR.[209]

6. Violation of a Limited Driving Privilege

A person who has been granted a restrictive or limited driving privilege under G.S. 20-16.1(b) who violates any of its conditions commits the offense of driving while license revoked under G.S. 20-28(a).[210] Whenever a person is charged with operating a motor vehicle in violation of applicable restrictions, the person's limited driving privilege must be suspended pending final disposition of the charge.[211]

7. Driving While License Revoked for an Offense Involving Impaired Driving

A person whose driver's license has been revoked for an impaired driving revocation who drives a motor vehicle on a street or highway commits the offense of driving while license revoked (DWLR) for an offense involving impaired driving under G.S. 20-28(a1), a Class 1 misdemeanor. This offense contains one additional element beyond what is required for commission of DWLR under G.S. 20-28(a), namely, that the person be revoked for an *impaired driving license revocation*, defined in G.S. 20-28.2(a) as a revocation made under any of the following statutes:

- G.S. 20-13.2: consuming alcohol/drugs or willful refusal by driver under 21
- G.S. 20-16(a)(8b): military driving while impaired
- G.S. 20-16.2: refused chemical test
- G.S. 20-16.5: pretrial civil license revocation
- G.S. 20-17(a)(2): impaired driving or impaired driving in a commercial motor vehicle
- G.S. 20-138.5: habitual impaired driving
- G.S. 20-17(a)(12): transporting open container
- G.S. 20-17.2: court order not to operate (repealed effective December 1, 2006)
- G.S. 20-16(a)(7): impaired driving out of state resulting in North Carolina revocation
- G.S. 20-17(a)(1): manslaughter or second-degree murder involving impaired driving
- G.S. 20-17(a)(3): felony involving use of motor vehicle, involving impaired driving
- G.S. 20-17(a)(9): felony or misdemeanor death or serious injury by vehicle involving impaired driving
- G.S. 20-17(a)(11): assault with motor vehicle involving impaired driving
- G.S. 20-28.2(a)(3): the laws of another state and the offense for which the person's license is revoked prohibit substantially similar conduct which, if committed in North Carolina, would result in a revocation listed under any of the above statutes

The last category of revocation listed above warrants some discussion. G.S. 20-28(a1) borrows its definition of an "impaired driving revocation" from the statutory provisions providing for seizure, impoundment, and forfeiture of motor vehicles driven in the commission of an impaired driving offense by a person with an impaired driving license revocation.[212] Thus, revocation of a person's

---

209. *See* State v. Cannon, 38 N.C. App. 322 (1978) (concluding that defendant's guilty plea to driving without an operator's license precluded his subsequent prosecution for DWLR on the same occasion).
210. G.S. 20-16.1(b)(4).
211. *Id.*
212. *See* G.S. 20-28.2(a).

driver's license by another state for an impaired driving event may render the motor vehicle driven by the person in the commission of an impaired driving offense in North Carolina subject to seizure, impoundment, and forfeiture.[213] As discussed earlier, it is unclear whether revocation by another state with no corresponding action by NCDMV constitutes a revocation for purposes of driving while license revoked pursuant to G.S. 20-28.[214]

As previously noted, DWLR for impaired driving is a more serious misdemeanor offense (a Class 1 misdemeanor) than the related charge of driving while license revoked (a Class 3 misdemeanor). Moreover, persons convicted of DWLR for an impaired driving offense are subject to an additional period of revocation: one year for the first offense, two years for the second offense, and permanently for a third or subsequent offense.[215]

Driving in violation of the terms of a limited driving privilege, as previously mentioned, constitutes the offense of DWLR. If the limited driving privilege was issued to permit driving during an impaired driving revocation, then violation of its terms constitutes DWLR for an impaired driving revocation.[216]

8. Violation of an Ignition Interlock Privilege

Certain persons convicted of impaired driving may have their licenses restored only in conjunction with an ignition interlock restriction (meaning that the only vehicle the person may operate is one that has been equipped with a DMV-approved working ignition interlock device).[217] A person whose license is revoked as a result of a conviction of impaired driving pursuant to G.S. 20-138.1 who had (1) an alcohol concentration of 0.15 or higher, (2) a prior conviction for an offense involving impaired driving, that offense having occurred within seven years immediately preceding the date of the offense for which the person's license is revoked, or (3) was sentenced at Aggravated Level One pursuant to G.S. 20-179.3(f3) may have his or her license restored only with an ignition interlock restriction.[218]

A person who violates an ignition interlock restriction commits the offense of driving while license revoked (DWLR) for impaired driving under G.S. 20-28(a1) and is subject to punishment and license revocation as provided in that section.[219] If a law enforcement officer has reasonable grounds to believe that a person subject to this section has consumed alcohol while driving or has driven while he or she has remaining in his or her body any alcohol previously consumed, the suspected offense of DWLR is an alcohol-related offense subject to the implied-consent provisions of G.S. 20-16.2.[220]

If a person subject to an ignition interlock restriction is charged with DWLR for impaired driving based on his or her violation of the ignition interlock restriction and a judicial official finds probable cause for the charge, the person's license is suspended pending the resolution of the case and the judicial official must require that the person surrender his or her driver's license.[221]

---

213. G.S. 20-28.2(a)(3).

214. *See supra* section II.E.5.a.

215. G.S. 20-28(a1).

216. G.S. 20-179.3(j).

217. G.S. 20-17.8.

218. G.S. 20-17.8(l) sets forth a medical exception to the ignition interlock requirement for people subject to the requirement solely because of an alcohol concentration of 0.15 or higher who establish that they are not capable of personally activating the ignition interlock system.

219. G.S. 20-17.8(f).

220. *Id.*

221. *Id.*

III. Vehicle Registration and Inspection Requirements in North Carolina

A. Registration Requirements

A vehicle must be registered with DMV, or specifically exempted from registration requirements, to be lawfully driven on a street or highway in North Carolina.[222] The owner of a vehicle subject to registration must apply to DMV for a certificate of title, a registration plate, and a registration card for the vehicle.[223] As part of the application process, the vehicle's owner must state that he or she is an eligible risk for insurance coverage.[224]

Under G.S. 20-51, the following types of vehicles are exempted from the registration requirement:

- a vehicle driven or moved on a highway in conformance with the provisions of Article 3 of G.S. Chapter 20 relating to manufacturers, dealers, or nonresidents
- a vehicle driven or moved on a highway for the sole purpose of crossing the highway from one property to another
- an implement of husbandry, farm tractor, road construction or maintenance machinery, or other vehicle which is not self-propelled that was designed for use in work off the highway and which is operated on the highway for the purpose of going to and from such nonhighway projects
- a vehicle owned and operated by the U.S. government
- farm tractors equipped with rubber tires and trailers or semitrailers when attached thereto and when used by a farmer, his or her tenant, agent, or employee in transporting his or her own farm implements, farm supplies, or farm products from place to place on the same farm, from one farm to another, from farm to market, or from market to farm; this exemption extends to any tractor, implement of husbandry, and trailer or semitrailer while on any trip within a radius of ten miles from the point of loading, so long as the vehicle does not exceed a speed of 35 miles per hour[225]
- a trailer or semitrailer attached to and drawn by a licensed motor vehicle when used by a farmer, his or her tenant, agent, or employee in transporting unginned cotton, peanuts, soybeans, corn, hay, tobacco, silage, cucumbers, potatoes, all vegetables, fruits, greenhouse and nursery plants and flowers, Christmas trees, livestock, live poultry, animal waste, pesticides, seeds, fertilizers, or chemicals purchased or owned by the farmer or tenant for personal use in implementing husbandry, irrigation pipes, loaders, or equipment owned by the farmer or tenant from place to place on the same farm, from one farm to another, from farm to gin, from farm to dryer, or from farm to market, and when not operated on a for-hire basis
- small farm trailers known generally as tobacco-handling trailers, tobacco trucks or tobacco trailers when used by a farmer, his or her tenant, agent, or employee when transporting or otherwise handling tobacco in connection with the pulling, tying, or curing thereof

---

222. G.S. 20-50(a).

223. *Id.*

224. G.S. 20-52(a)(4) (requiring a statement that the owner is an eligible risk for insurance coverage as defined in G.S. 58-37-1(4a)).

225. This exemption *does not extend* to farm tractors, implements of husbandry, and trailers or semitrailers that are operated on a for-hire basis. G.S. 20-51(5).

- a vehicle driven or moved on a highway for the sole purpose of crossing or traveling on the highway from one side to the other, provided the owner or lessee of the vehicle owns the fee or a leasehold in all the land along both sides of the highway at the place or crossing
- devices known as "tow dollies" that are designed for towing private passenger motor vehicles or vehicles not exceeding 5,000 pounds gross weight[226]
- devices generally called converter gear or dollies consisting of a tongue attached to a single or tandem axle upon which is mounted a fifth wheel and which are used to convert a semitrailer to a full trailer for the purpose of being drawn behind a truck tractor and semitrailer
- motorized wheelchairs or similar vehicles not exceeding 1,000 pounds gross weight when used for pedestrian purposes by a handicapped person with a mobility impairment as defined in G.S. 20-37.5
- a vehicle registered in another state and operated temporarily within this state by a public utility, a governmental or cooperative provider of utility services, or a contractor for one of these entities for the purpose of restoring utility services in an emergency outage
- electric personal assistive mobility devices[227]
- any vehicle that
  - is designed for use in work off the highway,
  - is used for agricultural quarantine programs under the supervision of the Department of Agriculture and Consumer Services,
  - is driven or moved on the highway for the purpose of going to and from nonhighway projects,
  - is identified in a manner approved by DMV, and
  - is operated by a person who possesses an identification card issued by the Department of Agriculture and Consumer Services
- A header trailer when transported to or from a dealer, or after a sale or repairs, to the farm or to another dealership

A vehicle that meets all of the following conditions is also exempt from the requirement of registration and certificate of title. The provisions of G.S. 105-449.117 continue to apply to the vehicle and to the person in whose name the vehicle would be registered.

- The vehicle is an agricultural spreader vehicle. An "agricultural spreader vehicle" is a vehicle that is designed for off-highway use on a farm to spread feed, fertilizer, seed, lime, or other agricultural products.
- The vehicle is driven on the highway for the sole purpose of going from the location of its supply source for fertilizer or other products to and from a farm.
- The vehicle does not exceed a speed of 45 miles per hour.
- The vehicle does not drive outside a radius of 50 miles from the location of its supply source for fertilizer and other products.
- The vehicle is driven by a person who has a license appropriate for the class of the vehicle.

---

226. G.S. 20-51(10). A tow dolly is "a two-wheeled device without motive power designed for towing disabled motor vehicles and is drawn by a motor vehicle in the same manner as a trailer." *Id.*

227. G.S. 20-4.01(7b) defines "electric personal assistive mobility device" as a "self-balancing nontandem two-wheeled device, designed to transport one person, with a propulsion system that limits the maximum speed of the device to 15 miles per hour or less."

- The vehicle is insured under a motor vehicle liability policy in the amount required under G.S. 20-309.
- The vehicle displays a valid federal safety inspection decal if the vehicle has a gross vehicle weight rating of at least 10,001 pounds.

A vehicle that is leased to an individual who is a resident of North Carolina is a vehicle intended to be operated upon a highway of this state.

B. Commonly Charged Vehicle Registration Offenses

G.S. 20-111 defines several registration-related offenses.

1. Driving an Unregistered Vehicle

G.S. 20-111(1) makes it unlawful to

(1) drive
(2) a vehicle
(3) on a highway
(4) when the vehicle is not registered or does not display a current registration plate.

a. Punishment

Driving an unregistered vehicle in violation of G.S. 20-111(1) is a Class 3 misdemeanor.

2. Knowingly Permitting Unregistered Vehicle to Be Driven

G.S. 20-111(1) also prohibits a person from

(1) knowingly permitting
(2) a vehicle owned by that person
(3) to be driven on a highway
(4) when the vehicle is not registered or does not display a current registration plate.

a. Punishment

Knowingly permitting another to drive one's unregistered vehicle on a highway in violation of G.S. 20-111(1) is a Class 3 misdemeanor.

3. Failure of Owner to Obtain Registration

A person violates G.S. 20-50 if he or she

(1) owns a vehicle
(2) that is required to be registered and
(3) that is intended to be operated on a highway and
(4) the owner fails to apply for and obtain each of the following:
    (a) a registration card,
    (b) a registration plate, and
    (c) a certificate of title.

a. Punishment

Owning a vehicle (including a moped) that is not registered with DMV or that is not displaying a current registration plate is a Class 3 misdemeanor.[228]

4. Giving, Lending, or Borrowing a License Plate for Use on Another Motor Vehicle

A license plate may be lawfully displayed only upon the motor vehicle for which it is issued. It is unlawful under G.S. 20-111(3) for a person to

(1) give, lend, or borrow
(2) a license plate
(3) for use on a motor vehicle other than the one for which it is issued.

a. Punishment

Giving, lending, or borrowing a license plate for the purpose of using it on a motor vehicle other than the one for which it is issued is a Class 3 misdemeanor.[229] When such improper use of a license plate is discovered, the plate must be revoked and a new license plate must be purchased. A person's failure to surrender to DMV a license plate that has been suspended, canceled, or revoked is a Class 2 misdemeanor.[230]

C. Vehicle Inspection Requirements

1. Safety Inspections

A motor vehicle that is required to be registered with DMV must be inspected for safety as provided in Article 3A of G.S. Chapter 20 unless it qualifies under one of the following exceptions: (1) it is subject to inspection under federal motor carrier safety regulations, (2) it is a trailer whose gross weight is less than 4,000 pounds or is a house trailer, (3) it is a historic vehicle,[231] or (4) it is a bus titled to a local board of education and subject to school bus inspection requirements.[232]

A safety inspection of a motor vehicle consists of an inspection of the following equipment to see if the vehicle has the required equipment and if the equipment is in a safe operating condition:[233]

- brakes
- lights
- horn
- steering mechanism
- windows and windshield wipers[234]
- directional signals
- tires

---

228. G.S. 20-111(1).

229. G.S. 20-111(3).

230. G.S. 20-111(4); 20-176(a), (c). It likewise is a Class 2 misdemeanor to fail to surrender a title certificate or registration card that has been suspended, canceled, or revoked. G.S. 20-111(4); 20-176(a), (c).

231. Historic vehicles are defined in G.S. 20-79.4(b)(91) as motor vehicles that are "at least 35 years old measured from the date of manufacture."

232. G.S. 20-183.2(a), (a1).

233. G.S. 20-183.3(a).

234. To determine if a vehicle window meets North Carolina's window tinting restrictions, a safety inspection mechanic must first determine whether after-factory tint has been applied to the windows. If after-factory tint has been applied, the mechanic must use a light meter to determine if the window meets the window tinting restrictions.

- mirrors
- exhaust systems and emissions control devices

A vehicle must be inspected by the last day of the month in which the vehicle's registration expires.[235] The vehicle may be inspected ninety days prior to midnight of the last day of the month in which its registration expires.[236] An inspection authorization expires at midnight of the last day of the month designated by the vehicle registration sticker of the following year.[237]

2. Emissions Inspections

Motor vehicles meeting each of the following requirements are subject to an emissions inspection:[238]

(1) the motor vehicle is required to be registered with DMV or is operated on a federal installation[239] in an emissions county and is not a tactical military vehicle;

(2) it is

    (a) a 1996 or later model and older than the three most recent model years or

    (b) a 1996 or later model and has 70,000 miles or more on its odometer;

(3) it is

    (a) required to be registered in an emissions county,[240]

    (b) part of a fleet that is operated primarily in an emissions county,

    (c) offered for rent in an emissions county,

    (d) a used vehicle offered for sale by a dealer in an emissions county, or

    (e) otherwise required by federal environmental regulations to be subjected to an emissions inspection; and

(4) it is not a new motor vehicle[241] and has been a used motor vehicle[242] for twelve months or more.[243]

---

235. G.S. 20-183.4C(a)(6).

236. G.S. 20-183.4C(a)(7).

237. G.S. 20-183.4D(e).

238. G.S. 20-183.2(b).

239. A "federal installation" is an "installation that is owned by, leased to, or otherwise regularly used as the place of business of a federal agency." G.S. 20-183.2(c)(3).

240. The following counties are designated in G.S. 143-215.107A(c) as counties in which motor vehicle emissions inspections must be performed: Alamance, Brunswick, Buncombe, Burke, Cabarrus, Caldwell, Carteret, Catawba, Chatham, Cleveland, Craven, Cumberland, Davidson, Durham, Edgecombe, Forsyth, Franklin, Gaston, Granville, Guilford, Harnett, Haywood, Henderson, Iredell, Johnston, Lee, Lenoir, Lincoln, Mecklenburg, Moore, Nash, New Hanover, Onslow, Orange, Pitt, Randolph, Robeson, Rockingham, Rowan, Rutherford, Stanly, Stokes, Surry, Union, Wake, Wayne, Wilkes, and Wilson.

241. "New motor vehicle" is defined in G.S. 20-286(10)a. as "a motor vehicle that has never been the subject of a completed, successful, or conditional sale that was subsequently approved other than between new motor vehicle dealers, or between a manufacturer and a new motor vehicle dealer of the same franchise." This provision further states that "the use of a new motor vehicle by a new motor vehicle dealer for demonstration or service loaner purposes does not render the new motor vehicle a used motor vehicle, notwithstanding (i) the commencement of the manufacturer's original warranty as a result of the franchised dealer's use of the vehicle for demonstration or loaner purposes, or (ii) the dealer's receipt of incentive or warranty compensation or other reimbursement or consideration from a manufacturer, factory branch, distributor, distributor branch or from a third-party warranty, maintenance, or service contract company relating to the use of a vehicle as a demonstrator or service loaner."

242. "Used motor vehicle" is defined in G.S. 20-286(10)b. as any motor vehicle other than a "new motor vehicle."

243. A motor vehicle that has been leased or rented, or offered for lease or rent, is subject to an emissions inspection when (1) it has been leased or rented, or offered for lease or rent, for twelve months or more or (b) it is sold to a consumer-purchaser. G.S. 20-183.2(b)(7).

The following types of motor vehicles are, notwithstanding the general rules stated above, excepted from emissions inspection requirements:

- vehicles licensed at the farmer rate under G.S. 20-88(b)
- trailers whose gross weight is less than 4,000 pounds, house trailers, and motorcycles[244]

An emissions inspection includes "a visual inspection of the vehicle's emissions control devices to determine if the devices are present, are properly connected, and are the correct type for the vehicle."[245] The inspector must also analyze the data provided by the on-board diagnostic (OBD) equipment installed by the vehicle manufacturer to identify any deterioration or malfunction that violates environmental standards for that vehicle's model year.[246] A vehicle must pass both the visual inspection and the OBD analysis to pass an emissions inspection.[247] A safety inspection must accompany any emissions inspection.[248]

When a vehicle successfully passes inspection, an inspection authorization is generated electronically through an electronic accounting system.[249] That system creates a unique authorization number that is assigned to the vehicle's inspection receipt. The inspections information is transmitted electronically to DMV.[250]

D. Infraction Violations of Inspection Requirements

G.S. 20-183.8 defines several inspection-related violations. Each of these violations is an infraction punishable by a penalty of up to $50.[251]

1. Driving Without a Current Inspection

A person violates G.S. 20-183.8(a)(1) if he or she

(1) operates
(2) a motor vehicle
(3) that is subject to inspection
(4) on a highway or public vehicular area
(5) when the vehicle has not been inspected, as evidenced by the lack of a current electronic inspection authorization for the vehicle or otherwise.

2. Allowing an Electronic Inspection Authorization to Be Issued Without a Proper Inspection

A person violates G.S. 20-183.8(a)(2) if he or she

(1) allows
(2) an electronic inspection authorization to be issued
(3) to a vehicle owned or operated by that person

---

244. G.S. 20-183.2(b)(6), (2), respectively.
245. G.S. 20-183.3(b1).
246. *Id.*
247. *Id.*
248. *Id.*
249. G.S. 20-183.2(c)(1) (defining "electronic inspection authorization"); 20-183.4D(b) (requiring inspection mechanic to issue electronic inspection authorization to vehicle that passes inspection).
250. G.S. 20-183.4(b)(4) (safety inspection); 20-183.4A(b)(3) (emissions inspection).
251. G.S. 20-183.8(a).

(4) knowing that the vehicle
    (a) was not inspected before the electronic inspection authorization was issued or
    (b) was not inspected properly.

3. Issuing an Electronic Inspection Authorization Without a Proper Inspection

A person violates G.S. 20-183.3(a)(3) if he or she

(1) issues an electronic inspection authorization on a vehicle
(2) knowing or having reasonable grounds to know that
    (a) an inspection was not performed on that vehicle or
    (b) it was performed improperly.[252]

4. Altering a Vehicle to Prevent On-Board Diagnostic (OBD) Analysis

A person violates G.S. 20-183.8(a)(4) if he or she

(1) "[a]lters the original certified configuration or data link connectors of a vehicle"
(2) in a manner that makes an emissions inspection by analysis of data from OBD equipment inaccurate or impossible.

5. Defenses

The following defenses apply to the infractions defined in G.S. 20-183.8(a)(1)–(4) and discussed above:

(1) The vehicle was out of state continuously for at least the thirty days preceding the date on which the electronic inspection authorization expired and a current electronic inspection authorization was obtained within ten days after the vehicle returned to North Carolina.
(2) The vehicle displays a dealer license plate or transporter plate, the vehicle was repossessed or otherwise acquired by the dealer within the last ten days, and the vehicle is being driven from the place it was acquired to the dealer's place of business or to an inspection station.
(3) The charged infraction is driving without a current inspection in violation of G.S. 20-183.8(a)(1) and the vehicle owner establishes in court that the vehicle was inspected after the citation was issued and within thirty days of the former inspection's expiration date.[253]

IV. Financial Responsibility Requirements in North Carolina

As discussed earlier in this chapter, DMV may not issue a driver's license to a person until the person has furnished proof of financial responsibility.[254] In addition, an application to register a vehicle must contain a statement that the owner is an eligible risk for insurance coverage as defined in G.S. 58-37-1(4a).[255] The owner of a motor vehicle registered in North Carolina must maintain financial responsibility continuously throughout the period of registration.[256] When liability insurance for a

---

252. Anyone who is cited for a civil penalty under G.S. 20-183.8B for an emissions violation in connection with the inspection of a vehicle may not be charged with an infraction under G.S. 20-183.8(a)(3) based on that same vehicle.
253. G.S. 20-183.8(b).
254. G.S. 20-7(c1).
255. G.S. 20-52(a)(4).
256. G.S. 20-309(a).

motor vehicle is terminated, the owner must surrender the registration certificates and license plates for the vehicle to DMV, unless financial responsibility is maintained in some other way that complies with statutory requirements.[257] These requirements are designed to ensure that the operators of motor vehicles are properly insured in the event of an accident. Article 9A of G.S. Chapter 20 sets forth the requirements for liability insurance for motor vehicles. Proof of financial responsibility is defined as proof of ability to respond in damages for liability for motor vehicle accidents in the amount of $30,000 for bodily injury to, or for death of, one person in any one accident; $60,000 for bodily injury or death of two or more persons in any one accident; and $25,000 for injury or destruction of property of others in any one accident.[258]

A. Operating a Vehicle Without Insurance

G.S. 20-313 makes it unlawful to

(1) own
(2) a motor vehicle
(3) registered or required to be registered in North Carolina and
(4) operate the vehicle (or permit its operation)
(5) without the required financial responsibility.

1. Punishment

Owning and operating a vehicle without insurance is a Class 3 misdemeanor.[259]

B. Making a False Certification Concerning Insurance

G.S. 20-313.1(a) makes it unlawful for a person to

(1) own
(2) a motor vehicle
(3) registered or required to be registered in North Carolina and
(4) make a false certification concerning his or her financial responsibility for the operation of such motor vehicle.

1. Punishment

Making a false certification concerning insurance is a Class 1 misdemeanor.[260]

---

257. G.S. 20-309(d). Insurers are required to notify DMV when they issue a new or replacement motor vehicle liability policy or when they terminate a policy without simultaneously issuing a replacement policy. G.S. 20-309.2(a). When DMV receives notice that the owner of a motor vehicle registered in North Carolina does not have financial responsibility for the operation of the vehicle, it must send a letter notifying the owner that it has received such information. *Id.* § 20-311(a). A lapse in financial responsibility may result in a financial penalty and/or the revocation of the vehicle's registration, depending upon the circumstances. *Id.*

258. G.S. 20-279.1(11). Special rules govern the liability insurance requirements for commercial motor vehicles. *Id.* § 20-309(a1).

259. G.S. 20-313(a).

260. G.S. 20-313.1(a).

C. Giving False Information Concerning Another's Financial Responsibility

G.S. 20-313.1(b) makes it unlawful to

(1) give
(2) false information
(3) to DMV
(4) concerning another person's financial responsibility for the operation of a motor vehicle registered or required to be registered in North Carolina
(5) knowing or having reason to believe
(6) that such information is false.

1. Punishment

Giving false information to DMV about another's vehicle liability insurance knowing or having reason to believe the information is false is a Class 1 misdemeanor.[261]

D. Safe Driver Incentive Plan

Automobile insurance policies for North Carolina drivers are governed by the Safe Driver Incentive Plan, or SDIP, established pursuant to G.S. 58-36-65. The SDIP distinguishes among classes of drivers that have a record of at-fault accidents, a record of convictions of major moving traffic violations, a record of convictions of minor moving traffic violations, or a combination thereof, and provides for premium differentials among those classes of drivers. Insurers learn of traffic convictions and adjudications of responsibility for infractions by obtaining records from DMV.[262]

The North Carolina Department of Insurance (DOI) publishes a guide to the SDIP that sets forth the insurance points assigned to each type of conviction for a traffic violation and the corresponding rate of increase for those convictions and adjudications.[263] Insurance points are different from driver's license points assigned by DMV pursuant to G.S. 20-16. Driver's license points matter because DMV may revoke the driver's license of a person who accumulates 12 or more license points within three years.[264] Insurance points matter because of rate increases. A single insurance point, which can result from conviction of a minor moving violation, results in a 30 percent rate increase.[265]

The SDIP provides for certain exceptions to rate increases. For example, no insurance points are charged for a single prayer for judgment continued (PJC) entered per household every three years.[266] And no insurance points are assessed for conviction of speeding 10 m.p.h. or less over the posted speed limit, so long as the violation did not occur in a school zone and the driver has not been convicted of another moving traffic violation within the three-year *experience period*.[267]

---

261. G.S. 20-313.1(b).

262. *See* G.S. 58-36-65(e) (providing that "[r]ecords of convictions for moving traffic violations to be considered under this section shall be obtained at least annually from [DMV]"); *see also id.* § 20-4.24(a) (requiring a state that is a member of the Drivers License Compact to report to another member state a conviction for any offense "that the member states agree to report").

263. N.C. Dep't of Ins., Safe Driver Incentive Plan, www.ncdoi.com/_Publications/It%20Pays%20 to%20Be%20a%20Safe%20Driver%20Insurance%20Points_CAU1.pdf.

264. G.S. 20-16(a)(5).

265. *See* N.C. Dep't of Ins., *supra* note 263.

266. *Id.*

267. *Id.* (defining the "experience period" as the three-year span preceding (a) the date on which an individual applies for insurance coverage or (b) the date on which the individual's insurer makes preparations to renew an existing policy).

V. Equipment Violations

Part 9 of Article 3 of G.S. Chapter 20, G.S. 20-115 through -137.5, sets forth numerous requirements governing the size, weight, construction, and equipment of vehicles moved on streets or highways in North Carolina. This section reviews the elements of offenses that arise from faulty or improper vehicle equipment.

A. Safe Equipment

As noted earlier in the section on safety inspections, equipment central to the safe operation of a vehicle must be inspected and deemed in safe operating condition for a vehicle to pass inspection and be registered by DMV. Not surprisingly, related provisions of Chapter 20 prohibit driving a vehicle with certain types of faulty equipment.

1. Driving with Unsafe Tires

G.S. 20-122.1 requires that motor vehicles that are subject to safety equipment inspection and are operated on streets and highways have safe tires. A tire is considered unsafe under this statute if any of the following conditions is met:

- The tire is cut, cracked, or worn in a manner that exposes tire cord.[268]
- There is visible tread[269] separation or chunking.[270]
- The tire has less than 2/32-inch tread depth[271] at two or more places around the tire in two adjacent major tread grooves.[272]
- The tread wear indicators are in contact with the roadway at two or more locations around the tire in two adjacent major tread grooves.[273]

Additional requirements apply to the tires of any motor vehicle that has a gross vehicle weight rating (GVWR) of at least 10,001 pounds and is operated on a North Carolina street or highway.[274]

a. Punishment

Driving with unsafe tires in violation of G.S. 20-122.1 is an infraction punishable by a fine of not more than $100.[275]

b. Compliance Period

The driver of any vehicle who is charged with violating G.S. 20-122.1 is permitted fifteen calendar days to bring the vehicle's tires into conformance with the requirements for safe tires.[276] It is a defense to a charge of violating G.S. 20-122.1 that the person so charged produced in court or submitted to the prosecuting attorney before trial a certificate from an official safety inspection equipment station

---

268. "Cord" is defined as the "strands forming a ply in a tire." G.S. 20-122.1(a)(2).

269. "Tread" is the portion of the tire that comes into contact with the road. G.S. 20-122.1(a)(3).

270. "Chunking" is defined as "separation of the tread from the carcass in particles" that may range in size. G.S. 20-122.1(a)(1).

271. "Tread depth" is "the distance from the base of the tread design to the top of the tread." G.S. 20-122.1(a)(4).

272. The 2/32-inch requirement does not apply to dual wheel trailers. G.S. 20-122.1(a).

273. *Id.*

274. G.S. 20-122.1(a1).

275. G.S. 20-176(a), (b); *id.* § 20-115.

276. G.S. 20-122.1(b).

showing that, within fifteen calendar days after the charge, the tires on the vehicle were made to conform with the statutory requirements or the vehicle was sold, destroyed, or permanently removed from the highways.[277]

2. Failing to Maintain Steering Mechanism in Good Working Order

G.S. 20-123.1 requires that the steering mechanism of every self-propelled motor vehicle driven on a street or highway in North Carolina be maintained in "good working order, sufficient to enable the [driver] to control the vehicle's movements and to maneuver it safely."

a. Punishment

Violation of G.S. 20-123.1 is an infraction punishable by a fine of not more than $100.[278]

3. Operating a Motor Vehicle Without Working Speedometer

G.S. 20-123.2(a) requires that every self-propelled motor vehicle driven on a street or highway in North Carolina be equipped with a speedometer that is "maintained in good working order."

a. Punishment

Violation of G.S. 20-123.2(a) is an infraction punishable by a fine of not more than $25.[279]

b. Lesser-Included Offense of Speeding

Operating a motor vehicle without a working speedometer is statutorily defined as a lesser-included offense of speeding, with the exception of charges of speeding more than 25 m.p.h. over the posted speed limit.[280]

4. Inadequate Brakes

G.S. 20-124(a)–(g) define several offenses related to the absence of sufficient brakes on a motor vehicle. Each of these offenses is an infraction, punishable by a fine of not more than $100.[281]

a. Failing to Maintain Brakes in Conformity with Regulations

G.S. 20-124(a) requires that every motor vehicle driven on a highway in North Carolina be equipped with brakes that are "adequate to control the movement of and to stop such vehicle." The brakes must be "maintained in good working order" and must conform to the requirements in G.S. 20-124.

b. Failure to Maintain Originally Equipped Brakes

G.S. 20-124(c) requires that every motor vehicle driven on a highway in North Carolina be equipped with brakes "adequate to control the movement of and to stop and hold such vehicle." This subsection further requires that all originally equipped brakes be "in good working order, including two separate means of applying the brakes." If the two separate means of applying the brakes are connected, they must be constructed so that the "failure of any one part of the operating mechanism [does] not leave the motor vehicle without brakes."[282]

---

277. *Id.*
278. G.S. 20-176(a), (b); *id.* § 20-115.
279. G.S. 20-123.2(b).
280. G.S. 20-141(o)(2).
281. G.S. 20-176(a), (b); *id.* § 20-115.
282. G.S. 20-124(c).

c. Absence of at Least One Brake on Motorcycle Used on Highway

G.S. 20-124(d) requires that every motorcycle and motor-driven cycle operated on a highway in North Carolina be equipped with at least one brake that can be operated by hand or by foot. This requirement does not apply to autocycles, which are subject to the requirements for motor vehicles under G.S. 20-124.[283]

d. Absence on Trucks of Brakes Sufficient to Stop Vehicle Within Required Distances

G.S. 20-124(e) requires that motor trucks and tractor-trucks[284] with semitrailers attached "be capable of stopping on a dry, hard, . . . level highway free from loose material at a speed of 20 miles per hour within the following distances":

- thirty feet when both the hand and the service brake are applied simultaneously and
- fifty feet when either brake is applied separately.[285]

e. Absence of Brakes Acting on All Wheels on Specified Trucks or Truck-Trailers with Tractors

G.S. 20-124(e1) requires that every motor truck and truck-tractor[286] with semitrailer attached "be equipped with brakes acting on all wheels." An exception applies to trucks and truck-tractors with three or more axles manufactured before July 25, 1980.[287] Such trucks are not required to have brakes on the front wheels but are required to meet the performance requirements of G.S. 20-124(e).[288]

5. Motor Vehicle Not Equipped with Directional Signals

G.S. 20-125.1 makes it unlawful for the owner of a motor vehicle to register that vehicle, or to cause the vehicle to be registered, in North Carolina if it is not "equipped with a mechanical or electrical signal device by which the [driver] may indicate to the operator of another vehicle, approaching from . . . the front or rear . . . within a distance of 200 feet, his [or her] intention to turn from a direct line."[289] The signal device must be of a type approved by DMV.[290]

G.S. 20-125.1(b) makes it unlawful for any dealer to sell or deliver a motor vehicle that is not equipped with a mechanical or electrical signal device that meets the aforementioned requirements if the dealer knows or has reason to know that the purchaser intends to register the vehicle or sell it to another person for registration and use on the streets and highways of North Carolina.

Under G.S. 20-125.1(c), trailers that meet both of the following conditions are not required to be equipped with directional signal devices:

---

283. G.S. 20-124(d).

284. The terms "motor truck" and "tractor-truck" are not defined by statute. Presumably, however, those terms refer to the same machinery as a "truck-tractor", which is defined as a vehicle "designed and used primarily for drawing other vehicles" and is not built to carry any load independent of the drawn vehicle. G.S. 20-4.01(48).

285. Under G.S. 20-127(e), different requirements apply to certain trucks registered before 1929.

286. A "truck-tractor" is a vehicle that is "designed and used primarily for drawing other vehicles" and is not built to carry any load independent of the drawn vehicle. G.S. 20-4.01(48).

287. G.S. 20-124(e1).

288. *Id.*

289. G.S. 20-125.1(a). This requirement applies to any motor vehicle manufactured or assembled after July 1, 1953.

290. *Id.*

- The trailer and its load do not block the directional signals of the towing vehicle from the view of any driver who is approaching from the rear of the trailer and is within a distance of 200 feet.
- The gross weight of the trailer and its load does not exceed 4,000 pounds.

a. Punishment

Violation of G.S. 20-125.1 is an infraction punishable by a fine of not more than $100.[291]

6. Windows and Windshields

a. Window Tinting Restrictions

G.S. 20-127(b) makes it unlawful to

(1) drive
(2) a vehicle
(3) on a street, highway, or public vehicular area
(4) in violation of North Carolina's window or windshield tinting restrictions.

i. Punishment

Violation of the tinting application restrictions of, or the prohibition on driving a vehicle that does not meet the tinting restrictions laid out in, G.S. 20-127 is a Class 3 misdemeanor.[292]

The window and windshield tinting restrictions are described below.

ii. Windshields

Generally, a vehicle's windshield may only be tinted along the top portion of the windshield, and the tinting cannot extend more than the longer of (1) five inches from the top of the windshield or (2) below the windshield's AS-1 line.[293] An untinted clear film that does not obstruct vision but reduces or eliminates ultraviolet radiation may be applied to the windshield.

iii. Windows

Under G.S. 20-127(b), any window of a vehicle other than the windshield may be tinted as follows:

- "The total light transmission of the tinted window [must] be at least [35] percent . . . . A vehicle window that, by use of a [DMV-approved light meter], measures a total light transmission of more than [32] percent is conclusively presumed to meet this restriction."
- "The light reflectance of the tinted window [must] be [20] percent or less."
- The "material used to tint the window [must] be nonreflective and [may] not be red, yellow, or amber."

iv. Exceptions

The window and windshield of commercial motor vehicles must comply with federal regulations governing tinting.[294]

---

291. G.S. 20-176(a), (b); *id.* § 20-115.

292. G.S. 20-127(d).

293. G.S. 20-127(b). According to AAA, an AS-1 line is "a line extending from the letters AS-1, found on most motor vehicle windshields, running parallel to the top of the windshield or shall mean a line 5 inches below and parallel to the top of the windshield, whichever is closer to the top of the windshield." *Digest of Motor Laws*, AAA.com, http://drivinglaws.aaa.com/?s=%22AS-1+line%22.

294. G.S. 20-127(b1).

Moreover, the window tinting requirements set out in G.S. 20-127(b) do not apply to the following vehicle windows:[295]

- a window of an "excursion passenger vehicle", as defined in G.S. 20-4.01(27)a1.;
- a window of a "motor home", as defined in G.S. 20-4.01(27)d2.;
- a window of an "ambulance", as defined in G.S. 20-4.01(27)f.;
- the rear window of a "property-hauling vehicle", as defined in G.S. 20-4.01(31);
- a window of a limousine;
- a window of a law enforcement vehicle;
- a window of a "multipurpose vehicle"[296] behind the driver of the vehicle;
- a window of a vehicle registered in another state that meets the requirements of the registering state;[297]
- a window of a vehicle for which DMV has issued a medical exception permit under G.S. 20-127(f).

v. Defense

It is a defense to a charge of driving a vehicle with an unlawfully tinted window that the tinting was removed within fifteen days following the charge and the window now meets G.S. 20-127's window tinting restrictions.[298] To successfully assert this defense, the person charged must produce in court, or must before trial submit to the prosecuting attorney, a certificate from DMV or from the State Highway Patrol showing that the window complies with the statute's restrictions.[299]

vi. After-Market Tinting

State law also prohibits the application to a vehicle's window of tinting that does not comply with the restrictions described above. A person violates G.S. 20-127(d)(1) if he or she

(1) applies tinting
(2) to the window of a vehicle that is subject to safety inspection in North Carolina
(3) and the resulting tinted window
(4) does not meet the window tinting restrictions set out in G.S. 20-127.

(a) Punishment

A violation of this provision is a Class 3 misdemeanor.[300]

---

295. G.S. 20-127(c).

296. Under G.S. 20-127(c)(9), "[a] multipurpose vehicle is a passenger vehicle that is designed to carry [ten] or fewer passengers and either is constructed on a truck chassis or has special features designed for occasional off-road operation." Minivans and pickup trucks are multipurpose vehicles.

297. There is no corresponding exception for the *windshields* of vehicles registered in other states. *See* State v. Schiffer, 132 N.C. App. 22, 28 (1999).

298. G.S. 20-127(e).

299. *Id.*

300. G.S. 20-127(d).

b. Driving a Vehicle Without Windshield Wipers

G.S. 20-127(a) makes it unlawful to operate a vehicle that has a windshield on a street or highway in North Carolina without a "windshield wiper to clear rain or other substances from the windshield in front of the driver of the vehicle." The windshield wiper must be in "good working order."[301] If a vehicle is equipped with more than one windshield wiper as described above, then all windshield wipers must be in good working order.[302]

i. Punishment

A violation of these provisions is an infraction punishable by a fine of not more than $100.[303]

7. Mirrors

The requirements for mirrors on vehicles are set forth in G.S. 20-126. The statute requires inside rearview mirrors for most motor vehicles,[304] at least one outside driver's side mirror for vehicles registered in North Carolina,[305] and rearview mirrors for motorcycles.[306] A violation of any of these mirror requirements is an infraction.

a. Driving Motor Vehicle Without Rearview Mirror

G.S. 20-126(a) prohibits

(1) driving
(2) a motor vehicle
(3) on a street or highway
(4) when the motor vehicle is not equipped with an inside rearview mirror
(5) located so as to reflect to the driver a view of the highway to the rear of the vehicle.[307]

Farm tractors, self-propelled implements of husbandry, and construction equipment, along with self-propelled vehicles not subject to registration under G.S. Chapter 20, are exempted from the rearview mirror requirements of G.S. 20-126.[308] Pickup trucks that have DMV-approved outside rearview mirrors are exempt from the statute's inside rearview mirror requirements.

8. Improper Muffler

G.S. 20-128 renders unlawful several acts related to mufflers and emissions control devices. G.S. 20-128(a) prohibits the driving of, on a street or highway, a motor vehicle that is not equipped with a muffler, or other exhaust system of the type installed at the time the vehicle was manufactured, that is in good working condition and in constant operation to prevent excessive noise, "annoying smoke," and smoke screens.

---

301. G.S. 20-127(a).
302. *Id.*
303. G.S. 20-176(a), (b); *id.* § 20-115.
304. G.S. 20-126(a).
305. G.S. 20-126(b).
306. G.S. 20-126(c).
307. Under G.S. 20-126(a), any manufacturer-installed inside mirror is deemed to comply with the statute's requirements.
308. G.S. 20-126(a).

G.S. 20-128(b) makes it unlawful to use a "muffler cut-out"[309] on any motor vehicle upon a highway.

G.S. 20-128(c) prohibits the driving of any motor vehicle that is registered in North Carolina and that was manufactured after 1967 unless it is equipped with the emissions control devices that were installed on the vehicle when it was manufactured. The emissions control devices also must be properly connected.[310] These requirements do not apply if the emissions control devices were removed to convert the motor vehicle to operate on natural or liquefied petroleum gas or if other state-approved modifications have been made to reduce air pollution.[311]

a. Punishment

Violation of G.S. 20-128 is an infraction punishable by a fine of not more than $100.[312]

B. Seat Belt Use

Under G.S. 20-135.2A, all occupants of a motor vehicle that has been manufactured with seat belts must "have a seatbelt properly fastened about his or her body . . . when the vehicle is in forward motion on a street or highway in [North Carolina].[313] Thus, the driver and all front and rear seat passengers generally are required to be restrained by a properly fastened seat belt.[314]

There are a few exceptions to this seat-belts-for-all-occupants requirement. They are set out in G.S. 20-135.2A(c) and apply to the following persons and motor vehicles:

- drivers or occupants of noncommercial motor vehicles with medical or physical conditions that prevent them from being restrained by seat belts;
- rural letter carriers;
- newspaper delivery persons while delivering newspapers;
- drivers and passengers who frequently stop and leave their vehicles or who deliver property from their vehicles, provided the vehicle's speed between stops is 20 m.p.h. or less;
- property-carrying vehicles used for agricultural purpose in intrastate commerce;
- motor vehicles that are not required to be equipped with seat belts under federal law;
- occupants of a motor home other than the driver and front seat passengers;
- persons in the custody of a law enforcement officer who are being transported in the back of a law enforcement vehicle; and
- passengers of a residential garbage or recycling truck that is making collection rounds.

1. Failure to Wear a Seat Belt

A person commits the offense of failure to wear a seat belt if he or she

(1) is a driver or occupant

(2) of a motor vehicle that has been manufactured with seat belts and

---

309. *See* ENGINEERING-DICTIONARY.ORG, Cut-Out, http://www.engineering-dictionary.org/wiki/A/A/AM/Cutout (defining "cut-out" as a "form of bypass valve, located in the exhaust line, that can be used to divert the flow of exhaust from one pipe to another. Often used to bypass the muffler into a straight pipe. See exhaust cutout.").

310. G.S. 20-128(c).

311. G.S. 20-128(d).

312. G.S. 20-176(a), (b); *id.* § 20-115.

313. G.S. 20-135.2A(a).

314. *Id.* A separate statute, G.S. 20-137.1(a), requires that drivers with passengers who are under 16 years of age have such passengers "properly secured in a child passenger restraint system or seat belt."

(3) is in forward motion

(4) on a North Carolina street or highway and

(5) the person does not have a seat belt properly fastened about his or her body.[315]

A driver's or front seat passenger's failure to wear a seat belt as required by G.S. 20-135.2(a) is an infraction punishable by a penalty of $25.50 and designated court costs.[316] A rear seat passenger's failure to wear a seat belt is also an infraction and is punishable by a penalty of $10 but no court costs.[317]

A law enforcement officer who has reasonable suspicion to believe that a driver or front seat passenger of a vehicle does not have a seat belt properly fastened about his or her body may stop the vehicle to investigate this violation of law, just as the officer may stop a vehicle for other traffic misdemeanors and infractions.[318] A law enforcement officer who has reasonable suspicion to believe that *a rear seat occupant* is not wearing a seat belt may not, however, stop the vehicle. That's because the failure of a rear seat occupant to have a seat belt properly fastened is categorized as a secondary violation for which a vehicle may not be stopped.[319] A law enforcement officer who has lawfully stopped a vehicle for another reason and who, in the process of doing so, learns of a rear seat belt violation may, of course, cite the driver for this offense.

2. Riding in Bed of Pickup Truck

G.S. 20-135.2B(a) prohibits the driver of a vehicle with an open bed or cargo area from transporting a child under the age of 16 in that area of the vehicle. An open bed or cargo area is an area, such as the open bed of a pickup truck, that lacks a "permanent overhead restraining construction."[320] The statute does not specify whether its provisions apply only on streets or on streets and public vehicular areas.

a. Exceptions

G.S. 20-135.2B(a) does not apply if any of the following circumstances are present:[321]

(1) There is an adult in the bed or cargo area of the vehicle and he or she is supervising the child.

(2) The child is secured or restrained by a DMV-approved seat belt that is manufactured in compliance with federal standards and "installed to support a load strength of not less than 5,000 pounds for each belt."

(3) There is an emergency situation.

(4) The vehicle in which the child is riding is being operated in a parade.

(5) The vehicle in which the child is riding is "being operated in an agricultural enterprise, including providing transportation to and from the principal place of the agricultural enterprise."

---

315. G.S. 20-135.2A(a).

316. G.S. 20-135.2A(e).

317. *Id.*

318. G.S. 20-135.2A(d). *See also* State v. Parker, 183 N.C. App. 1, 7 (2007) ("A law enforcement officer may stop a motorist when the officer has 'probable cause' to believe that the motorist has committed a readily observed traffic infraction."); State v. Styles, 362 N.C. 412, 415 (2008) (footnote omitted) (holding that "reasonable suspicion is the necessary standard for traffic stops, regardless of whether the traffic violation was readily observed or merely suspected").

319. G.S. 20-135.2A(d1).

320. G.S. 20-135.2B(a).

321. G.S. 20-135.2B(b).

b. Punishment

Violation of G.S. 20-135.2B(a) is an infraction punishable by a penalty of not more than $25. This maximum fine applies even when more than one child under 16 is riding in the vehicle's open bed or open cargo area.[322] No court costs may be assessed for a person found responsible for violating G.S. 20-135.2B(a).

C. Child Passenger Restraints

A driver who is transporting one or more passengers under the age of 16 must have all of these passengers "secured in a child passenger restraint system or a seat belt."[323] A child who is younger than 8 years old and who weighs less than 80 pounds must be "properly secured in a weight-appropriate child passenger restraint system."[324] In any vehicle that has an active passenger-side front airbag and a rear seat, a child who is under 5 and who weighs less than 40 pounds must be "properly secured in a rear seat, unless the child restraint system is designed [to be used] with air bags."[325] If there is no seating position available with a lap and shoulder belt to "properly secure the weight-appropriate child passenger restraint system," a child younger than 8 years old and weighing between 40 and 80 pounds "may be restrained by a properly fitted lap belt only."[326]

Under G.S. 20-137.1(b), the child-restraint requirements set out above do not apply to the following vehicles:

(1) ambulances and other emergency vehicles,
(2) vehicles in which "all seating positions equipped with child passenger-restraint systems or seat belts are occupied;" or
(3) vehicles that are not required to be equipped with seat belts under federal laws or regulations.

Violation of any of the child-restraint system requirements is an infraction punishable by a penalty of not more than $25.[327] A single infraction will be charged and a maximum penalty of $25 applies even when more than one child is not properly secured. No driver charged with failure to have a child under 8 properly secured in a child-restraint system may be found responsible if the driver produces at the time of trial proof that he or she has subsequently obtained an approved child passenger-restraint system for a vehicle in which the child usually rides.[328]

The child-restraint system statute fails to specify when its provisions apply. Thus, it is unclear whether they apply in public vehicular areas as well as on public roadways or, if, as in the case of the seat belt statute, a vehicle must be in forward motion for the requirements to apply.

---

322. G.S. 20-135.2B(c).
323. G.S. 20-137.1(a).
324. G.S. 20-137.1(a1).
325. *Id.*
326. *Id.*
327. G.S. 20-137.1(c).
328. *Id.*

D. Lighting Requirements

1. Lighted Headlamps and Rear Lamps

Vehicles on streets or highways in North Carolina must be equipped with lighted headlamps and rear lamps during the period between sunset and sunrise and when any of the following conditions exists:[329]

- the light outside is not sufficient to "render clearly discernable any person on the highway at a distance of 400 feet ahead;"[330]
- the vehicle's windshield wipers are in use due to smoke, fog, rain, sleet, or snow;[331] or
- "inclement weather or environmental factors severely reduce the ability to clearly discern persons and vehicles on the street and highway at a distance of 500 feet ahead."[332]

2. Headlamps, Generally

G.S. 20-129(b) mandates that all self-propelled motor vehicles other than motorcycles, road machinery, and farm tractors "be equipped with at least two headlamps, all in good operating condition with at least one on each side of the front of the motor vehicle." Headlamps must, "under normal atmospheric conditions and on a level road, produce a driving light sufficient to render clearly discernable a person 200 feet ahead."[333]

a. Dimming Light from Headlamps

Any person operating a motor vehicle on a street or highway must, upon encountering another vehicle, control the lights of his or her vehicle "by shifting, depressing, deflecting, tilting, or dimming the headlight beams in such a manner [so as not to] project a glaring or dazzling light to persons within . . . 500 feet" of the headlamp.[334] A person who fails to dim his or her headlights as required

---

329. G.S. 20-129(a). *See* State v. Hopper, 205 N.C. App. 175 (2010) (finding testimony from officer sufficient to establish that the road on which the defendant's motor vehicle was stopped in the rain was a public road and rejecting, in light of broad definition of "highway" or "street" in G.S. 20-4.01(13), defendant's argument that provisions of G.S. 20-129 apply only to highways or streets that form part of the state highway system).

330. G.S. 20-129(a)(2).

331. G.S. 20-129(a)(4). Lighted headlamps and rear lamps are not required when windshield wipers are being used "intermittently in misting rain, sleet, or snow." *Id.*

332. *Id.* An exception applies for vehicles parked on highways. *Id.* § 20-129(a). The rules governing lighting for those vehicles are set forth in G.S. 20-134.

333. G.S. 20-131(a). Whenever a street or highway is "sufficiently lighted to reveal a person on the [roadway] at a distance of 200 feet ahead of the vehicle," the driver may "dim the headlamps or . . . tilt the beams downward or . . . substitute . . . the light from an auxiliary driving lamp or . . . lamps." *Id.* § 20-131(c).

334. G.S. 20-131(a) (headlamps are deemed to comply with the prohibition against "glaring and dazzling lights if none of the main bright portion of the headlamp beams rises above a horizontal plane passing through the lamp centers parallel to the level road upon which the loaded vehicle stands, and in no case higher than 42 inches, 75 feet ahead of the vehicle," *id.* § 20-131(b)).

when meeting another vehicle or when following another vehicle at a distance of less than 200 feet commits an infraction punishable by a penalty of not more than $10.[335] Such a driver is not subject to this penalty, however, when he or she is "engaged in the act of overtaking and passing."[336]

b. Motorcycle Headlamps

Every motorcycle in North Carolina must be equipped with at least one, and with no more than two, headlamps.[337] A motorcycle's headlamps must be lighted whenever the motorcycle is being operated on highways or public vehicular areas.[338]

c. Rear Lamps, Generally

Under G.S. 20-129(d), all motor vehicles, along with all trailers or semitrailers attached to motor vehicles and all vehicles "drawn at the end of a combination of vehicles," must have "all originally equipped rear lamps or the equivalent in good working order."[339] Those lamps must "exhibit a red light plainly visible under normal atmospheric conditions from a distance of 500 feet to the rear of [the] vehicle."[340] The statute also requires that one rear lamp, or a separate rear lamp, be constructed and placed so that the number plate on the rear of the vehicle is "illuminated by a white light [that can] be read from a distance of 50 feet to the rear of the vehicle."[341] In addition to the "originally equipped rear lamps" mentioned above, trailers and semitrailers must carry at the rear a DMV-approved red reflector that is "visible for at least 500 feet when approached by a motor vehicle displaying . . . undimmed lights at night on an unlighted highway."[342]

d. Motorcycle Rear Lamps

As with headlamps, the rear lamps of a motorcycle must be lighted whenever the motorcycle is being operated on a highway or public vehicular area.[343]

e. Bicycle Lamps

When operated at night on any public street, public vehicular area, or public greenway, a bicycle must be equipped with (1) a lighted lamp on the front, "visible under normal atmospheric conditions from a distance of at least 300 feet in front of [the] bicycle" and (2) either a lamp on the rear, "exhibiting a

---

335. G.S. 20-181.

336. *Id.*

337. G.S. 20-129(c).

338. *Id.* Autocycles are not subject to the motorcycle headlamp requirements. Instead, they are subject to the requirements for motor vehicles. *Id.*

339. G.S. 20-129(d).

340. *Id.*

341. *Id. See* State v. Ford, 208 N.C. App. 699, 702 (2010) (deeming evidence (1) that officers pulled within 50 feet of the rear of the defendant's vehicle around 1:45 a.m. and were unable to read his license plate, despite having their patrol car's headlights on, and (2) that one officer then turned off the patrol car's lights to verify his suspicion that the defendant's tag light was out sufficient to support the trial court's finding that the defendant's vehicle's tag light was not functioning properly in violation of G.S. 20-129(d)).

342. G.S. 20-129(d). There is an exception for any trailer weighing less than 4,000 pounds or for any farm trailer of the type described in G.S. 20-51(6) weighing less than 6,500 pounds. Such trailers do not have to be equipped with a rear lamp if they are equipped with two DMV-approved rear red reflectors of a specified diameter that are "visible for at least 500 feet when approached by a motor vehicle displaying lawful undimmed headlights at night on an unlighted highway." *Id.*

343. *Id.*

red light visible . . . from a distance of at least 300 feet to the rear of such bicycle, or the operator must wear clothing or a vest that is bright and visible from" the same distance.[344]

3. Lighting for Other Vehicles

All vehicles not otherwise covered by the provisions of G.S. 20-129 must carry on their left sides "one or more lighted lamps or lanterns projecting a white light, visible under normal atmospheric conditions from a distance of [at least] 500 feet [in] front of [the] vehicle and . . . at least 500 feet to the rear of [the] vehicle."[345] A vehicle may be equipped with DMV-approved reflectors in place of such lights.[346] Any farm tractor operated on a highway at night "must be equipped with at least one white lamp visible at a distance of 500 feet from the front of the tractor and . . . at least one red lamp visible at a distance of 500 feet to the rear of the tractor."[347] Two red reflectors with a minimum diameter of four inches may be substituted for the red lamp at the rear of the tractor.[348]

4. No Sale or Operation Without a Stop Lamp

G.S. 20-129(g) prohibits the sale or operation on a North Carolina street or highway of any motor vehicle manufactured after December 31, 1970, that it is not equipped with one stop lamp on each side of the rear of the vehicle. The sale or operation on a street or highway in the state of a motorcycle or motor-driven cycle manufactured after December 31, 1955, that does not have a stop lamp on the rear is also prohibited.[349] The stop lamps mandated by the statute must "emit, reflect, or display a red or amber light visible from a distance of not less than 100 feet to the rear in normal sunlight, and [must] be actuated upon application of the . . . foot . . . brake. The stop lamps may be incorporated into a unit with one or more other rear lamps."[350]

5. Additional Lighting

Buses, trucks, truck-tractors,[351] and certain trailers and semitrailers are required to have additional lighting equipment. Those requirements are set forth in G.S. 20-129.1 and are not discussed herein.

All wreckers[352] operated on North Carolina highways must be equipped with an amber-colored flashing light that must be "mounted and located [so] as to be clearly visible in all directions from a distance of 500 feet."[353] The light must be activated whenever the wrecker is (1) at the scene of an accident, (2) taking part in a recovery operation, or (3) towing a vehicle that either has a total outside width of more than 96 inches or that exceeds the width of the towing vehicle.[354]

---

344. G.S. 20-129(e).
345. G.S. 20-129(f).
346. *Id.*
347. *Id.*
348. *Id.*
349. G.S. 20-129(g).
350. *Id.*
351. A "truck-tractor" is a vehicle that is "designed and used primarily for drawing other vehicles" and is not built to carry any load independent of the drawn vehicle. G.S. 20-4.01(48).
352. A "wrecker" is a vehicle that has a "permanently attached crane [and that is] used to move other vehicles." G.S. 20-4.01(50).
353. G.S. 20-130.2.
354. *Id.*

Other types of vehicles are also authorized to have similar amber warning lights, including N.C. Department of Transportation equipment that is performing road maintenance or construction work.[355]

Motor vehicles are also permitted to have certain kinds of additional lighting beyond what is required by statute:

- Motor vehicles other than motorcycles may have up to two spot lamps; motorcycles may have one spot lamp.[356]
- All lighted spot lamps must be "aimed and used upon approaching another vehicle [so] that no part of the beam will be directed to the left of the center of the highway nor more than 100 feet ahead of the vehicle." Spot lamps may not be used on the rear of a vehicle.[357]
- A motor vehicle may have up to two auxiliary driving lamps on its front.[358]
- Any device, other than headlamps, spot lamps, or auxiliary driving lamps, that "projects a beam of light of an intensity greater than 25 candlepower [must] be . . . directed [so] that no part of the beam will strike the level of the surface on which the vehicle stands at a distance of more than 50 feet from the vehicle."[359]

a. White or Clear Lights on Rear of Vehicle Prohibited

A person may not "willfully drive a motor vehicle in forward motion" on North Carolina's highways displaying a white or clear light on the rear of the vehicle.[360] This provision does not apply to the white light that is required to illuminate a vehicle's license plate.[361] It likewise does not apply to white or clear lights that are lighted when a vehicle is in reverse gear or is backing up.[362]

b. Red Lights Prohibited

A person may not install, activate, or operate a "red light" in or on any vehicle in North Carolina.[363] For purposes of this prohibition, the term "red light" means "an operable red light not sealed in the manufacturer's original package" that is designed to be used by emergency vehicles or is similar in appearance to such a light and that can be operated using the vehicle's battery or electrical system or

---

355. *Id.*

356. G.S. 20-130(a). Autocycles are considered motor vehicles for purposes of the spot lamp provisions. *Id.*

357. *Id.*

358. G.S. 20-130(b).

359. G.S. 20-130(c). Electronically modulated headlamps are permissible on motorcycles, law enforcement, and emergency vehicles so long as the headlamps and light modulator are of a type approved by DMV. *Id.* § 20-130(d). Public transit vehicles may be equipped with amber, high-mounted, flashing deceleration lamps on the rear of the vehicles. G.S. 20-130(e). On or after October 1, 2017, a person may not drive a motor vehicle on a street or highway while using a "light bar lighting device", defined as a "bar-shaped lighting device comprised of multiple lamps capable of projecting a beam of light at an intensity greater than [25 candlepower]." *See* S.L. 2017-112 (enacting new G.S. 20-130(f)). Violation of this provision is an infraction. The light bar ban does not apply to motorcycles, school buses, ambulances, law enforcement vehicles, fire department vehicles, or other types of vehicles described in G.S. 20-130(d) and 20-130.1(b). G.S. 20-130(f) does not apply to or restrict the use of a light bar lighting device with strobing lights.

360. G.S. 20-130.3.

361. *Id.*

362. *Id.*

363. G.S. 20-130.1(a).

by using a dry cell battery.[364] The term "red light" also means any red light installed on a vehicle after its initial manufacture.[365] Violation of the red light prohibition is a Class 1 misdemeanor.[366]

Several types of vehicles are excepted from the red light prohibition, including law enforcement vehicles, emergency vehicles, fire-fighting vehicles, and school buses.[367]

c. Blue Lights Prohibited

A person may not possess a "blue light" or install, activate, or operate a blue light in or on any vehicle in North Carolina. The term "blue light" means any blue light that is installed on a vehicle after its initial manufacture or an operable blue light that (1) is not being (a) "installed on, held in inventory for the purpose of being installed on, or held in inventory for the purpose of sale for installation on a vehicle on which it may be lawfully operated" or (b) installed on a vehicle [that] is used solely for the purpose of demonstrating the blue light for sale to law enforcement personnel;" (2) "is designed for use by an emergency vehicle, or is similar in appearance to a blue light designed for use by an emergency vehicle;" and (3) can be operated using the vehicle's battery or electrical system or by using a dry cell battery.[368] Violation of the blue light provision is a Class 1 misdemeanor.[369]

Publicly owned vehicles that are used for law enforcement purposes and other vehicles that are being used by law enforcement officers who are performing their official duties are excepted from the blue light prohibition.[370]

The blue light prohibition also does not apply to the "possession and installation of an inoperable blue light[371] on a vehicle that is inspected by and registered with [DMV] as a specially constructed vehicle and that is used primarily for participation in shows, exhibitions, parades, or holiday/weekend activities, and not for general daily transportation."[372]

E. Equipment-Related Offenses

Several equipment-related offenses are described in detail below.

1. Vehicles Resembling Law Enforcement Vehicles

G.S. 20-137.2(a) makes it unlawful

(1) for any person who is not a law enforcement officer of the state or of any county, municipality, or other political subdivision of the state to,

(2) with the intent to impersonate a law enforcement officer,

(3) operate any vehicle that

---

364. *Id.*

365. *Id.*

366. G.S. 20-130.1(e).

367. G.S. 20-130.1(b). Refer to the statute for a complete listing of exempted vehicles.

368. G.S. 20-130.1(c).

369. G.S. 20-130.1(e).

370. G.S. 20-130.1(c).

371. The term "inoperable blue light" for purposes of G.S. 20-130.1 is a "blue-colored lamp housing or cover that does not contain a lamp or other mechanism having the ability to produce or emit illumination." G.S. 20-130.1(c1).

372. *Id.*

(4) by its coloration, insignia, lettering, and blue or red light resembles a vehicle that is owned, possessed, or operated by a law enforcement agency.

Violation of G.S. 20-137.2(a) is a Class 1 misdemeanor.[373]

2. Altering a Vehicle to Raise or Lower Height

G.S. 20-135.4(d) imposes limitations on the elevating or lowering of the manufacturer's specified height for a passenger motor vehicle.[374] Under this provision, a person may not elevate or lower the manufacturer's specified height for a passenger vehicle, in front or back, more than six inches by modifying, altering, or changing the physical structure of the vehicle without prior written approval of DMV. It is also unlawful to operate a self-propelled vehicle that has been altered in violation of this provision on a street, highway, or public vehicular area without the prior written approval of DMV.[375]

3. Unlawful Smoke Screens

G.S. 20-136(a) makes it unlawful to

(1) drive, operate, equip, or possess
(2) a motor vehicle
(3) that contains a device designed, used, or capable of being used to discharge from the device or motor vehicle
  (a) an unusual amount of smoke, gas, or other substance
  (b) that is not necessary to the actual propulsion or care of the vehicle.

Under G.S. 20-136(a), a person's possession of such a device, regardless of whether or not it is attached to a motor vehicle, is prima facie evidence of the person's guilt for a violation of the statute.

Violation of G.S. 20-136(a) is a Class I felony.[376]

4. Location of Television, Computer, or Video Players in Vehicles

G.S. 20-136.1 makes it unlawful to

(1) drive
(2) a motor vehicle
(3) on a street, highway, or public vehicular area
(4) while viewing any television, computer, or video player in the motor vehicle
  (a) that is located "at any point forward of the back of the driver's seat" and
  (b) that is visible to the driver while he or she is operating the motor vehicle.

The use of the following types of systems, displays, and devices are exempted from the broad prohibition in G.S. 20-136.1:

---

373. G.S. 20-137.2(b).

374. The term "private passenger vehicle" is defined in G.S. 20-4.01(27)g. as consisting of all passenger vehicles that are not otherwise specifically defined in G.S. 20-4.01(27). The latter subsection defines, for example, "autocycle", "child care vehicle", "school bus", "ambulance", and other types of vehicles used to transport passengers. G.S. 20-135.4(a) defines "private passenger automobile" as "a four-wheeled motor vehicle designed principally for carrying passengers, for use on public roads and highways, except a multipurpose passenger vehicle which is constructed either on a truck chassis or with special features for occasional off-road operation."

375. G.S. 20-135.4(d).

376. G.S. 20-136(b).

- global positioning systems (GPS);
- turn-by-turn navigation displays or similar navigation devices;
- any factory-installed or after-market GPS or wireless communications devices that are used to transmit or receive data as part of a digital dispatch system;
- any equipment that displays audio system information, functions, or controls, or that displays weather, traffic, and safety information;
- information regarding vehicle safety or equipment; and
- image displays that enhance the view of the driver in any direction, whether inside or outside of the vehicle.

In addition, the provisions of G.S. 20-136.1 *do not apply* to

- law enforcement or emergency personnel who are performing their official duties or
- the operator of any vehicle that is lawfully parked or stopped.

5. Restrictions on Mobile Phone Use

G.S. Chapter 20 imposes several restrictions on the use of mobile telephones. Whether a driver may lawfully use such a device while operating a motor vehicle on a street, highway, or public vehicular area depends upon the driver's age, the type of vehicle he or she is driving, and the manner in which the device is being used.[377]

a. Use of a Mobile Phone by a Person under 18

G.S. 20-137.3(b) makes it unlawful for

(1) a person under the age of 18
(2) to operate a motor vehicle
(3) on a street, highway, or public vehicular area
(4) while using either
    (a) a mobile telephone or
    (b) any type of "additional technology associated with a mobile telephone"
(5) while the vehicle is in motion.

i. Mobile Telephone

The term "mobile telephone" is defined in G.S. 20-137.3(a)(2) as a "device used by subscribers and other users of wireless telephone service[378] to access the service." The term includes

- a device with which a user, while using at least one hand, engages in a call and
- a device with an internal feature or function, or one that is equipped with some type of attachment or addition, by which a user, without using either hand, engages in a call.

---

377. Local governments in North Carolina may not enact jurisdiction-specific rules governing the use of mobile phones. *See* King v. Town of Chapel Hill, 367 N.C. 400, 412 (2014) (quoting G.S. 160A-174(b)(5)) (holding that the North Carolina General Assembly's enactment of various statutory provisions to reduce the dangers associated with mobile phone use while driving indicated its " 'intent to provide a complete and integrated regulatory scheme to the exclusion of local regulation.' ").

378. "Wireless telephone service" is defined as "[a] service that is a two-way real-time voice telecommunications service that is interconnected to a public switched telephone network and is provided by a commercial mobile radio service," as the latter term is defined by federal regulation. G.S. 20-137.3(a)(3).

ii. Additional Technology

The "additional technology" referenced in G.S. 20-137.3 is "[a]ny technology that provides access to digital media including, but not limited to, a camera, music, the Internet, or games."[379] The statute expressly excludes electronic mail and text messaging from this definition.[380]

iii. Exceptions

The prohibition against mobile phone use by drivers under 18 does not apply when the young driver is using the mobile phone for the sole purpose of communicating with

- his or her parent, legal guardian, or spouse or
- any of the following individuals/places regarding an emergency situation:
  - an emergency response operator;
  - a hospital, physician's office, or health clinic;
  - a public or privately owned ambulance company or service;
  - a fire department; or
  - a law enforcement agency.[381]

iv. Penalty

Violation of G.S. 20-137.3 is an infraction punishable by a fine of $25.[382]

b. Unlawful Use of a Mobile Phone by School Bus Driver

G.S. 20-137.4(b) makes it unlawful for any person to

(1) operate a school bus
(2) on a street, highway, or public vehicular area
(3) while using either
  (a) a mobile telephone or
  (b) any type of "additional technology associated with a mobile telephone"
(4) while the school bus is in motion.

i. School Bus

The term "school bus" is defined for purposes of this provision as "[a] vehicle whose primary purpose is to transport school students over an established route to and from school for the regularly scheduled school day, that is equipped with alternately flashing red lights on the front and rear and a mechanical stop signal, that is painted primarily yellow below the roofline, and that bears the plainly visible words "School Bus" on the front and rear."[383] Public, private, or parochial vehicles that meet this description

---

379. G.S. 20-137.3(a)(1).
380. *Id.*
381. G.S. 20-137.3(d).
382. G.S. 20-137.3(e). While chief district court judges normally exercise discretion regarding the traffic offenses for which a defendant may waive the right to hearing or trial and admit responsibility, G.S. 20-137.3(e) requires that such waivers be permitted for charges under G.S. 20-137.3. The subsection further specifies that no driver's license points, insurance surcharges, or court costs may be assessed against a person for violating G.S. 20-137.3.
383. G.S. 20-137.4(a)(4) (incorporating definition of "school bus" from G.S. 20-4.01(27)d4.).

are included in the definition,[384] as are any school activity buses as defined in G.S. 20-4.01(27)d3.[385] and any vehicles transporting public, private, or parochial school students for compensation.[386]

ii. Exception

An exception to the prohibition against mobile phone use by school bus drivers applies in situations where the driver is using a mobile telephone or some type of additional technology associated with a mobile phone for the sole purpose of communicating in an "emergency situation." An emergency situation consists of "[c]ircumstances such as medical concerns, unsafe road conditions, matters of public safety, or mechanical problems that create a risk of harm for the operator or passengers of a school bus."[387]

iii. Penalty

A violation of G.S. 20-137.4 is a Class 2 misdemeanor punishable by a fine of not less than $100.[388] No driver's license points or insurance surcharges may be assessed against a person for violating G.S. 20-137.4.[389]

c. Using a Mobile Phone for Text Messaging or Electronic Mail

G.S. 20-137.4A(a) makes it unlawful for a person to

(1) operate
(2) a vehicle
(3) on a street, highway, or public vehicular area
(4) while using a mobile telephone to either
   (a) manually key into the device multiple letters or text as a way to communicate with another person or
   (b) read any electronic mail or text message that has been transmitted to the device or stored within it.[390]

i. Exceptions

The provisions of G.S. 20-137.4A do not apply to the operator of any vehicle that is lawfully parked or stopped, nor do they apply to the use of a mobile telephone by any law enforcement officer, fire department member, or ambulance operator who is performing his or her official duties. G.S. 20-137.4A does not prohibit the use of (1) GPS or wireless communications devices that are used to transmit or receive data as part of a digital dispatch system[391] or (2) voice-operated technology.[392]

---

384. G.S. 20-4.01(27)d4.

385. G.S. 20-4.01(27)d3. defines the term "school activity bus" as "[a] vehicle, generally painted a different color from a school bus, whose primary purpose is to transport school students and others to or from a place for participation in an event other than regular classroom work." The term includes any public, private, or parochial vehicle meeting this description. *Id.*

386. G.S. 20-137.4(a)(4).

387. G.S. 20-137.4(a)(2).

388. G.S. 20-137.4(f).

389. *Id.*

390. This prohibition does not apply to any name or number stored in the device or to caller identification information. G.S. 20-137.4A(a)(2).

391. G.S. 20-137.4A(b)(3).

392. G.S. 20-137.4A(b)(4).

ii. Penalty

A violation of G.S. 20-137.4A for using a mobile phone while operating a school bus, as defined in G.S. 20-137.4(a)(4), is a Class 2 misdemeanor punishable by a fine of not less than $100; any other violation of the statute is an infraction punishable by a fine of $100 plus court costs.[393] No driver's license points or insurance surcharges may be assessed against a person for violating G.S. 20-137.4A.[394]

d. Use of Mobile Phone by a Motor Carrier

G.S. 20-137.4A(a1) makes it unlawful for a person to

(1) operate
(2) a commercial motor vehicle that is subject to either Part 390 or Part 392 of Title 49 of the Code of Federal Regulations
(3) on a street, highway, or public vehicular area
(4) while using a mobile telephone or another electronic device in violation of Part 390 or Part 392.

i. Federal Regulations

Federal regulations prohibit the driver of a qualifying commercial motor vehicle from "us[ing] a hand-held mobile telephone while driving."[395] "Driving" is defined broadly in the regulations as "operating a commercial motor vehicle on a highway, including while temporarily stationary because of traffic, a traffic control device, or other momentary delays."[396] Driving in this context does not include "operating a commercial motor vehicle when the driver has moved the vehicle to the side of, or off, a highway and has halted in a location where the vehicle can safely remain stationary."[397] An exception applies to allow the driver of a commercial motor vehicle to use a hand-held mobile telephone "when necessary to communicate with law enforcement officials or other emergency services."[398]

Drivers of qualifying commercial motor vehicles also are prohibited under federal regulations from texting while driving.[399] The term "driving" in this context means "operating a commercial motor vehicle, with the motor running, including while temporarily stationary because of traffic, a traffic control device, or other momentary delays."[400] Driving for purposes of the regulation prohibiting texting "does not include operating a commercial motor vehicle with or without the motor running when the driver has moved the vehicle to the side of, or off, a highway[401] . . . and halted in a location where the vehicle can safely remain stationary."[402] An emergency exception permits drivers of commercial motor vehicles to text while driving when doing so is "necessary to communicate with law enforcement officials or other emergency services."[403]

While the federal regulations discussed above apply only to commercial motor vehicles operated in *interstate* commerce, North Carolina's administrative rules extend the prohibition to for-hire motor

---

393. G.S. 20-137.4A(c).
394. *Id.*
395. 49 C.F.R. § 392.82(a)(2).
396. 49 C.F.R. § 392.82(b).
397. *Id.*
398. 49 C.F.R. § 392.82(c).
399. 49 C.F.R. § 392.80.
400. 49 C.F.R. § 392.80(c).
401. As defined in 49 C.F.R. § 390.5.
402. 49 C.F.R. § 392.80(c).
403. 49 C.F.R. § 392.80(d).

carriers, for-hire motor carrier vehicles, private motor carriers, and private motor carrier vehicles operated entirely *within* North Carolina, provided the vehicle is

(1) a vehicle having the greater of
    (a) a gross vehicle weight rating (GVWR) of 26,001 pounds or more,
    (b) a gross combination weight rating (GCWR) of 26,001 pounds or more,
    (c) a gross vehicle weight (GVW) of 26,001 pounds or more, or
    (d) a gross combination weight (GCW) of 26,001 pounds or more;
(2) designed or used to transport sixteen or more passengers, including the driver; or
(3) used to transport a large enough quantity of hazardous material so as to require a placard pursuant to 49 C.F.R. Parts 170 through 185.[404]

Neither the federal nor the North Carolina rules barring hand-held mobile phone use apply to commercial motor vehicles operated by federal, state, or local governments.[405]

VI. Rules of the Road

A. Generally

Part 10 of Article 3 of G.S. Chapter 20 sets forth numerous requirements for the operation of vehicles within North Carolina, which collectively are referred to as rules of the road. This part of Chapter 20 defines several of the most commonly charged motor vehicle offenses, including impaired driving, reckless driving, and speeding. The offense of driving while impaired and other alcohol- or impairment-related offenses are not discussed herein. The elements, penalties, and special rules that apply to the investigation and prosecution of those offenses are reviewed in detail in *The Law of Impaired Driving and Related Implied Consent Offenses in North Carolina.*[406]

B. Offenses

1. Reckless Driving

Reckless driving is among the most commonly charged, and most broadly defined, motor vehicle offenses. Three types of reckless driving, all Class 2 misdemeanors, are defined in G.S. 20-140.

a. Reckless Driving—Wanton Disregard

G.S. 20-140(a) makes it unlawful to

(1) drive
(2) a vehicle
(3) on a street, highway, or public vehicular area
(4) "carelessly and heedlessly" and
(5) "in willful or wanton disregard of the rights or safety of others."

---

404. 14B N.C.A.C. 07C, § .0101.
405. 49 C.F.R. § 390.3(f)(2); G.S. 20-137.4A(a1).
406. This School of Government publication is cited in full *supra* note 1.

b. Reckless Driving to Endanger

The second type of reckless driving, which is by far the most frequently charged version of the offense, is set forth in G.S. 20-140(b). That subsection makes it unlawful to

(1) drive
(2) a vehicle
(3) on a street, highway, or public vehicular area
(4) "without due caution and circumspection" and
(5) at a speed or in a way that endangers, or is likely to endanger, people or property.

A person who violates both G.S. 20-140(a) and (b) in "one continuous operation of [a] vehicle" is guilty of but one offense of reckless driving.[407]

i. Culpable Negligence Required

Reckless driving is defined in terms that equate to the common law concept of *culpable negligence*. Thus, the analysis required to determine when negligent driving rises to the level of reckless driving is the same utilized in determining when actionable negligence becomes culpable, or criminal, negligence. The state supreme court employed this parallel analysis in *State v. Cope*,[408] ordering a new trial on manslaughter charges based on the trial court's erroneous instruction to the jury that "'if one violates any of the laws that were passed for the protection of the traveling public on the highways, and that violation of the law on his part causes the death of another, he will be guilty of manslaughter at least whether he intended to do so or not.'"[409] In distinguishing civil negligence based upon violation of a safety statute from the culpable negligence required to support a conviction for manslaughter, *Cope* noted a similar distinction in the definition of reckless driving: "Under this definition, the simple violation of a traffic regulation, which does not involve actual danger to life, limb, or property, while importing civil liability if damage or injury ensue, would not perforce constitute the criminal offense of reckless driving."[410]

Beyond the *Cope* principle that proof of a simple traffic violation that does not involve actual danger, without more, is insufficient to establish reckless driving,[411] North Carolina's appellate courts have developed no other generalities about the kind of driving that qualifies as reckless. Given the statute's broad language, it is not surprising that efforts to define it in more concrete terms have been unsuccessful.[412]

Reckless driving may best be understood by reviewing factual scenarios in which the courts have evaluated the sufficiency of the State's evidence. Consider the following illustrative cases.

---

407. *See* State v. Lewis, 256 N.C. 430, 432 (1962).

408. 204 N.C. 28 (1933).

409. *Id.* at 29.

410. *Id.* at 31 (citations omitted).

411. *See, e.g.,* State v. Dupree, 264 N.C. 463, 466 (1965) ("mere fact that defendant's automobile was on the left of the center line . . . . when the collision occurred, without any evidence that it was being operated at a dangerous speed or in a perilous manner" insufficient to establish reckless driving).

412. *See, e.g.,* State v. Teel, 180 N.C. App. 446, 450 (2006) (quoting State v. Floyd, 15 N.C. App. 438, 440 (1972)) ("[T]o send a charge of reckless driving to the jury the State must introduce sufficient evidence as to 'whether [defendant's] speed, or his manner of driving, endangered or was likely to endanger any person or property including himself, his passenger, his property or the person or property of others[.]' ").

- State v. Davis, 163 N.C. App. 587, 591 (2004) (evidence that defendant drove "well over the posted speed limit," swerved into the opposing lane of traffic, and subsequently "braked his vehicle sharply and slid for approximately twenty feet near an occupied residence" sufficient to establish reckless driving).
- State v. Smith, 178 N.C. App. 134, 138 (2006) (sufficient evidence of reckless driving when, during a high-speed chase on a rainy day, defendant "came extremely close to hitting an oil tanker at speeds in excess of sixty miles per hour," and crossed double yellow lines).
- State v. Teel, 180 N.C. App. 446 (2006) (evidence that defendant drove a motorcycle at 90 m.p.h. in a 45 m.p.h. zone, followed an unmarked police car two to three feet from the rear end of the officer's vehicle, attempted to pass the officer on the left across a double yellow line in a curve (crossing the double yellow line two or three times), and later tried to pass the officer on the shoulder of the road (touching the white line two or three times) sufficient to establish reckless driving under G.S. 20-140(b)).
- State v. Coffey, 189 N.C. App. 382 (2008) (evidence that defendant drove while impaired and traveled 92 m.p.h. in a 45 m.p.h. zone sufficient to establish reckless driving under G.S. 20-140(b)).
- State v. Jackson, 212 N.C. App. 167 (2011) (evidence that defendant drove 82 m.p.h. in a 55 m.p.h. zone, maneuvered from one lane to another to go around slower vehicles, and crossed double yellow lines sufficient to establish reckless driving).
- *In re* A.N.C., Jr., 225 N.C. App. 315 (2013) (evidence that a juvenile unlicensed driver ran off the road and collided with a utility pole was insufficient to establish reckless driving).
- State v. Geisslercrain, 233 N.C. App. 186 (2014) (evidence that the defendant drove while intoxicated, that all four tires of the vehicle she drove went off the road, that distinctive yaw marks were left on the road indicating that she lost control of the vehicle, that the vehicle overturned twice, that it traveled 131 feet from the point it went off the road before it flipped and another 108 feet after it flipped was sufficient to establish reckless driving under G.S. 20-140(b)).

c. Reckless Driving in a Commercial Motor Vehicle

The third type of reckless driving is limited to commercial motor vehicles carrying oversize or overweight loads. G.S. 20-140(f) makes it unlawful to

(1) drive
(2) a commercial motor vehicle
(3) carrying a load that is subject to the permit requirements of G.S. 20-119
(4) upon a street, highway, or public vehicular area either
  (a) "carelessly and heedlessly in willful or wanton disregard of the rights or safety of others" or
  (b) "without due caution and circumspection" and at a speed or in a way that endangers, or is likely to endanger, people or property.

i. Commercial Motor Vehicle

A "commercial motor vehicle" is defined as one of the motor vehicles listed below that are designed or are used to transport passengers or property:

- a Class A motor vehicle with a combined gross vehicle weight rating (GVWR) of at least 26,001 pounds that includes as part of the combination a towed unit with a GVWR of at least 10,001 pounds;
- a Class B motor vehicle;
- a Class C motor vehicle that either
  - is designed to transport at least sixteen passengers, including the driver, or
  - is transporting hazardous materials and is required by federal regulations to carry a placard.[413]

ii. Permits under G.S. 20-119

G.S. 20-119(a) authorizes the N.C. Department of Transportation (DOT) to issue special permits that allow applicants to operate or move vehicles of a size or weight that exceeds otherwise applicable state size and weight limits on any highway that DOT is responsible for maintaining. A municipality may issue permits authorizing the movement of oversize or overweight vehicles on streets of the municipality under this same statute.

2. Speeding

A person can violate the speed restrictions that apply on North Carolina roads pursuant to G.S. 20-141 in one of seven ways:

1. by driving at a speed "greater than is reasonable and prudent" under existing conditions,[414]
2. by failing to reduce speed to avoid a collision,[415]
3. by exceeding maximum speed limits,[416]
4. by operating a vehicle at less than a minimum posted speed,[417]
5. by speeding on school property,[418]
6. by speeding in a highway work zone,[419] or
7. by driving at such a slow speed as to impede the movement of traffic.[420]

Generally speaking, speeding is an infraction punishable by a penalty of not more than $100.[421] Driving on a highway at a speed of more than 15 m.p.h. over the speed limit or over 80 m.p.h., however, is a Class 3 misdemeanor.[422] A violation of G.S. 20-123.2, the law requiring that every self-propelled motor vehicle operated on the highway have a speedometer that is "maintained in good working order," is deemed by statute to be a lesser-included offense of any violation of G.S. 20-141 other than a charge of speeding in excess of 25 m.p.h. over the posted speed limit.[423]

---

413. G.S. 20-4.01(3d). For additional discussion of vehicle classifications, see *supra* section II.D.1.
414. *See* G.S. 20-141(a).
415. *See* G.S. 20-141(m).
416. *See* G.S. 20-141(b).
417. *See* G.S. 20-141(c).
418. *See* G.S. 20-141(e1).
419. *See* G.S. 20-141(j2).
420. *See* G.S. 20-141(h).
421. G.S. 20-176(a), (b).
422. G.S. 20-141(j1).
423. G.S. 20-141(o).

a. Driving Too Fast for Conditions

G.S. 20-141(a) makes it unlawful to

(1) drive
(2) a vehicle
(3) on a street, highway, or public vehicular area
(4) at a speed "greater than is reasonable and prudent" under existing conditions.

Driving below the speed limit is not a defense to a charge of driving at a speed greater than is reasonable and prudent under existing conditions.[424]

b. Failure to Reduce Speed to Avoid a Collision

G.S. 20-141(m) states that "[t]he fact that the speed of a vehicle is lower than the [speed limits established in G.S. 20-141] shall not relieve the operator of a vehicle from the duty to decrease speed as may be necessary to avoid colliding with any person, vehicle or other conveyance on or entering the highway, and to avoid injury to any person or property." This provision has been interpreted to not only eliminate a defense to driving too fast for conditions in violation of G.S. 20-141(a), but also to impose upon drivers a duty to reduce speed if necessary to avoid a collision.[425] This requirement applies regardless of the posted speed limit or the speed actually driven.[426]

A person violates G.S. 20-141(m) if he or she

(1) drives
(2) a vehicle
(3) on a street or highway and
(4) fails to decrease speed in order to
    (a) avoid colliding with any person, vehicle, or other conveyance that is on or is entering the highway and
    (b) avoid injury to people or property.

c. Exceeding the Posted Speed

G.S. 20-141(b) makes it unlawful to

(1) drive
(2) a vehicle
(3) on a street or highway
(4) at a speed that exceeds
    (a) 35 m.p.h. inside municipal corporate limits or
    (b) 55 m.p.h. outside municipal corporate limits.[427]

If a local authority has adopted a higher or lower speed limit, then it is likewise unlawful to drive a vehicle at a speed that exceeds the established limit.[428]

---

424. *See* State v. Stroud, 78 N.C. App. 599, 602–03 (1985) (so interpreting G.S. 20-141(m), quoted in text *infra* section VI.B.2.b).

425. *Stroud*, 78 N.C. App. at 603.

426. *Id.* Thus, G.S. 20-141(m) does not "protect a driver proceeding at precisely the posted speed from responsibility for a rear-end collision with another vehicle." *Stroud*, 78 N.C. App. at 603.

427. The 55 m.p.h. restriction does not apply to school buses or school activity buses. G.S. 20-141(b)(2).

428. *See* G.S. 20-141(e) (providing that higher or lower speed limits authorized by local authorities are effective so long as "appropriate signs giving notice" are placed at the parts of all affected streets).

i. Local Authority

For purposes of this statute, a "local authority" is a county, municipality, or other territorial district with a local board or body that is authorized to adopt local police regulations.[429]

d. Driving Slower than Posted Minimum Speed

G.S. 20-141(c) makes it unlawful to

(1) drive
(2) a passenger vehicle
(3) on an interstate or primary highway
(4) at less than the following speeds:
    (a) 40 m.p.h. in a 55 m.p.h. speed zone or
    (b) 45 m.p.h. in a speed zone of 60 m.p.h. or greater.

Under this provision, the minimum speeds are effective only when "appropriate signs" that indicate the minimum speed are posted.

i. Passenger Vehicle

The term "passenger vehicle" is defined in G.S. 20-4.01(27) to include the following types of vehicles:

- autocycles
- excursion passenger vehicles
- for-hire passenger vehicles
- common carriers of passengers
- child care vehicles
- motor-driven bicycles
- motorcycles
- mopeds
- motor homes
- school activity buses
- school buses
- "U-drive-it" passenger vehicles
- ambulances
- private passenger vehicles
- low-speed vehicles

ii. Penalty

Driving slower than the posted minimum speed in violation of G.S. 20-141(c) is an infraction punishable by a fine of not more than $100.[430]

G.S. 20-141(g) permits DOT or local authorities to "determine on the basis of an engineering and traffic investigation that slow speeds on any part of a highway considerably impede the normal and reasonable movement of traffic." In such a case, DOT or a local authority may declare a minimum speed below which a person may not operate a motor vehicle, except when driving below this speed

---

429. G.S. 20-4.01(18).
430. G.S. 20-176(a), (b).

is necessary for safe and lawful operation.[431] These minimum speed limits are effective so long as "appropriate signs giving notice" of the speed limit are placed at affected parts of the highway.[432] These minimum speed limits do not apply to farm tractors or to any other motor vehicle that is operating at a speed that is reasonable for the type and nature of the particular vehicle.[433] Violation of G.S. 20-141(g) is an infraction punishable by a fine of not more than $100.[434]

e. Speeding on School Property

G.S. 20-141(e1) permits local authorities to enact ordinances setting lower speed limits on school property within their jurisdictions than those limits set by G.S. 20-141(b). Speed limits established pursuant to this subsection are effective so long as "appropriate signs giving notice" of the speed limits are placed at all affected property. A person violates G.S. 20-141(e1) if he or she

(1) drives
(2) a motor vehicle
(3) on school property
(4) at a speed greater than the speed limit set and posted under G.S. 20-141(e1).

i. Punishment

A violation of G.S. 20-141(e1) is an infraction punishable by a fine of $250.

f. Impeding Traffic by Slow Speed

G.S. 20-141(h) makes it unlawful to

(1) drive
(2) a motor vehicle
(3) on a street or highway
(4) "at such a slow speed as to impede the normal and reasonable movement of traffic,"
(5) except when driving at a reduced speed is necessary for the safe operation of the vehicle or is in compliance with law.

i. Exceptions

G.S. 20-141(h) does not apply to farm tractors or to any other motor vehicle that is operating at a speed that is reasonable for the type and nature of the particular vehicle.

ii. Punishment

A violation of G.S. 20-141(h) is an infraction punishable by a fine of up to $100.[435]

g. Exceeding the Speed Limit by 15 m.p.h. or Driving Over 80 m.p.h.

G.S. 20-141(j1) makes it unlawful to

(1) drive
(2) a vehicle
(3) on a street or highway

---

431. G.S. 20-141(g).
432. *Id.*
433. *Id.*
434. G.S. 20-176(a), (b).
435. *Id.*

(4) at a speed that is either
   (a) more than 15 m.p.h. over the applicable speed limit or
   (b) more than 80 m.p.h.

i. Punishment

Violation of G.S. 20-141(j1) is a Class 3 misdemeanor. A driver charged with speeding more than 25 m.p.h. over the posted speed limit is ineligible to have his or her case disposed of by entry of a prayer for judgment continued.[436]

h. Speeding in a Work Zone

G.S. 20-141(j2) makes it unlawful to

(1) drive
(2) a motor vehicle
(3) in a highway work zone
(4) at a speed greater than the posted speed limit.

i. Punishment

Speeding in a highway work zone under G.S. 20-141(j2) is an infraction,[437] unless the driver was traveling more than 15 m.p.h. over the speed limit or more than 80 m.p.h., in which case the offense is a Class 3 misdemeanor.[438] A fine of $250, on top of any other fines authorized by G.S. Chapter 20, will be imposed in cases of speeding in a highway work zone when "signs are posted at the beginning and end of any segment of the highway work zone stating the penalty for speeding in that segment of the work zone."[439]

ii. Charging Language

Any law enforcement officer who issues a citation for speeding in a highway work zone must note the offending vehicle's speed and the speed limit posted in the segment of the work zone where the violation occurred and must determine whether the driver violated G.S. 20-141(j1) (prohibiting driving more than 15 m.p.h. over the speed limit or more than 80 m.p.h.).[440] Whenever a person is convicted of speeding in a highway work zone, the clerk of court must report to DMV that the person's vehicle was in a work zone, the vehicle speed, and the speed limit in the work zone.[441]

i. Speeding by an Oversize or Overweight Commercial Motor Vehicle

G.S. 20-141(j3) makes it unlawful to

(1) drive
(2) a commercial motor vehicle
(3) carrying a load that is subject to the permit requirements of G.S. 20-119

---

436. G.S. 20-141(p); *see also* Shea Denning, *Charges? What Charges?* N.C. Crim. L., UNC Sch. of Gov't Blog (Apr. 9, 2009) (expressing the view that the "charge" properly considered by the judge is the charge to which the person pleads guilty or responsible or upon which the defendant is tried), https://nccriminallaw.sog.unc.edu/charges-what-charges/.
437. G.S. 20-176(a), (b).
438. G.S. 20-141(j1).
439. G.S. 20-141(j2).
440. G.S. 20-141(j2).
441. *Id.*

(4) on a street, highway, or public vehicular area

(5) at a speed of 15 m.p.h. or more above

    (a)   the posted speed or

    (b)   the restricted speed of the permit obtained or,

(6) if no permit was obtained, at the speed that would be applicable to the load had a permit been obtained.

i. Punishment

Violation of G.S. 20-141(j3) is a Class 2 misdemeanor.

j. Speeding in a School Zone

The Board of Transportation or local authorities may enact ordinances that set speed limits lower than those designated in G.S. 20-141 for areas that are near any public, private, or parochial school.[442] However, the speed limit may not be set below 20 m.p.h.[443] These reduced speed limits are effective so long as signs are erected that give notice of the school zone, the authorized speed limit, and the days and hours when the lower limit is effective.[444] Alternatively, the reduced speed limit is effective when signs are erected that give notice of the school zone, the authorized speed limit, and the days and hours that the lower limit is effective "by an electronic flasher operated with a time clock."[445]

Lower speed limits for school zones may be enforced only on days when school is in session.[446]

A person violates G.S. 20-141.1 when he or she

(1) drives

(2) a motor vehicle

(3) in a school zone

(4) at a speed greater than the speed limit set and posted under G.S. 20-141.1

(5) during the days and hours while the school zone speed limit is effective and

(6) on a day when school is in session.

i. Punishment

A violation of G.S. 20-141.1 is an infraction punishable by a penalty of $250.

3. Unlawful Racing

North Carolina law prohibits two types of racing: prearranged speed competitions and willful speed competitions.[447]

a. Engaging in Prearranged Racing

G.S. 20-141.3(a) makes it unlawful to

(1) drive

(2) a motor vehicle

(3) on street or highway

---

442. G.S. 20-141.1.
443. *Id.*
444. *Id.*
445. *Id.*
446. *Id.*
447. G.S. 20-141.3.

(4) willfully

(5) in a prearranged speed competition with another motor vehicle.

i. Punishment

A violation of G.S. 20-141.3(a) is a Class 1 misdemeanor.

b. Allowing One's Vehicle to Be Used in Prearranged Racing

G.S. 20-141.3(c) makes it unlawful for a person to

(1) authorize or knowingly permit

(2) a motor vehicle

(3) that he or she owns or controls

(4) to be operated

(5) on a street or highway

(6) in a prearranged speed competition with another motor vehicle.

i. Punishment

A violation of G.S. 20-141.3(c) is a Class 1 misdemeanor.

c. Betting on Prearranged Racing

G.S. 20-141.3(c) also makes it unlawful to place or to receive a bet, wager, or "other thing of value" on the outcome of a prearranged speed competition on a street or highway.

i. Punishment

Betting on prearranged racing in violation of G.S. 20-141.3(c) is a Class 1 misdemeanor.

d. Willful Speed Competitions

Prosecutions for willful racing in violation of G.S. 20-141.3(b) far outnumber those for prearranged racing.

G.S. 20-141.3(b) makes it unlawful to

(1) drive

(2) a motor vehicle

(3) on a street or highway

(4) willfully

(5) in a speed competition with another motor vehicle.

i. Punishment

A violation of G.S. 20-141.3(b) is a Class 2 misdemeanor.

ii. Willfully

To prove willfulness for purposes of a prosecution for a willful speed competition or a prearranged speed competition, the State must establish that the defendant "purposely and deliberately" engaged in a race with the other motor vehicle.[448]

---

448. *Cf.* Hord v. Atkinson, 68 N.C. App. 346, 350 (1984) (concluding that a driver's statement that the car following him could not outrun his car did not establish his intent to willfully engage in a speed competition).

4. Operating a Motor Vehicle to Flee or Attempt to Elude a Law Enforcement Officer

G.S. 20-141.5(a) makes it unlawful to

(1) drive
(2) a motor vehicle
(3) on a street, highway, or public vehicular area
(4) while fleeing or attempting to elude a law enforcement officer who is lawfully performing his or her duties.

a. Punishment

Violation of G.S. 20-141.5(a) is a Class 1 misdemeanor.

A person's violation of G.S. 20-141.5(a) is elevated to a Class H felony, however, if two or more of the following aggravating factors are present at the time of the offense:[449]

- speeding more than 15 m.p.h. over the legal speed limit;
- the person's faculties are grossly impaired while driving due to
  - his or her consumption of an impairing substance or
  - a blood alcohol concentration of 0.14 or more within a "relevant time after the driving;"[450]
- reckless driving as prohibited under G.S. 20-140;
- negligent driving leading to an accident that causes
  - property damage of more than $1,000 or
  - personal injury;
- driving while driver's license is revoked;[451]
- driving on school property or in any area designated as a school zone (see G.S. 20-141.1) or in a highway work zone (see G.S. 20-141(j2)) in excess of the posted speed limit during the days and hours when the posted limit is in effect;
- Passing a stopped school bus as prohibited under G.S. 20-217; or
- driving with a child under the age of 12 in the vehicle.

Further, whenever a violation of G.S. 20-141.5(a) (operating motor vehicle while fleeing or attempting to elude law enforcement officer) is the proximate cause of the death of any person, the misdemeanor offense is elevated to a Class H felony.[452] Whenever a person violates G.S. 20-141.5(b) (fleeing or attempting to elude accompanied by two or more aggravating factors) and proximately causes the death of another, he or she commits a Class E felony.[453]

When evidence is presented that a vehicle was operated in violation of G.S. 20-141.5, it is considered to be prima facie evidence that the vehicle was operated by the person in whose name the vehicle was registered with DMV at the time of the offense.[454] If the vehicle involved in the statutory violation was rented, then proof of the rental is considered prima facie evidence that the vehicle was operated

---

449. G.S. 20-141.5(b).

450. The term "relevant time after the driving" is defined as "[a]ny time after the driving in which the driver still has in his body alcohol consumed before or during the driving." G.S. 20-4.01(33a).

451. The court of appeals held in *State v. Dewalt*, 209 N.C. App. 187, 191–92 (2011), that the aggravating factor of driving while license revoked, when used to elevate misdemeanor fleeing to elude arrest to a felony offense, does not require proof that the defendant drove on a street or highway.

452. G.S. 20-141.5(b1).

453. *Id.*

454. G.S. 20-141.5(c).

by the renter at the time of the offense.[455] Before relying on either of these prima facie evidence rules to establish probable cause, a law enforcement officer must make a reasonable effort to contact the vehicle's registered owner before he or she initiates criminal process.[456]

Each law enforcement agency in North Carolina must adopt a policy governing the pursuit of fleeing or eluding motorists.[457] Each such policy must include factors for officers to consider in determining whether to initiate or to terminate a pursuit.[458]

b. Double Jeopardy Considerations

The court of appeals held in *State v. Mulder*, 233 N.C. App. 82 (2014), that the defendant was unconstitutionally subjected to double jeopardy when he was convicted of speeding and reckless driving in addition to felony fleeing to elude arrest based on speeding and reckless driving.[459] The court deemed speeding and reckless driving to be lesser-included offenses of felony fleeing to elude aggravated by the factors of speeding and reckless driving.[460] It reasoned that the legislature intended for those offenses, which seek to deter driving on public roads in ways that might endanger public safety or property, to permit alternative and not cumulative punishments.[461]

5. Aggressive Driving

G.S. 20-141.6(a) makes it unlawful for a person to

(1) drive
(2) a motor vehicle
(3) "carelessly and heedlessly in willful or wanton disregard of the rights or safety of others"
(4) on a street, highway, or public vehicular area
(5) in violation of the speed restrictions set forth in G.S. 20-141 or the speed restrictions in school zones set forth in G.S. 20-141.1.

a. Punishment

Violation of G.S. 20-141.6(a) is a Class 1 misdemeanor.[462] The offense of reckless driving under G.S. 20-140 is a lesser-included offense of aggressive driving in violation of G.S. 20-141.6(a).[463]

b. Carelessly and Heedlessly in Willful or Wanton Disregard of the Rights or Safety of Others

In order to prove that a person drove "carelessly and heedlessly in willful or wanton disregard of the rights or safety of others," the State must show that the person committed two or more of the following offenses while speeding in violation of G.S. 20-141 or 20-141.1:

- running a red light in violation of G.S. 20-158(b)(2) or (b)(3) or 20-158(c)(2) or (c)(3);
- running a stop sign in violation of G.S. 20-158(b)(1) or (c)(1);
- illegally passing in violation of G.S. 20-149 or 20-150;

---

455. *Id.*
456. G.S. 20-141.5(e).
457. G.S. 20-141.5(f).
458. *Id.*
459. 233 N.C. App. at 94–95.
460. *Id.* at 94.
461. *Id.*
462. G.S. 20-141.6(c).
463. G.S. 20-141.6(d).

- failing to yield the right-of-way in violation of G.S. 20-155, 20-156, 20-158(b)(4) or (c)(4), or 20-158.1; or
- following too closely in violation of G.S. 20-152.[464]

6. Rules Governing Operation of Motorcycles

G.S. 20-146.1 sets forth rules governing the operation of motorcycles.

Under G.S. 20-146.1(a), every motorcycle is entitled to full use of a lane and no motor vehicle may be driven in a way that deprives any motorcycle of such full use of a lane. This rule does not apply to "motorcycles operated two abreast in a single lane."[465]

Under G.S. 20-146.1(b), motorcycles may not be operated more than two abreast in a single lane.

a. Motorcycles, Defined

For purposes of G.S. 20-146.1, the term "motorcycle" does not include autocycles.[466] But autocycles, just like motorcycles, may not be operated more than one abreast in a single lane under G.S. 20-146.1(b). Motorcycles are defined for purposes of G.S. Chapter 20 as vehicles that have a saddle for the rider and that are designed to travel on no more than three wheels.[467] Motor scooters and motor-driven bicycles are classified as motorcycles; mopeds are not.[468]

b. Exceeding Authorized Number of Riders

G.S. 20-140.4(a)(1) makes it unlawful to

(1) drive
(2) a motorcycle or moped
(3) on a street, highway, or public vehicular area
(4) when the number of persons riding on or within the motorcycle or moped, including the driver, exceeds the number of persons the vehicle was designed to carry.

i. Punishment

A violation of G.S. 20-140.4(a)(1) is an infraction punishable by a penalty of $25.50 and the assessment of specified court costs.[469]

c. Failure to Wear a Helmet

G.S. 20-140.4(a)(2) makes it unlawful to

(1) drive
(2) a motorcycle or moped
(3) on a street, highway, or public vehicular area
(4) unless the driver and all passengers are wearing federally-approved safety helmets with properly secured retention straps.

---

464. G.S. 20-141.6(b).
465. G.S. 20-146.1(a).
466. An autocycle is a "three-wheeled motorcycle that has a steering wheel, pedals, seat safety belts for each occupant, antilock brakes, completely or partially enclosed seating that does not require the operator to straddle or sit astride, and is otherwise manufactured to comply with federal safety requirements for motor-cycles." G.S. 20-4.01(27)a.
467. G.S. 20-4.01(27)d.
468. *Id.*
469. G.S. 20-140.4(c).

The requirements of this section do not apply to the operator of or passengers in an autocycle with "completely enclosed seating".[470]

i. Punishment

A violation of G.S. 20-140.4(a)(2) is an infraction punishable by a penalty of $25.50 and the assessment of specified court costs.[471]

7. Passing a Vehicle Traveling in the Same Direction

Three statutory provisions, G.S. 20-149, 20-150, and 20-150.1, establish rules governing a driver's overtaking of a vehicle that is proceeding in the same direction as the driver's vehicle. With the exception of the offense of failure to give way to a passing vehicle, discussed below, a violation of the rules governing passing is an infraction punishable by a penalty of not more than $100.[472]

a. Two Feet to the Left

To properly overtake another vehicle traveling in the same direction, the driver of the overtaking vehicle must pass at least two feet to the left of the slower-moving vehicle.[473] The driver of the overtaking vehicle may not again drive to the right side of the street or highway until his or her vehicle is safely clear of the vehicle that he or she has passed.[474]

The driver of the overtaking vehicle may not drive to the left of the center of the street or highway unless the left side is clearly visible and free of oncoming traffic "for a sufficient distance," thereby ensuring that the overtaking and passing can be safely made.[475]

b. No-Passing Zones

G.S. 20-150 sets forth several areas in which passing another vehicle is prohibited.[476]

A driver may not pass another vehicle proceeding in the same direction on the crest of a grade or on a curve in the street or highway unless the passing driver has an unobstructed view of the street or highway for a distance of at least 500 feet.[477]

A driver may not pass another vehicle proceeding in the same direction at any railway grade crossing or at any "intersection of highway" unless a traffic or police officer has authorized the driver to do so.[478] The term "intersection of highway" means an intersection "designated and marked by [DOT] by appropriate signs, and street intersections in cities and towns."[479]

A driver may not drive to the left side of a highway's centerline on the crest of a grade or on a curve in a highway if the centerline has been placed on the highway by DOT and is visible.[480]

---

470. G.S. 20-140.4(a)(2).
471. G.S. 20-140.4(c).
472. G.S. 20-176(a), (b).
473. G.S. 20-149(a).
474. *Id.*
475. G.S. 20-150(a). This restriction does not apply (1) on a one-way street or (2) to the driver of a vehicle that is turning left into or out of an alley, a private road, or a driveway. *Id.* § 20-150(f).
476. None of the restrictions in G.S. 20-150 apply (1) on one-way streets or (2) to drivers of vehicles that are turning left into or out of alleys, private roads, or driveways. G.S. 20-150(f).
477. G.S. 20-150(b).
478. G.S. 20-150(c).
479. *Id.*
480. G.S. 20-150(d).

A driver may not overtake another vehicle on any segment of a street or highway that is marked by signs, markers, or markings that have been placed by DOT and that state that passing is prohibited.[481] A double yellow line painted on the roadway is an example of such a marking by DOT that prohibits passing.[482]

The prohibition against passing in an area marked as a no-passing zone does not apply if each of the following conditions is satisfied.

- The slower-moving vehicle to be passed is a moped or bicycle.
- The slower-moving vehicle is traveling in the same direction as the faster-moving vehicle.
- The driver of the faster-moving vehicle (1) provides a minimum distance of four feet between his or her vehicle and the slower-moving vehicle or (2) "completely enters the left lane of the highway."
- The driver of the slower-moving vehicle is neither (1) making a left turn nor (2) signaling, in accordance with G.S. 20-154, an intention to make a left turn.[483]

c. Passing on the Right

A faster-moving vehicle is permitted to pass a vehicle proceeding in the same direction upon the right only in the following circumstances:

- when the vehicle being overtaken is driving in a lane that has been designated for left turns;
- when both vehicles are being operated on a street or highway that has "unobstructed pavement of sufficient width [that has] been marked for two or more lanes of moving vehicles in each direction and [these lanes] are not occupied by parked vehicles;"
- when both vehicles are being operated on a one-way street or a street or highway where traffic is restricted to one direction of movement, provided the street or highway is free from obstructions, is sufficiently wide, and is marked for at least two lanes of moving vehicles that are not occupied by parked vehicles; and
- when the vehicles are driving in a lane that designates a right turn on a red traffic signal light.[484]

In all other circumstances, passing on the right is prohibited.

d. Failure to Give Way

Except when passing on the right is authorized, the driver of an overtaken vehicle must under G.S. 20-149(b) give way to the right in favor of the overtaking vehicle, "on audible signal,"[485] and must not increase his or her vehicle's speed until that vehicle has been completely passed by the overtaking vehicle.

---

481. G.S. 20-150(e).
482. State v. Wade, 161 N.C. App. 686, 691 (2003).
483. G.S. 20-150(e).
484. G.S. 20-150.1.
485. G.S. 20-149(b). Note that the driver of an overtaking vehicle is not required to sound his horn, though this was once a statutory requirement. *See* Perry v. Aycock, 68 N.C. App. 705, 708 (1984).

An overtaken vehicle's failure to give way to the right pursuant to G.S. 20-149(b) is a Class 1 misdemeanor if it is the proximate cause of a collision that results in serious bodily injury.[486] If the failure to give way is the proximate cause of a collision that results in bodily injury or property damage, the offense is a Class 2 misdemeanor.[487] In all other cases, the failure to give way in violation of G.S. 20-149(b) is an infraction punishable by a penalty of not more than $100.[488]

8. Lane Violations

G.S. 20-146 sets forth requirements for the portion of a street or highway on which a vehicle may be driven.

a. Right Half of the Highway

G.S. 20-146(a) requires that, "upon all highways of sufficient width," a vehicle must be driven on the right half of the highway except

1. when lawfully overtaking and passing another vehicle proceeding in the same direction;
2. when there is an obstruction that makes it necessary to drive to the left of the highway's center, in which case the driver must yield the right-of-way to any vehicle traveling in the proper direction on the unobstructed portion of the highway;
3. on a highway that is divided into three marked lanes for traffic; or
4. on a highway posted for one-way traffic.

Drivers of vehicles that are traveling in opposite directions must pass each other to the right, with each driver giving the other "at least one[-]half of the main-traveled portion of the roadway as nearly as possible."[489]

b. Slower-Moving Vehicles

Any vehicle traveling on a highway at less than the legal maximum speed limit must be driven in "the right-hand lane then available for thru traffic" or as close as possible to the highway's right-hand curb or edge, "except when overtaking and passing another vehicle proceeding in the same direction or when preparing for a left turn."[490]

c. Four-Lane Roads

On any street or highway that has at least four lanes for moving traffic and that provides for two-way movement of traffic, no vehicle may be driven to the left of the highway's centerline, except when doing so is "authorized by official traffic-control devices designating certain lanes to the left side of the center of the highway for use by traffic not otherwise permitted to use such lanes" or when there is an obstruction that makes it necessary to drive to the left of the center of the roadway.[491]

---

486. G.S. 20-149(b)(1).
487. G.S. 20-149(b)(2).
488. G.S. 20-149(b)(3); *see also id.* §§ 20-176(a), (b).
489. G.S. 20-148.
490. G.S. 20-146(b).
491. G.S. 20-146(c).

d. Two-Lane Roads

When a street is divided into at least two lanes for traffic, the following rules apply:

- A vehicle must be driven "as nearly as practicable entirely within a single lane."[492] The vehicle may not move from that lane until the driver has determined that the movement is safe.[493]
- On a street that is divided into at least three lanes and that has two-way traffic, a vehicle may not be driven in the center lane, except when (1) the vehicle is overtaking or passing another vehicle proceeding in the same direction when the center lane is free of traffic within a safe distance, (2) the vehicle is preparing to make a left turn, or (3) the center lane is "at the time allocated exclusively to traffic moving in the same direction that the vehicle is proceeding and such allocation is designated by [an] official traffic-control device."[494]
- Official traffic-control devices that direct certain traffic to use a designated lane or that designate certain lanes to be used by traffic proceeding in a specific direction regardless of the center of the street may be installed, and drivers must obey the direction of such devices.[495]
- Traffic-control devices may also prohibit the changing of lanes on certain sections of streets, and drivers must obey the directions of such devices.[496]

When "appropriate" signs, such as "Slower Traffic Keep Right," have been posted, G.S. 20-146(e) makes it unlawful to operate a motor vehicle on the inside lane next to the median of any dual-lane highway at a speed less than the posted speed limit when doing so impedes the steady flow of traffic. This provision does not apply to vehicles that are preparing to turn left. Violation of G.S. 20-146(e) is an infraction punishable by a penalty of not more than $100.[497]

9. Following Too Closely

G.S. 20-152(a) prohibits the driver of a motor vehicle on a street or highway from following another vehicle "more closely than is reasonable and prudent." G.S. 20-152(b) requires the driver of a motor vehicle on a street or highway outside a business or residential district who is following another vehicle to, when conditions permit, leave sufficient space so that an overtaking vehicle can safely enter and occupy the space. The requirement does not apply to prevent a motor vehicle from overtaking and passing another motor vehicle, and it does not apply to funeral processions. A violation of the provisions of G.S. 20-152 is an infraction punishable by a penalty of not more than $100.[498]

---

492. G.S. 20-146(d)(1).
493. *Id.*
494. G.S. 20-146(d)(2).
495. G.S. 20-146(d)(3).
496. G.S. 20-146(d)(4). The court of appeals in *State v. Osterhoudt*, 222 N.C. App. 620 (2012), determined that the defendant violated G.S. 20-146(d)(1), (3), and (4) when, while turning right, he crossed a double yellow line separating the turn lane from the straight travel lane. *Id.* at 629. By crossing the line, the defendant failed to stay in his lane and failed to obey a traffic-control device. *Id.*
497. G.S. 20-176(a), (b).
498. *Id.*

10. Unsafe Movement

G.S. 20-154(a) requires the driver of a vehicle on a street, highway, or public vehicular area to ascertain before starting, stopping, or turning from a direct line that such a movement may be safely made. The act of changing lanes is treated as a turn for purposes of G.S. 20-154(a).[499]

If a pedestrian could be affected by any of the movements described above, the driver must signal his or her intention to make the movement by sounding the vehicle's horn.[500] If the movement could affect the operation of another vehicle, the driver must provide an appropriate and "plainly visible" mechanical, electrical, or hand signal indicating his or her intention to carry out the movement.[501] The failure to ascertain that a movement may be safely made or to signal to a potentially affected pedestrian or driver is commonly termed an "unsafe movement."

a. Affecting the Operation of Another Vehicle

The operation of another vehicle is "affected" within the meaning of G.S. 20-154(a) when the surrounding circumstances provide a driver reasonable grounds to conclude that the movement of his or her vehicle may affect the operation of another vehicle.[502] Thus, in *State v. Styles*,[503] the North Carolina Supreme Court concluded that reasonable suspicion of a violation of G.S. 20-154(a) existed when the defendant, whose car was immediately in front of an officer's patrol car, changed lanes on a highway without signaling.[504] The court stated that "it is clear that changing lanes immediately in front of another vehicle may affect the operation of the trailing vehicle."[505] Similarly, the court of appeals in *State v. McRae*[506] concluded that an officer had reasonable suspicion to stop a driver for a violation of G.S. 20-154(a) after the driver, who was driving in medium traffic about 100 feet ahead of the police vehicle, turned right into a parking lot without signaling. No vehicle may be affected, and thus no signal is required, however, when a driver turns at an intersection that permits travel in only one direction.[507]

b. Signals

The signals required by G.S. 20-154(a) may be given by way of a mechanical or electrical signal or by a hand signal that is visible from the front and rear of the vehicle.[508] Regarding this last signal form, a driver properly indicates his or her intention to start, stop, or turn by extending his or her hand and arm from and beyond the left side of the vehicle as follows:

---

499. State v. Styles, 185 N.C. App. 271, 273 (2007) (citing Sass v. Thomas, 90 N.C. App. 719, 723 (1988)), *aff'd*, 362 N.C. 412 (2008). Given that a lane change is the equivalent of a turn under the statute, a driver must signal his or her intent to change lanes when another vehicle might be affected.

500. G.S. 20-154(a).

501. *Id.*

502. Sass v. Thomas, 90 N.C. App. 719, 723 (1988).

503. 362 N.C. 412 (2008).

504. *Id.* at 416–17.

505. *Id.* at 417.

506. 203 N.C. App. 319, 323 (2010).

507. *See* State v. Ivey, 360 N.C. 562, 565, 566 (2006) (concluding that officer unlawfully stopped defendant for a violation of G.S. 20-154(a) for his failure to signal a right hand turn at a T-intersection where a concrete median blocked a left turn, giving defendant no choice but to turn right), *abrogated on other grounds by State v. Styles*, 362 N.C. 412 (2008).

508. G.S. 20-154(b). If the distance from the center of the steering post top to the left outside limit of the motor vehicle's body, cab, or load is more than 24 inches, or if the distance from the center of the steering post top to the rear limit of the vehicle's body or load is more than 14 feet, the signal must be given by a signal lamp or lamps or by a mechanical signal device. *Id.* The more-than-14-feet measurement requirement

- Left turn—hand and arm are horizontal, forefinger is pointing
- Right turn—hand and arm are pointed upward
- Stop—hand and arm are pointed downward[509]

The operator of a bicycle signals his or her intention to make a right turn by "extending his or her hand and arm horizontally, with the forefinger pointing, from beyond the right side of the bicycle."[510]

All hand and arm signals must be given continuously for the last 100 feet traveled before the driver stops or makes a turn.[511] If the speed limit is at least 45 m.p.h. and the driver intends to turn from a direct line of travel, the driver must continuously signal his or her intention to turn for the last 200 feet traveled before turning.[512]

c. Backing

G.S. 20-154(a) further prohibits a driver from backing a vehicle unless he or she can do so safely and without interfering with other traffic.

d. Punishment

A violation of G.S. 20-154(a) generally is an infraction punishable by a penalty of not more than $100.[513] If, however, the rider of a bicycle or motorcycle is affected by a violation of G.S. 20-154, the offending driver may be subject to additional punishment, as discussed below.

e. Unsafe Movement That Causes a Motorcyclist or Cyclist to Change Lanes or Leave the Roadway

If a driver's violation of G.S. 20-154(a) causes the rider of a motorcycle or bicycle to change travel lanes or to leave the travel lane of a street or highway, the driver is responsible for an infraction punishable by a fine of not less than $200.[514]

f. Unsafe Movement That Causes a Crash

If a driver's unsafe movement results in a crash that causes property damage or personal injury to the operator or passenger of a motorcycle or bicycle, the driver is responsible for an infraction punishable by a penalty of $500,[515] unless the property damage exceeds $5,000 or the crash causes serious bodily injury,[516] in which case stiffer penalties apply.[517]

11. Rules for Railroad Crossings

Drivers are required by G.S. 20-142.1 to stop their vehicles at railroad crossings in certain circumstances.

---

applies to any single vehicle and to any combination of vehicles, with the exception of combinations driven by farmers hauling farm products. *Id.*

509. *Id.*

510. G.S. 20-154(b1).

511. G.S. 20-154(b).

512. *Id.*

513. G.S. 20-176(a), (b).

514. G.S. 20-154(a1).

515. *Id.*

516. G.S. 20-154(a2) incorporates the definition of "serious bodily injury" set out in G.S. 20-160.1(b): "bodily injury that involves a substantial risk of death, extreme physical pain, protracted and obvious disfigurement, or protracted loss or impairment of the function of a bodily member, organ, or mental faculty."

517. G.S. 20-154(a2). In such cases, the driver is responsible for an infraction punishable by a fine of not less than $750.

First, the driver of a vehicle approaching a railroad grade crossing must stop within 15 to 50 feet of the intersection when any of the following circumstances exist.

- There is a clearly visible electrical or mechanical signal device warning of an immediately approaching train.
- A crossing gate has been lowered, or a flagman has given a signal, indicating the approach or passage of a train.
- A train that is approaching within 1,500 feet of the crossing is emitting a signal that is audible from that distance, and the train is an immediate hazard due to its speed or its proximity to the crossing.
- An approaching train is "plainly visible and is in hazardous proximity to the crossing."[518]

Second, a person is prohibited from driving a vehicle through, around, or under a crossing gate or barrier at a railroad crossing while such gate or barrier is closed or is being opened or closed.[519]

When stopping at a railroad crossing per any of the requirements outlined above, a driver must keep as far to the right of the highway as possible. The driver may not form two lanes of traffic unless the roadway is marked for at least four lanes.[520]

Violation of any of the aforementioned provisions is an infraction punishable by a penalty of not more than $100.[521] Any employer who "knowingly allows, requires, permits, or otherwise authorizes" an employee driving a commercial motor vehicle to violate any of these provisions is guilty of an infraction.[522] Employers likewise are subject to a civil penalty for any such violation.[523]

When a stop sign is erected at a railroad crossing,[524] the driver of a vehicle that approaches the crossing must stop within 15 to 50 feet from the nearest rail of the crossing and may proceed "only upon exercising due care."[525] Failure to comply with these requirements, which are set forth in G.S. 20-142.2, is an infraction punishable by a penalty of not more than $100.[526] Any employer who "knowingly allows, requires, permits, or otherwise authorizes" an employee driving a commercial motor vehicle to violate this statute commits an infraction and is subject to additional civil penalties.[527]

Drivers of the following types of vehicles are required by G.S. 20-142.3(a) to stop at railroad crossings, even when no signal or signage requires vehicles generally to stop:

- school buses,
- activity buses,
- motor vehicles carrying passengers for compensation,
- commercial motor vehicles listed in 49 C.F.R. § 392.10, and
- motor vehicles that seat sixteen or more.

---

518. G.S. 20-142.1(a).

519. G.S. 20-142.1(b). Pedestrians are similarly prohibited from passing through, around, or under a crossing gate or barrier at a railroad crossing while such gate or barrier is being opened or closed. *Id.*

520. G.S. 20-142.1(c).

521. G.S. 20-142.1(d); *id.* §§ 20-176(a), (b).

522. G.S. 20-142.1(e).

523. *Id.* (providing for imposition of a civil penalty under G.S. 20-37.21).

524. DOT is authorized to designate certain highway crossings of railroads as "particularly dangerous" and to place stop signs at such crossings. G.S. 20-142.2.

525. *Id.*

526. G.S. 20-176(a), (b).

527. G.S. 20-142.2.

Drivers of such vehicles must stop within 15 to 50 feet from the nearest rail of the railroad.[528] The driver must, while so stopped, listen and look in both directions along the track for any train that might be approaching and may not proceed until he or she can do so safely.[529] The driver must cross the track with the vehicle in a gear that permits crossing without changing gears; he or she may not, in fact, change gears while crossing.[530]

Under G.S. 20-142.3, with the exception of school buses and activity buses, the vehicles mentioned in the bulleted list above are not required to stop at the following locations:

- railroad tracks that are used solely for industrial switching purposes within a business district;
- any railroad grade crossing through which a police officer or a crossing flagman directs traffic to proceed;
- railroad grade crossings protected by gates or flashing signals that are designed to stop traffic when a train is approaching, when such a gate or flashing signal does not indicate the approach of a train;
- abandoned railroad grade crossings that are marked with signs indicating that the rail line has been abandoned; or
- any industrial or spur line railroad grade crossing that is marked with a sign reading "Exempt" that has been posted either by or with the consent of "the appropriate State or local authority."[531]

A violation of G.S. 20-142.3 is an infraction punishable by a fine of not more than $100.[532] Any employer who "knowingly allows, requires, permits, or otherwise authorizes" an employee driving a commercial motor vehicle to violate G.S. 20-142.3 commits an infraction and also is subject to a civil penalty.[533]

G.S. 20-142.4(a) prohibits the operation or movement of any crawler-type tractor, crane, or roller or any sort of equipment or structure having a normal operating speed that does not exceed 5 m.p.h. on or across any tracks at a railroad crossing unless the operator or mover has complied with special requirements. First, notice of any intended crossing of such equipment or structure must be provided to the railroad superintendent and the railroad must be given a reasonable amount of time to provide protection at the crossing.[534] Second, before making any crossing of this sort, the person operating or moving the vehicle or equipment must do the following.

1. Stop the vehicle or equipment between 15 and 50 feet from the nearest rail of the railroad.
2. While stopped, the operator or mover must listen and look in both directions along the track for any approaching train and for signals indicating that a train is approaching.
3. The operator or mover may not proceed until it is safe to make the crossing.[535]

---

528. G.S. 20-142.3(a).
529. *Id.*
530. *Id.*
531. G.S. 20-142.3(b).
532. G.S. 20-142.3(c); *id.* §§ 20-176(a), (b).
533. G.S. 20-142.3(f).
534. G.S. 20-142.4(b).
535. G.S. 20-142.4(c). These requirements do not apply at any railroad crossing where State or local authorities have posted an official sign "carrying the legend 'Exempt'" based on a determination that trains are not running during certain times or seasons of the year. G.S. 20-142.4(e).

No crossing by heavy equipment or structures as described in G.S. 20-142.4(a) may be made when a warning signal has been given indicating the immediate approach of a railroad train or car.[536]

A violation of G.S. 20-142.4 is an infraction punishable by a penalty of not more than $100.[537] Any employer who "knowingly allows, requires, permits, or otherwise authorizes" an employee driving a commercial motor vehicle to violate G.S. 20-142.4 is guilty of an infraction and also is subject to a civil penalty.[538]

12. Duty to Stop When Traffic Obstructed

G.S. 20-142.5 makes it unlawful to

(1) drive
(2) a vehicle
(3) into an intersection, a marked crosswalk, or onto any railroad grade crossing
(4) unless there is sufficient space on the other side of such intersection, crosswalk, or railroad crossing to accommodate the vehicle
(5) without obstructing the passage of other vehicles, pedestrians, or trains,
(6) "notwithstanding the indication of any traffic control signal to proceed."

a. Punishment

Violation of G.S. 20-142.5 is an infraction punishable by a penalty of not more than $100.[539]

Any employer who "knowingly allows, requires, permits, or otherwise authorizes" an employee driving a commercial motor vehicle to violate G.S. 20-142.5 commits an infraction and also is subject to a civil penalty.[540]

13. Turning at Intersections

G.S. 20-153(a) requires that a person make (1) the approach for a right turn and (2) the right turn itself "as close as practicable" to the right-hand curb or the edge of a roadway.[541] G.S. 20-153(b) requires any driver of a vehicle who intends to turn left at an intersection to approach that intersection in the "extreme left-hand lane lawfully available to traffic moving in the direction of travel of that vehicle." After entering the intersection, the vehicle must make the left turn in a manner that results in the vehicle leaving the intersection in a "lane lawfully available to traffic moving in the direction upon the roadway being entered."[542] Local authorities and DOT may, in their respective jurisdictions, modify this method of turning at intersections by clearly indicating within an intersection the course to be followed by turning vehicles; drivers who fail to turn in the manner directed will be in violation of law.[543]

---

536. G.S. 20-142.4(d).
537. G.S. 20-142.4(f); *id.* §§ 20-176(a), (b).
538. G.S. 20-142.5(g).
539. G.S. 20-142.5; *id.* §§ 20-176(a), (b).
540. G.S. 20-142.5.
541. The court of appeals in *State v. Osterhoudt*, 222 N.C. App. 620 (2012), determined that the defendant violated G.S. 20-153(a) when he made a wide right turn that caused him to veer over the roadway's double yellow line defining the turn lane when there was no obstacle in the roadway. *Id.* at 629.
542. G.S. 20-153(b).
543. G.S. 20-153(c).

a. Punishment

Violation of G.S. 20-153 is an infraction punishable by a penalty of not more than $100.[544]

14. Rules Governing the Right-of-Way

G.S. 20-155 sets forth the rules governing the right-of-way when vehicles meet at an intersection.

a. Meeting at an Intersection

G.S. 20-155(a) provides that whenever two vehicles "approach or enter an intersection from different highways at approximately the same time," the driver of the vehicle on the left must yield the right-of-way to the driver of the vehicle on the right. This rule applies regardless of whether the intersection requires a four-way stop or is unmarked by traffic signals.[545] The North Carolina Supreme Court held in *Dawson v. Jennette*[546] that vehicles "approach or enter an intersection at approximately the same time" within the meaning of G.S. 20-155(a) when, considering their distances from the intersection, their speeds, and other circumstances, "the driver of the vehicle on the left should reasonably apprehend danger of collision" were he not to wait until the vehicle on the right has passed.[547] The court also noted that the right-of-way "is *not* determined by a fraction of a second."[548]

Based on the rule set out in G.S. 20-155(a), at the intersection depicted in figures 1 and 2, below, the grey vehicle must yield the right-of-way to the white vehicle.

b. Turning Left

The rule in G.S. 20-155(a) does not apply to vehicles proceeding in opposite directions that meet at an intersection.[549] When that situation occurs, either vehicle may proceed straight ahead or turn right. The driver of a vehicle who intends to turn left at an intersection or turn into an alley, private road, or driveway, however, must yield the right-of-way to a vehicle that is approaching from the opposite direction and is in the intersection "or so close as to constitute an immediate hazard."[550]

In the circumstance depicted in figure 3, below, the driver of the white vehicle must yield the right-of-way to the driver of the grey car so long as that car is proceeding straight through the intersection or making a right turn.

c. Traffic Circles

G.S. 20-155(d) sets forth the right-of-way rules for drivers of vehicles entering a traffic circle. Such a driver must yield the right-of-way to a vehicle that is already in the traffic circle.

At the traffic circle depicted in figure 4, below, the white vehicle must yield the right-of-way to the grey vehicle that is already in the traffic circle.

---

544. G.S. 20-176(a), (b).

545. *Cf.* White v. Phelps, 260 N.C. 445, 446 (1963) (explaining that "[w]here by reason of automatic traffic lights, stop or caution signs or other devices one street at an intersection is favored over the other, and one street is thereby made permanently or intermittently dominant and the other servient, G.S. [ ]20-155 has no application").

546. 278 N.C. 438 (1971).

547. *Id.* at 445.

548. *Id.*

549. Fleming v. Drye, 253 N.C. 545, 549 (1960).

550. G.S. 20-155(b).

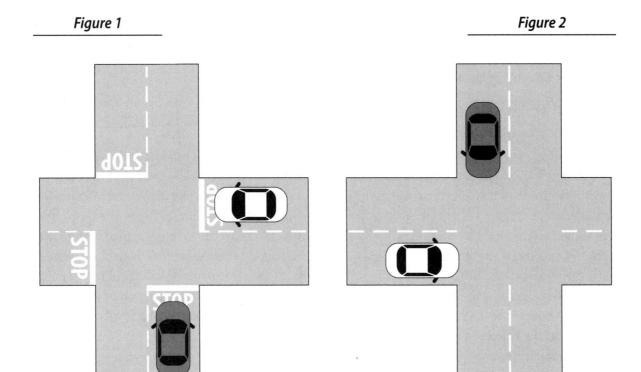

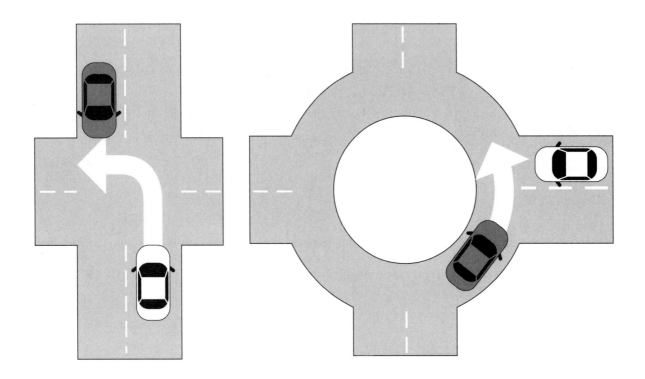

d. Exceptions

G.S. 20-156 sets forth several exceptions to the right-of-way rule.

- The driver of a vehicle that is about to enter or cross a street or highway from an alley, a building entrance, a private road, or a driveway must yield the right-of-way to vehicles that are approaching on the street or highway to be entered.[551]
- The driver of a vehicle on a highway must yield the right-of-way to any of the following types of vehicles when the driver of such a vehicle is giving a warning signal by an "appropriate light and by bell, siren or exhaust whistle audible under normal conditions from a distance of [at least] 1,000 feet":
  - police vehicles;
  - fire department vehicles;
  - ambulances;
  - vehicles used by an organ procurement organization to recover or transport human tissues and organs for transplantation;
  - vehicles used by a transplant coordinator working for an organ procurement organization for the purpose of responding to a call to recover or transport human tissues or organs for transplantation;
  - rescue squad emergency service vehicles;
  - vehicles used by county fire marshals and civil preparedness coordinators;
  - vehicles used by the Division of Marine Fisheries or the Division of Parks and Recreation for law enforcement, firefighting, or other emergency response purposes; and
  - vehicles used by the N.C. Forest Service for law enforcement, firefighting, or other emergency response purposes.[552]

When an "appropriate warning signal" is given, any of these types of emergency vehicles may proceed through an intersection or other place when the vehicle is facing a stop sign, a yield sign, or a traffic light that is emitting either a flashing strobe signal or a beam of steady or flashing red light.[553]

e. Pedestrian Crossing

G.S. 20-155(c) requires vehicles to yield the right-of-way to pedestrians in certain circumstances. For example, the driver of a vehicle on a street or highway within a business or residential district must yield the right-of-way to any pedestrian who is crossing the street or highway within a clearly marked crosswalk.[554] The driver of a vehicle must also yield the right-of-way to a pedestrian crossing that is "included in the prolongation of the lateral boundary lines of the adjacent sidewalk at the end of a block, except at intersections where the movement of traffic is . . . regulated by traffic officers or traffic direction devices."[555]

Additional provisions governing the rights of pedestrians in relation to vehicles are set forth in Part 11 of Article 3 of G.S. Chapter 20.

---

551. G.S. 20-156(a).
552. G.S. 20-156(b).
553. *Id.*
554. G.S. 20-155(c).
555. *Id.*

f. Pedestrian-Control Signals

Whenever pedestrian-control signals have been installed on a street or highway, pedestrians are obligated by law to comply with them. When a pedestrian is facing a signal that indicates "WALK", he or she may proceed across the street or highway in the direction of the signal and must be accorded the right-of-way by all vehicle drivers.[556] When the signal faced by a pedestrian indicates "DON'T WALK", he or she may not begin to cross the street or highway in the direction of the signal. However, a pedestrian who has partially completed his or her crossing on the "WALK" signal may proceed to a sidewalk or safety island while the "DON'T WALK" sign is displayed.[557]

g. Traffic-Control Signals

When a system of traffic-control signals or devices does not include special pedestrian-control signals, all pedestrians are subject to the vehicular traffic-control signals or devices as they apply to pedestrian traffic.[558]

h. No Signals in Crosswalk

When there are no traffic-control signals in a given location on a roadway, or when any signals present are not in operation, a vehicle must yield the right-of-way to a pedestrian crossing the roadway within a marked crosswalk or within an unmarked crosswalk at or near an intersection by "slowing down or stopping if need be."[559] An "unmarked crosswalk" is the "area within an intersection which also lies within the lateral boundaries of a sidewalk projected across the intersection."[560] Thus, to have an unmarked crosswalk, there must be a sidewalk or "sidewalk like area" on at least one side of the intersection.[561]

i. Alleys, Driveways, and Other Entrances

In addition, the driver of any vehicle entering or exiting an alley, a building entrance, a private road, or a driveway must yield the right-of-way to a pedestrian or bicycle rider who is approaching on any sidewalk or walkway that extends across the alley, entrance, road, or driveway.[562]

j. Drivers Must Exercise Due Care

Pedestrians crossing the road at any place other than a crosswalk must "yield the right-of-way to all vehicles upon the roadway."[563] Notwithstanding this rule, vehicle drivers are required to "exercise due care" to prevent collisions with pedestrians on roadways and must, "when necessary," provide warning by sounding their horns.[564] Drivers also must "exercise proper precaution upon observing any child or any confused or incapacitated person upon a roadway."[565]

---

556. G.S. 20-172(b)(1).
557. G.S. 20-172(b)(2).
558. G.S. 20-172(c).
559. G.S. 20-173(a).
560. Anderson v. Carter, 272 N.C. 426, 430 (1968).
561. Tucker v. Bruton, 102 N.C. App. 117, 120 (1991).
562. G.S. 20-173(c).
563. G.S. 20-174(a).
564. G.S. 20-174(e).
565. *Id.*

k. Pedestrians Must Use Sidewalks

"Where sidewalks are provided," it is unlawful for a pedestrian to walk on a roadway adjacent to a sidewalk.[566] When there are no sidewalks, a pedestrian must walk "on the extreme left of the roadway or its shoulder facing traffic which may approach from the opposite direction;"[567] a pedestrian in these circumstances must yield the right-of-way to approaching traffic.[568]

Violation of any of the above-cited right-of-way rules by a driver or pedestrian is an infraction punishable by a penalty of not more than $100.[569]

l. Approach of Emergency Vehicles

When any of the following vehicles are approaching and are giving a warning signal, a driver must under G.S. 20-157(a) immediately drive "as near as possible and parallel to the right-hand edge or curb" of a street or highway and stop his or her vehicle:

- law enforcement vehicle
- fire department vehicle
- ambulance
- rescue squad emergency service vehicle
- Division of Marine Fisheries vehicle
- Division of Parks and Recreation vehicle
- N.C. Forest Service vehicle traveling in response to a fire alarm or other emergency response purpose

The driver must stop his or her vehicle clear of any intersection and must remain stopped until the emergency vehicle has passed, "unless otherwise directed by a law enforcement or traffic officer."[570]

Vehicles traveling in the opposite direction of an emergency vehicle of the type listed above that is giving an appropriate signal are not required to pull to the right-hand edge of the roadway and stop if they are traveling on a four-lane limited access highway that has a median divider that divides the highway for vehicles traveling in opposite directions.[571]

A violation of G.S. 20-157(a) is a Class 2 misdemeanor.[572]

15. Move-Over Law

If an emergency vehicle of the type listed in section VI.B.14.j, above, or a public service vehicle is parking or is standing within 12 feet of a roadway and is "giving a warning signal by appropriate light, the driver of every other vehicle approaching shall, as soon as it is safe and when not otherwise directed by an individual lawfully directing traffic," take one of the following actions under G.S. 20-157:

---

566. G.S. 20-174(d).
567. *Id.*
568. *Id.*
569. G.S. 20-176(a), (b).
570. *Id.*
571. *Id.*
572. *Id.*

1. Move his or her vehicle into any lane other than the lane closest to the parked or standing authorized emergency or public service vehicle and keep driving in that lane "until safely clear of the authorized emergency vehicle." This requirement applies only when the roadway "has at least two lanes for traffic proceeding in the direction of the approaching vehicle and if the approaching vehicle may change lanes safely and without interfering with . . . traffic."[573]

Or

2. Slow his or her vehicle, maintaining a safe speed, and then drive at reduced speed, prepared to stop, until the vehicle is "completely past" the authorized emergency vehicle or public service vehicle. This requirement applies only when the roadway has just one lane for traffic proceeding in the direction of the approaching vehicle or when the approaching vehicle is unable to change lanes safely.[574]

a. Public Service Vehicle

A "public service vehicle," for purposes of G.S. 20-157, is a vehicle that "(i) is being used to assist motorists or law enforcement officers with wrecked or disabled vehicles, (ii) is being used to install, maintain, or restore utility service, including electric, cable, telephone, communications, and gas, (iii) is being used in the collection of refuse, solid waste, or recycling, or (iv) is a highway maintenance vehicle owned and operated by or contracted by the State or a local government and is operating an amber-colored flashing light authorized by G.S. 20-130.2."[575]

Failure to comply with the move-over law set out in G.S. 20-157 is an infraction punishable by a fine of $250, unless the more severe penalties described below apply.[576]

b. Violation of G.S. 20-157 Resulting in Property Damage or Injury

Any person who violates G.S. 20-157 and (1) causes damage to property in the immediate vicinity of the authorized emergency or public service vehicle totaling more than $500 or (2) injures a law enforcement officer, firefighter, emergency vehicle operator, Incident Management Assistance Patrol member, public service vehicle operator, or other emergency response personnel in the immediate vicinity of the authorized emergency or public service vehicle is guilty of a Class 1 misdemeanor.[577]

c. Violation of G.S. 20-157 Causing Serious Injury or Death

A person who violates G.S. 20-157 and causes serious injury or death to any law enforcement officer, firefighter, emergency vehicle operator, Incident Management Assistance Patrol member, public service vehicle operator, or other emergency response personnel in the immediate vicinity of the authorized emergency or public service vehicle is guilty of a Class I felony.[578]

d. Failure to Yield Causing Serious Bodily Injury

Under G.S. 20-160.1(a), any "person who commits the offense of failure to yield while approaching or entering an intersection, turning at a stop or yield sign, entering a roadway, upon the approach of an emergency vehicle, or at highway construction or maintenance" and who causes serious bodily

---

573. G.S. 20-157(f)(1).
574. G.S. 20-157(f)(2).
575. G.S. 20-157(f).
576. G.S. 20-157(g).
577. G.S. 20-157(h).
578. G.S. 20-157(i).

injury to another is subject to a fine of $500, unless the conduct is covered by another law providing greater punishment.

"Serious bodily injury", for purposes of this provision, is "bodily injury that involves a substantial risk of death, extreme physical pain, protracted and obvious disfigurement, or protracted loss or impairment of the function of a bodily member, organ, or mental faculty."[579]

16. Vehicle-Control Signs and Signals

a. Stop Signs

i. At an Intersection

When DOT or a local authority has placed a stop sign at an intersection, the driver of an approaching vehicle must stop and yield the right-of-way to vehicles driving on the "designated main-traveled or through highway."[580] When stop signs have been installed on at least three entrances to an intersection, a driver, after stopping, may proceed with caution.[581]

ii. At Other Places

When a stop sign has been placed at a site other than an intersection, the driver of an approaching vehicle must stop and must yield the right-of-way to pedestrians and other vehicles.[582]

b. Red Lights

i. At an Intersection

Whenever a traffic signal emits "a steady red circular light controlling traffic approaching an intersection, an approaching vehicle facing the red light [must] stop and [may] not enter the intersection. After coming to a complete stop and unless prohibited by an appropriate sign, that approaching vehicle may make a right turn."[583]

An approaching vehicle that turns right at a red light as described above must yield the right-of-way to other traffic and pedestrians using the intersection, as well as to pedestrians who are (1) moving towards the intersection, (2) "in reasonably close proximity to the intersection," and (3) preparing to cross in front of the traffic that must by law stop at the red light.[584]

A driver who fails to yield to a pedestrian while turning right at a red light commits an infraction punishable by a fine of between $100 and $500.[585] Otherwise, a driver's failure to stop at a red light is an infraction, punishable by a fine of not more than $100.[586]

ii. Motorcycle Defense

Under G.S. 20-158(e), the operator of a motorcycle[587] who can show all of the following has a defense to a violation of failure to stop at a red light:

---

579. G.S. 20-160.1(b).
580. G.S. 20-158(b)(1).
581. *Id.*
582. G.S. 20-158(c)(1).
583. G.S. 20-158(b)(2)a.
584. G.S. 20-158(b)(2)b.
585. G.S. 20-158(b)(2)c.
586. G.S. 20-176(a), (b).
587. For purposes of this provision, a "motorcycle" is a vehicle that has a saddle for the use of the rider and is designed to travel on a maximum of three wheels in contact with the ground. *See* G.S. 20-158(e) (incorporating definition of "motorcycle" in G.S. 20-4.01(27)d.). This definition includes autocycles, motor

"(1) The operator brought the motorcycle to a complete stop at the intersection or stop bar where a steady red light was being emitted in the direction of the operator.

(2) The intersection is controlled by a vehicle actuated traffic signal using an inductive loop to activate the traffic signal.

(3) No other vehicle that was entitled to have the right-of-way under applicable law was sitting at, traveling through, or approaching the intersection.

(4) No pedestrians were attempting to cross at or near the intersection.

(5) The motorcycle operator who received the citation waited a minimum of three minutes at the intersection or stop bar where the steady red light was being emitted in the direction of the operator before entering the intersection."

iii. At Other Places

When a traffic signal has been placed at a site other than an intersection and is emitting a steady red light, an approaching vehicle facing the red light must stop.[588]

c. Yellow and Green Lights

"When a traffic signal is emitting a steady yellow circular light on a traffic signal controlling traffic approaching an intersection or a steady yellow arrow light on a traffic signal controlling traffic turning at an intersection, vehicles facing the yellow light are warned that the related green light is being terminated or a red light will be immediately forthcoming."[589] When a traffic signal at an intersection or another location "is emitting a steady green light, vehicles may proceed with due care through the intersection subject to the rights of pedestrians and other vehicles."[590]

d. Flashing Red Lights

i. At an Intersection

"When a flashing red light has been erected or installed at an intersection, approaching vehicles facing the red light [must] stop and yield the right-of-way to vehicles in or approaching the intersection. The right to proceed [is] subject to the rules applicable to making a stop at a stop sign."[591]

ii. At Other Places

"When a flashing red light has been erected or installed at a place other than an intersection, approaching vehicles facing the light shall stop and yield the right-of-way to pedestrians or other vehicles."[592]

---

scooters, and motor-driven bicycles but excludes tractors and utility vehicles that are equipped with some additional device that is designed to transport property; three-wheeled vehicles used by law enforcement agencies; and mopeds as defined in G.S. 20-4.01(27)d1.

588. G.S. 20-158(c)(2).
589. G.S. 20-158(b)(2a).
590. *Id.*; *id.* § 20-158(c)(2).
591. G.S. 20-158(b)(3).
592. G.S. 20-158(c)(3).

e. Flashing Yellow Lights

i. At an Intersection

"When a flashing yellow light has been erected or installed at an intersection, approaching vehicles facing the yellow flashing light may proceed through the intersection with caution, yielding the right-of-way to vehicles in or approaching the intersection."[593]

ii. At Other Places

"When a flashing yellow light has been erected or installed at a place other than an intersection, approaching vehicles facing the light may proceed with caution, yielding the right-of-way to pedestrians and other vehicles."[594]

f. Where to Stop

i. At an Intersection

"When a stop sign, traffic signal, flashing light, or other traffic-control device . . . requires a vehicle to stop at an intersection, the driver [must] stop (i) at an appropriately marked stop line, or if none, (ii) before entering a marked crosswalk, or if none, (iii) before entering the intersection at the point nearest the intersecting street where the driver has a view of approaching traffic on the intersecting street."[595]

ii. At Other Places

"When a traffic signal, stop sign, or other traffic control device . . . requires a vehicle to stop at a place other than an intersection, the driver [must] stop at an appropriately marked stop line, or if none, before entering a marked crosswalk, or if none, before proceeding past the traffic control device."[596]

g. Light Outage

"When a traffic signal is not illuminated due to a power outage or other malfunction, vehicles [must] approach the intersection and proceed through the intersection as though [it] is controlled by a stop sign on all approaches to the intersection."[597] This rule does not apply if traffic at the intersection "is being directed by a law enforcement officer, another authorized person, or another type of traffic control device."[598]

h. Ramp Meters

Ramp meters are essentially stop lights (minus the yellow caution light) placed on highway entrance ramps.[599] Under G.S. 20-158(c)(6), when a ramp meter light is red, a vehicle facing the red light must stop. When a ramp meter light is green, "a vehicle may proceed for each lane of traffic facing the meter." When a ramp meter's display is dark or is not emitting either a red or a green light, "a vehicle may proceed without stopping." A violation of the rules governing the progress of traffic through ramp meters is an infraction.

---

593. G.S. 20-158(b)(4).
594. G.S. 20-158(c)(4).
595. G.S. 20-158(b)(5).
596. G.S. 20-158(c)(5).
597. G.S. 20-158(b)(6).
598. *Id.*
599. G.S. 20-4.01(32a).

17. Hit and Run

"Hit and run" is a term used to describe several felony and misdemeanor offenses set forth in G.S. 20-166, a statute in which neither the term "hit" nor "run" appears. The general rule for a driver involved in a crash in which a person is injured or at least $1,000 in property damages occurs is this: The driver must stop his or her vehicle at the scene and must remain there with the vehicle until a law enforcement officer completes a crash investigation or authorizes the driver to leave and the vehicle to be removed. An exception permits a driver to leave the scene of a crash in his or her vehicle to call for a law enforcement officer, to call for or obtain medical assistance or treatment, or to remove himself, herself, or others from significant risk of injury.[600] A driver who leaves for one of these purposes must return with the vehicle to the accident scene within a reasonable period of time, unless otherwise instructed by a law enforcement officer.[601]

G.S. 20-166 criminalizes (1) a driver's failure to stop at the scene of a crash in which the vehicle he or she is driving is involved; (2) a driver's failure to remain at the scene of such a crash; (3) a driver's facilitating of the premature removal of his or her vehicle from the scene; and (4) a driver's failure to provide identifying information to a person struck by a vehicle, the driver or occupants of any vehicle with which the driver collides, or any person whose property is damaged in a crash. These offenses and related provisions that govern the behavior of passengers at the scene of a crash are discussed in greater detail below.

a. Driver's Failure to Stop or Remain at the Scene of a Crash When Serious Bodily Injury or Death Occurs

G.S. 20-166(a) makes it unlawful to

(1) drive
(2) on a street, highway, or public vehicular area[602]
(3) a vehicle that is
(4) involved in a crash,
(5) causing serious bodily injury or death to any person,
(6) when the person driving knows or reasonably should know that the vehicle was involved in a crash that has caused serious bodily injury or death and
(7) willfully
    (a) fails to immediately stop the vehicle at the scene of the crash,
    (b) fails to remain with the vehicle at the crash scene until a law enforcement officer completes an investigation of the crash or authorizes the driver to leave and the vehicle to be removed, unless remaining at the scene places the driver or others at significant risk of injury, or
    (c) facilitates, allows, or agrees to the removal of the vehicle from the scene.

---

600. G.S. 20-166; State v. Scaturro, ___ N.C. App. ___, 802 S.E.2d 500 (explaining that a driver may lawfully leave a crash scene to *obtain* medical care for himself, herself, or another person even though G.S. 20-166(a) instructs that drivers may leave the scene merely *to call for* medical assistance or treatment), *temp. stay allowed*, ___ N.C. ___, 800 S.E.2d 421 (2017).

601. G.S. 20-166.

602. Though G.S. 20-166(a) is silent regarding the type of roadway on which the offense the statute sets out may be committed, the state supreme court held in *State v. Smith*, 264 N.C. 575, 576–77 (1965), that the requirements of G.S. 20-166 are not limited to streets and highways.

i. Crash

The term "crash" is defined as "[a]ny event that results in injury or property damage attributable directly to the motion of a motor vehicle or its load."[603] The terms "collision", "accident", and "crash" and their cognates share the same meaning.[604]

ii. Serious Bodily Injury

G.S. 20-166(a) defines "serious bodily injury" by reference to G.S. 14-32.4, the statute that defines the offense of assault inflicting serious bodily injury. Thus, "serious bodily injury" under G.S. 20-166(a) is "bodily injury that creates a substantial risk of death, or that causes serious permanent disfigurement, coma, a permanent or protracted condition that causes extreme pain, or permanent or protracted loss or impairment of the function of any bodily member or organ, or that results in prolonged hospitalization."[605]

iii. Exception That Permits Driver to Leave Scene and Remove Vehicle

A driver may lawfully facilitate, allow, or agree to the removal of his or her vehicle from a crash scene in order (1) to call for a law enforcement officer, (2) to call for or obtain medical assistance or treatment needed for or requested by an injured person, or (3) to remove himself or herself or others from significant risk of injury.[606] If the driver leaves the scene of a crash for any of the permitted reasons set out above, he or she must return to the accident scene with the vehicle within a reasonable period of time, unless a law enforcement officer instructs him or her otherwise.[607]

iv. Punishment

A willful violation of G.S. 20-166(a) is a Class F felony.

b. *Driver's Failure to Stop or Remain at the Scene of a Crash When Injury Occurs*

G.S. 20-166(a1) makes it unlawful to

    (1) drive
    (2) on a street, highway, or public vehicular area[608]
    (3) a vehicle that is
    (4) involved in a crash,
    (5) causing injury to any person,
    (6) when the person driving knows or reasonably should know that the vehicle was involved in a crash that has caused injury and
    (7) willfully
        (a) fails to immediately stop the vehicle at the scene of the crash,
        (b) fails to remain with the vehicle at the crash scene until a law enforcement officer completes an investigation of the crash or authorizes the driver to leave and the vehicle to

---

603. G.S. 20-4.01(4b).
604. *Id.*
605. G.S. 14-32.4(a).
606. G.S. 20-166(a); State v. Scaturro, ___ N.C. App. ___, 802 S.E.2d 500 (explaining that a driver may lawfully leave a crash scene to obtain medical care for himself, herself, or another person even though G.S. 20-166(a) instructs that drivers may leave the scene merely to call for medical assistance or treatment), *temp. stay allowed*, ___ N.C. ___, 800 S.E.2d 421 (2017).
607. G.S. 20-166(a).
608. *See supra* note 602.

> be removed, unless remaining at the scene places the driver or others at significant risk of injury, or

(c) facilitates, allows, or agrees to the removal of the vehicle from the scene.

i. Exception That Permits Driver to Leave Scene and Remove Vehicle

The exception discussed above that permits a driver to leave the scene of a crash involving serious bodily injury or death and remove his or her vehicle applies to drivers involved in crashes resulting in lesser injuries.[609]

ii. Punishment

A willful violation of G.S. 20-166(a1) is a Class H felony.

c. Driver's Failure to Give Information or Assistance When Injury, Serious Bodily Injury, or Death Occurs

G.S. 20-166(b) makes it unlawful to

(1) drive
(2) on a street, highway, or public vehicular area[610]
(3) a vehicle that is
(4) involved in a crash,
(5) causing injury, serious bodily injury, or death to any person,
(6) when the person driving knows or reasonably should know that the vehicle was involved in a crash that has caused injury, serious bodily injury, or death and
(7) the person driving fails to

    (a) give his or her name, address, driver's license number, and the license plate number of the vehicle involved in the crash to the person struck by his or her vehicle or to the driver or occupants of any vehicle with which he or she collided or

    (b) render "reasonable assistance" to any person injured, including by calling for medical assistance "if it is apparent that such assistance is necessary or is requested by the injured person."

i. Exception

A driver is not required to give his or her name, address, driver's license number, or the license plate number of his or her vehicle that has been involved in a crash to any person who is not physically and mentally capable of receiving it.[611]

ii. Punishment

A violation of G.S. 20-166(b) is a Class 1 misdemeanor.

---

609. *See supra* section VI.B.17.a.iii.

610. Though G.S. 20-166(a) is silent regarding the type of roadway on which the offense the statute sets out may be committed, the state supreme court held in *State v. Smith*, 264 N.C. 575, 576–77 (1965), that the requirements of G.S. 20-166 are not limited to streets and highways.

611. G.S. 20-166(b).

d. Driver's Failure to Stop When Injury or Death Is Not Apparent or Only Property Damage Occurs

G.S. 20-166(c) makes it unlawful to

(1) drive
(2) on a street, highway, or public vehicular area[612]
(3) a vehicle that is
(4) involved in a crash that caused
    (a) only property damage or
    (b) injury or death to any person that was not apparent and
(5) the driver knows or reasonably should know that the vehicle was involved in such a crash and
(6) willfully fails to immediately stop the vehicle at the scene of the crash,
(7) willfully fails to remain with the vehicle at the scene until a law enforcement officer completes an investigation or authorizes the driver to leave and the vehicle to be removed, unless remaining at the scene places the driver or others at significant risk of injury, or
(8) willfully facilitates, allows, or agrees to the removal of the vehicle before an investigation by law enforcement is completed or before receiving consent for the vehicle's removal from a law enforcement officer.

i. Reportable Crash

A "reportable crash" is a crash involving a motor vehicle that results in any of the following: death or injury to any person, property damage of $1,000 or more, or property damage of any amount to a vehicle that has been seized pursuant to G.S. 20-28.3.[613]

ii. Exceptions That Permit Driver to Leave Scene and Remove Vehicle

The exception discussed earlier that permits a driver to leave the scene of a crash involving serious bodily injury or death and remove his or her vehicle applies to drivers involved in crashes resulting in lesser injuries.[614]

In addition, if a crash occurs on any main lane, ramp, shoulder, median, or adjacent area of a highway and has not resulted in injury or death, or the drivers did not know or have reason to know of any injury or death, and each vehicle involved in the crash can be "normally and safely driven," each vehicle must, as soon as possible, be moved (1) out of the travel lane and onto the shoulder or (2) to a "designated accident investigation site".[615] A vehicle can be "normally and safely driven" under this provision "if it does not require towing and can be operated under its own power and in its usual manner, without additional damage or hazard to the vehicle, other traffic, or the roadway."[616]

---

612. *See supra* note 602.

613. G.S. 20-4.01(33b). G.S. 20-28.3(a), which is referenced in the definition of "reportable crash" set out in the text above, requires the seizure of a motor vehicle driven by a person charged with an offense involving impaired driving if the person was driving while his or her driver's license was revoked for an impaired driving license revocation or the person was driving without a valid driver's license and was not covered by an automobile liability policy.

614. *See supra* section VI.B.17.a.iii.

615. G.S. 20-166(c2).

616. *Id.*

iii. Punishment

Willful violation of G.S. 20-166(c) is a Class 1 misdemeanor.

e. Driver's Failure to Give Information When Injury or Death Is Not Apparent or Only Property Damage Occurs

G.S. 20-166(c1) makes it unlawful to

(1) drive

(2) on a street, highway, or public vehicular area[617]

(3) a vehicle that is

(4) involved in a crash that caused

    (a)   only property damage or

    (b)   injury or death to any person that was not apparent and

(5) the driver knows or reasonably should know that the vehicle was involved in such a crash and

(6) fails to give his or her name, address, driver's license number, and the license plate number of his or her vehicle to the driver or occupants of any other vehicle involved in the crash or to any person whose property has been damaged in the crash.

i. Damage to Parked and Unattended Vehicles

If the property damaged in a crash is a parked and unattended vehicle and the name and address of that vehicle's owner is not readily ascertainable, the driver of the vehicle that caused the property damage may (1) provide his or her name, address, driver's license number, and license plate number to the nearest officer or (2) "place a paper-writing containing the information in a conspicuous place upon or in the damaged vehicle."[618] If the driver chooses to provide his or her information via option (2), he or she must also send the owner of the parked or unattended vehicle a written report by certified mail within forty-eight hours.[619] That report must include the following information: (1) the time, date, and place of the accident; (2) the driver's name, address, and driver's license number; and (3) the registration plate number of the vehicle the driver used at the time of the accident.[620] The driver must send a copy of the report to DMV.[621]

ii. Punishment

Violation of G.S. 20-166(c1) is a Class 1 misdemeanor.

f. Failure to Report a Reportable Accident

G.S. 20-166.1(a) requires the driver of a vehicle involved in a "reportable accident" to immediately notify the "appropriate law enforcement agency" of the crash.[622] A "reportable accident" for purposes of this statute is a crash that results in (1) a person's injury or death, (2) property damage of at least

---

617. *See supra* note 602.

618. G.S. 20-166(c1).

619. *Id.* (requiring that a driver who leaves a paper-writing on a damaged vehicle comply with the requirements of G.S. 20-166.1(c) within forty-eight hours).

620. G.S. 20-166.1(c).

621. *Id.*

622. A plurality of the United States Supreme Court determined in *California v. Byers*, 402 U.S. 424 (1971), that California's hit and run statute, which required the driver of a motor vehicle involved in an accident to stop at the scene and give his or her name and address, did not violate the Fifth Amendment prohibition

$1,000, or (3) property damage to a vehicle seized pursuant to G.S. 20-28.3 in an impaired driving case.[623] If the accident occurred in a city, the "appropriate law enforcement agency" is the city police department. If the accident happened outside city limits, the appropriate agency is the State Highway Patrol or the sheriff's office or "other qualified rural police" in the county where the crash occurred.[624]

i. Punishment

Violation of G.S. 20-166.1 is a Class 2 misdemeanor.[625]

g. Passenger's Failure to Remain at Crash Scene or Unauthorized Removal of Vehicle When Serious Bodily Injury or Death Occurs

G.S. 20-166.2(a) makes it unlawful for a

(1) passenger
(2) in a vehicle that was
(3) involved in an accident or collision
(4) that caused serious bodily injury or death to any person,
(5) where such passenger knows or reasonably should know that the vehicle was involved in an accident or collision that caused serious bodily injury or death to any person,
(6) to willfully
    (a) leave the crash scene "by acting as the driver of a vehicle involved in the accident" before a law enforcement officer completes an investigation of the crash or authorizes the passenger to leave, unless remaining at the scene places the passenger or others at significant risk of injury or
    (b) facilitate, allow, or agree to the removal of the vehicle before a law enforcement officer completes an investigation of the crash or before receiving consent from the officer to leave.

i. Exception That Permits Removal of Vehicle

A passenger may lawfully facilitate, allow, or agree to the removal of a vehicle from a crash scene in order (1) to call for a law enforcement officer, (2) to call for or obtain medical assistance or treatment needed for or requested by an injured person, or (3) to remove himself or herself or others from significant risk of injury.[626] If the passenger leaves the scene of the crash for any of the permitted reasons set out above, he or she must return to the accident scene with the vehicle within a reasonable period of time, unless a law enforcement officer instructs him or her otherwise.[627]

---

against self-incrimination. The Court reached this conclusion on the basis that stopping and providing one's name and address was nontestimonial and that the government's regulatory and non-criminal interests in obtaining the information outweighed the potentially incriminating nature of the disclosures.

    623. G.S. 20-4.01(33b) (using the interchangeable term "reportable crash").

    624. G.S. 20-166.1(a).

    625. G.S. 20-166.1(k); *id.* §§ 20-176(a), (b).

    626. G.S. 20-166.2(a); *see also* State v. Scaturro, ___ N.C. App. ___, 802 S.E.2d 500 (explaining that a driver may lawfully leave a crash scene to *obtain* medical care for himself, herself, or another person even though G.S. 20-166(a), which contains an exception for drivers identical to that for passengers in G.S. 20-166.2(a), instructs that drivers may leave the scene merely *to call for* medical assistance or treatment), *temp. stay allowed*, ___ N.C. ___, 800 S.E.2d 421 (2017).

    627. G.S. 20-166.2(a).

ii. Punishment

Willful violation of G.S. 20-166.2(a) is either a Class H felony or a Class 1 misdemeanor, depending on the type of accident or collision involved.[628]

h. Passenger's Failure to Remain at Crash Scene or Unauthorized Removal of Vehicle When Serious Bodily Injury or Death Is Not Apparent or Only Property Damage Occurs

G.S. 20-166.2(a) makes it unlawful for a

(1) passenger
(2) in a vehicle that has been
(3) involved in a "reportable accident" that caused
  (a) only property damage or
  (b) injury or death that is not apparent,
(4) where the passenger knows or reasonably should know that the vehicle was involved in an accident or collision of this sort,
(5) to willfully
  (a) leave the crash scene "by acting as the driver of a vehicle involved in the accident" before a law enforcement officer completes an investigation of the crash or authorizes the passenger to leave, unless remaining at the scene places the passenger or others at significant risk of injury or
  (b) facilitate, allow, or agree to the removal of the vehicle before a law enforcement officer completes an investigation of the crash or before receiving consent from the officer to leave.

i. Reportable Accident

A "reportable accident" for purposes of this provision is a crash involving a motor vehicle that results in any of the following: death or injury to any person, property damage of $1,000 or more, or property damage of any amount to a vehicle seized pursuant to G.S. 20-28.3.[629]

ii. Exception That Permits Removal of Vehicle

The exception discussed above that permits a passenger to leave the scene of a crash involving serious bodily injury or death and remove his or her vehicle applies to passengers involved in crashes resulting in lesser injuries.[630]

iii. Punishment

Willful violation of G.S. 20-166.2(a) is either a Class H felony or a Class 1 misdemeanor, depending on the type of accident or collision involved.[631]

---

628. *Id.* ("A willful violation of this subsection is a Class H felony if the accident or collision is described in G.S. 20-166(a). A willful violation of this subsection is a Class 1 misdemeanor if the accident or collision is a reportable accident described in G.S. 20-166(c).")

629. G.S. 20-4.01(33b) (using the interchangeable term "reportable crash"). G.S. 20-28.3(a) requires the seizure of a motor vehicle driven by a person charged with an offense involving impaired driving if the person was driving while his or her driver's license was revoked for an impaired driving license revocation or the person was driving without a valid driver's license and was not covered by an automobile liability policy.

630. G.S. 20-166.2(a).

631. *Id. See supra* note 628.

(a) Passenger's Failure to Give Information or Assistance

G.S. 20-166.2(b) makes it unlawful for a

(1) passenger

(2) in a vehicle that was

(3) involved in an accident or collision,

(4) where the passenger knows or reasonably should know that the vehicle was involved in an accident or collision,

(5) to willfully

    (a) fail to give his or her name, address, driver's license number, and the license plate number of the vehicle in which he or she was a passenger, if possible, to the person struck in the crash or to the driver or occupants "of any other vehicle collided with" or

    (b) fail to provide "reasonable assistance" to anyone injured in the accident or collision.

(b) Exception

A passenger is not required to give his or her name, address, driver's license number, and vehicle license plate number to any person who is not "physically and mentally capable of receiving" it.[632]

(c) Punishment

Violation of G.S. 20-166.2(b) is a Class 1 misdemeanor.

18. Passing a Stopped School Bus

a. General Rule

Under G.S. 20-217(a), the driver of a vehicle that approaches a school bus from any direction on the same street, highway, or public vehicular area must stop and remain stopped when the bus (1) "is displaying its mechanical stop signal or flashing red lights" and (2) is stopped for the purpose of allowing passengers to board or leave the bus. The driver of the vehicle may not move, pass, or attempt to pass the bus until (1) the bus driver has withdrawn the mechanical stop signal, (2) the flashing red stoplights on the bus have been switched off, and (3) the bus has begun to move.[633]

b. School Bus, Defined

A school bus is defined in the General Statutes as a "vehicle whose primary purpose is to transport . . . students over an established route to and from school for the regularly scheduled school day."[634] To qualify as a school bus, the vehicle must be "equipped with alternately flashing red lights on the front and rear and a mechanical stop signal."[635] By law, a school bus must be "painted primarily yellow below the roofline" and must display, in a plainly visible way, the words "School Bus" on its front and rear.[636] Public, private, and parochial vehicles all may qualify as school buses under the law.[637]

---

632. G.S. 20-166.2(b).
633. G.S. 20-217(a).
634. G.S. 20-4.01(27)d4.
635. *Id.*
636. *Id.*
637. *Id.*

c. Exception for a Divided Roadway

An exception to the general rule set forth in section VI.B.18.a, above, applies to the driver of any vehicle that is traveling in the opposite direction of a school bus on a street that has been divided into two roadways that are separated by an "intervening space (including a center lane for left turns if the roadway consists of at least four or more lanes) or by a physical barrier."[638] Such a driver is not required to stop "upon meeting and passing any school bus that has stopped in the roadway across the dividing space or physical barrier."[639]

For their part, school bus drivers generally may not stop to allow passengers to board or leave a bus upon such a divided roadway if the passengers "would be required to cross the roadway to reach their destination or to board the bus."[640] Passengers may, however, board or leave a bus at points on a divided roadway that must be crossed if pedestrian and vehicle traffic is "controlled by adequate stop-and-go traffic signals."[641]

d. Punishment

Passing a stopped school bus in violation of G.S. 20-217(a) is a Class 1 misdemeanor that may not be disposed of by entry of a prayer for judgment continued.[642] A person convicted for such a violation must pay a fine of at least $500.[643]

A driver who willfully violates G.S. 20-217(a) and strikes another person is guilty of a Class I felony and must pay a fine of at least $1,250.[644]

A driver who willfully violates G.S. 20-217(a) and strikes another person, causing the death of that person, is guilty of a Class H felony and must pay a fine of at least $2,500.[645]

e. License Revocation

DMV must revoke for one year the driver's license of any person convicted of a second misdemeanor violation under G.S. 20-217 within a three-year period.[646]

DMV must revoke for two years the driver's license of any person convicted of a Class I felony under G.S. 20-217 and must revoke for three years the driver's license of any person convicted of a Class H felony under G.S. 20-217.[647] Any person whose license has been revoked for a first felony conviction under G.S. 20-217 may apply to the sentencing court for a limited driving privilege after six months of revocation.[648]

---

638. G.S. 20-217(c).

639. *Id.*

640. G.S. 20-217(d).

641. *Id.*

642. G.S. 20-217(e).

643. *Id.* Counties may adopt ordinances for the civil enforcement of G.S. 20-217. G.S. 153A-246(b). If a person is charged in a criminal pleading with violating G.S. 20-217, the charging law enforcement officer must so notify the "county office responsible for processing civil citations." G.S. 153A-246(b)(12)a. The county may not impose a civil penalty against the person charged arising out of "the same facts as those for which the person was charged in the criminal pleading." *Id.* § 153A-246(b)(12)b.

644. G.S. 20-217(g).

645. *Id.*

646. G.S. 20-217(g1).

647. *Id.*

648. *Id.*

DMV must permanently revoke the driver's license of any person convicted of a second felony under G.S. 20-217 or any person convicted of a third misdemeanor for passing a stopped school bus.[649]

DMV may restore a license permanently revoked under G.S. 20-217 after two years (in the case of revocation for a third misdemeanor) or three years (in the case of revocation for a second felony) of revocation.[650]

Any person whose driver's license is revoked under G.S. 20-217 is disqualified from driving a commercial motor vehicle for the entire period of the revocation.[651]

f. Registration Hold

The clerk of superior court must notify DMV of any person who has failed to pay, within twenty days of the date specified in a court judgment, a fine or costs ordered as a result of a conviction under G.S. 20-217.[652] Upon receiving such notice, DMV must refuse to register, issue a certificate of title for, or transfer registration for a motor vehicle registered in that person's name.[653] DMV will continue to withhold any registration and certificate of title until after the clerk of superior court notifies it that the person has paid the fine or costs or has otherwise satisfied all applicable conditions.[654]

g. Automated School Bus Safety Cameras

An "automated school bus safety camera" is defined as "a device affixed to a school bus . . . that is synchronized to automatically record photographs or video of a vehicle [that passes a stopped school bus]."[655] Any photographs or videos recorded by such a camera that capture a violation of G.S. 20-217 must be "provided to the investigating law enforcement agency for use as evidence in any proceeding alleging a violation of G.S. 20-217."[656] Such photographs and videos are admissible in any proceeding that alleges a violation of G.S. 20-217(a), provided they are "consistent with the North Carolina Rules of Evidence."[657] The State's failure to produce a photograph or video recorded by an automated school bus safety camera does not, however, preclude prosecution of a driver under G.S. 20-217.[658]

---

649. *Id.*
650. *Id.*
651. G.S. 20-17.4(o).
652. G.S. 20-217(g2).
653. *Id. See also id.* § 20-54(11).
654. G.S. 20-217(g2).
655. G.S. 115C-242.1(a).
656. G.S. 115C-242.1(d).
657. G.S. 20-217(h).
658. *Id.*

Subject Index

Case Index

North Carolina cases, United States Supreme Court cases, and cases from other states are listed in alphabetical order by case name. Federal appeals court cases are listed in numerical order by circuit. Federal district court cases are listed in alphabetical order by district.

Federal District Court Cases

Cases from Other States

Table of Statutes and Regulations

North Carolina General Statutes (G.S.)

North Carolina Session Laws (S.L.)

North Carolina Administrative Code (N.C.A.C.)

United States Code (U.S.C.)

Code of Federal Regulations (C.F.R.)